HOPE MILLS

Hope Mills

A NOVEL BY CONSTANCE PIERCE

WINNER OF THE EDITORS' BOOK AWARD

PUSHCART
Wainscott
New York 11975

ISBN 0-916366-82-0

LC - 97-65344

Winner of the Fifteenth Editors' Book Award

Published by Pushcart Press, PO Box 380, Wainscott, New York 11975
Distributed by W. W. Norton & Co. 500 Fifth Ave. New York, New York 10110

Founding editors for the Editors' Book Award are Simon Michael Bessie, James Charlton, Peter Davison, Jonathan Galassi, David Godine, Daniel Halpern, James Laughlin, Seymour Lawrence, Starling Lawrence, Robie Macauley, Joyce Carol Oates, Nan A. Talese, Faith Sale, Ted Solotaroff, Pat Strachan, Thomas Wallace.

Acknowledgments:

I would like to thank the Department of English, East Carolina University, for having me as its Writer in Residence several years ago. The generous terms of this appointment, as well as the opportunity to be back in "the Old Country" for a while, allowed this novel to evolve. I would also like to thank my home institution, Miami University, Oxford, Ohio, for summer support to make refinements. The manuscript of *Hope Mills* won the 1995 Pirates Alley Faulkner Prize for fiction, and I am most grateful to the prize's selection committee and to the patron who encouraged me so bountifully with that award. This story is set in the South Atlantic region of the United States where there is indeed a pretty little town on a lake with an irresistible name which I have not resisted. But the "Hope Mills" of this novel and all its citizens are works of my imagination; any relation to the real thing is in name only. CP

HOPE MILLS

1: Summer

That summer, the summer of 1959, the sun moved into the sky quickly, and for the rest of the day, it was hidden behind the white sheet of its own light. Nights were black, but illuminated fitfully by heat lightning, and sometimes there were a few hot drops of rain. Along the unpaved streets near the Mill, the parsimonious rainfall left its mark in thin layers on the locusts and sourwoods, the scraggly hawthorns and sweet gums, mottling the dust on the leaves until it looked like they had blight.

Several miles out of town, where the new Interstate met up with the old four-lane for a while before swinging out to by-pass it, nobody had thought to put up a caution light, and a crew of migrant cotton workers had been killed when a tractor-trailer plowed into the back of their bus. It had happened— significantly, Tollie thought—on the very last day of spring. The pictures had been on the front pages of the newspaper, twenty bodies, some covered and some not, spread out on the new asphalt's bone-white lines, and all around was the debris of the tractor-trailer's load: coconuts, dark and haired-over, round as heads. Tollie had thought they look like large stones too, like they'd been there a long time. Gathering moss.

It was the first time she'd seen pictures of dead people in the newspaper, and they'd given her a quick nauseating shock, as if an important tribal taboo had been broken. She hadn't talked to anybody about it yet, not even Lily, her best friend (she guessed). Especially not Lily. She wanted to tell the old Lily all about it, but the new Lily was

9

suffering from delusions of grandeur, about how things were going to be when she got out of high school and Hope Mills and got to Hollywood or New York. The new Lily wouldn't understand the first thing about being dead on a highway.

The blurry photographs were worse in their effects than older, clearer pictures Tollie had seen in her stepfather Les's magazines, though often these involved many more dead people. The magazines had names like *Argosy, True,* and *Stag,* and as you got nearer the bottom of the old footlocker where Les kept them: *Male, Man's Conquest, For Men Only,* and *Impact: Bold True Action for Men.* The footlocker was in a room that had been the baby's, but now it was just "the little room," empty except for the footlocker and a gun rack on the wall with zero to three hunting rifles, depending on how many Les had at the pawn shop, and a small wardrobe where Les kept his clothes. The crib and bathinette had been sold to a couple down the street.

Les's magazines had articles on sports and hunting and on the true-life adventures of regular soldiers and soldiers-of-fortune, usually in exotic locales. There were photographs and drawings from the War, and of things that had been found after the War, all mixed in with half-naked women, often bound hand and foot, but sometimes carrying a whip or a knife themselves. The articles had names like "Fishing in the High Chapparel," "Displaying Your Guns," and "Heroes of the Coral Sea," but also "The Adventurer Who Raped a Nation," "Sex-Starved SS Women," and "Bloodbath on the Isle of Hate." What interested Tollie most was the arrangement of pictures and photographs. It made her dizzy: the movement from naked skinny bodies stacked up like pick-up stix to curvy half-naked cartoon women bound hand and foot; from drawings of men that looked like Steve Canyon, letting a little buck-tooth Oriental in pajamas have it with a bayonet, to watercolors of beautiful hooked fish, suspended large and mournful in the air, and photographs of deer hanging from tree-limbs, their bodies opened in long, dark slits.

She was compelled to the footlocker, she wasn't sure why. It seemed like there was an important code in the arrangement of pictures that she couldn't decipher. It frustrated her, and yet she went back for more: Was she a glutton for punishment, as her mother used to say she was, back when Janice noticed things? The magazines gave Tollie something like the creeps. Not the real creeps, because the drawings were made-up and the photographs were of things that had happened, like in her mother's favorite song, "Long Ago and Far Away," not like the dead migrants, who were right now and right here. Their pictures gave her the real creeps. The magazines weren't meant for her, but for men like Les, to see or not see. The front page of the newspaper was for everybody.

Every day on the radio the disk jockey, Jack McLaurin—a.k.a. Big Mack—had been filling up the time between records with remarks on the weather, going on in a fake pitch about how it was the hottest summer in twenty years. "We're going out in a swelter folks," he kept saying, his voice ranging several dangerous-animal sounds. Tollie was lying on the bed in her room, where she had sneaked a couple of the magazines. She had just finished "The White Woman and the Headhunter" and "The Blonde Queen of the Comanches," which she'd been able to concentrate on as long as Big Mack played music, but his voice was a real distraction. She didn't need him reminding her about the heat, either. She had heat rash between her new breasts and between her legs and all around her waist, like the measles. She powdered herself all day long with cornstarch, which she shook from a large container that had been used for her baby brother's diaper rash before he died. At night, before going out with Ramírez, she would bathe and sneak some Chanel No. 5 bath powder from a box which was over fifteen years old and still half-full. Someone had given it to Janice before Tollie was born, and Janice had rationed it out like it was gold dust. The great cotton puff was so matted up by now there was no puffiness about it, but the powder still smelled good. In the evening, Tollie would rush past her mother and out the door, hoping Janice wouldn't pick up a whiff.

Not that her mother was noticing *anything* these days, Tollie thought, as she thought all the time now. She flipped past "Chewed to Bits by Giant Tropical Sea Turtles" and "The South Sea Harem of Sgt. Red Wirkus." Actually it was always a little depressing when, undetected, she sniffed the powder on her way to Ramírez's car. These days Janice didn't seem to notice enough to be alive.

But then there would be the car, idling in the driveway, distracting Tollie from Janice and Les. A hardtop-convertible with all its windows rolled down, looking cool in every way, except for the real rabbit's foot dangling from the rearview mirror on a short brassy chain.

Listening to Big Mack *trying* to be cool in the afternoons—but not able to talk about anything but the heat, the weather!—Tollie imagined him at the radio station, wiping the sweat off his forehead with a handkerchief and then running it, sopping wet, back under his collar. He should be sweating. He was screwing Lily every afternoon during something he'd made up just for the occasion, Platters Without Chatter, A Solid Hour of Rock 'n' Roll. Four to five o'clock, his voice would come on the air only once, to croak out the time and the heat "at the bottom of the hour." Then it was the absence of his voice that kept Tollie from concentrating. He should be sweating an ocean about Statutory Rape, something else she'd found mention of in the newspaper.

She'd seen Big Mack in the newspaper too, in the Sunday section called Living, which also included the Obituaries, though she'd noticed there weren't any for the dead migrants. He was about Les's age and he was heavy like Les used to be, but he wore his hair in a D.A. Les wore a short G.I. cut, though he'd never been in the service. During the War, he'd been turned down because of something in his lungs. In the picture, beside him on a couch at the radio station, were Big Mack's pretty wife and two little cotton-headed kids. Tollie wondered if it was the same couch where he was screwing Lily. It was so shiny it looked painted, unreal. No wonder he kept talking about the heat, she thought: that plastic was probably pulling the skin off his knees, the creep.

Fraud from the word Go. Not that you could tell Lily anything.

At night, when there was some choice, Tollie tuned Mack out in favor of the real disk jockeys far away, the ones he tried to imitate. She could hear them howling and whooping and growling from the Clear Channel stations in big cities everywhere east of the Rockies. She guessed they were doing the same thing on the other side of the Rockies too. She'd seen a big burly man from California growling like a wildcat on Dave Garroway. She didn't like the real deejays much better than she liked Big Mack, but at least one of them had to be the original. There must be a hundred phonies stretching out between the original in some bright faraway city and the phoney of phonies, Big Mack of Hope Mills.

Hopeless Mills. That's what people were beginning to call it.

She skimmed "Masculine Inadequacies Drive Women Nuts" and "Wyatt Earp, Hero or Heel?" Then she settled for a minute on "Five Places Where You Can Buy a Slave Girl." The five places were Saudi

Arabia, India, Mangalore, the Marquesas Islands, and "the hot, savage jungles of the Mato Grosso." *For a 9 mm Mauser,* she read, *a pocket knife, $10 Brazilian and a Primus Stove, I received a 16-year-old Quemada Virgin who came to me the way she came into the world. . . .*

Tollie reached for the Funk and Wagnalls, an old dictionary, 1939, that had belonged to her grandfather, one of Janice's few heirlooms from long ago and faraway Whiteville. She checked for Mauser, Primus, and Quemada, with no luck. Which she'd expected: They were all capitalized. Still, you never knew. She didn't let many new words go by her. That was a habit she'd got from her mother, who had an immense collection of words, even if she had more or less stopped talking by now.

Tollie put the dictionary back on the nightstand. For a moment she was wistful, remembering all the fun she and her mother used to have: Scrabble, crosswords. Wordgames in the car, back when Janice would get in a car. . . . Her mother had taught her the alphabet before she'd even gone to school, by singing "A You're Adorable," right up in Tollie's face. Giving her a quality for every letter, A to Z. Smiling. Tickling, kissing.

Tollie longed for the days when she and Janice had laughed over things in the newspaper, which they'd always divided and read together in the living room, even back when Tollie had just been interested in comics. Janice would poke fun at President Eisenhower, Estes Kefauver in his coonskin hat, the dumb sayings of John Foster Dulles, things like The Distant Early Warning System. She'd kidded Tollie that the two of them were "Commie-conspirators." Janice didn't do any of that anymore. She just leaves me to my own devices, Tollie thought with a little surge of anger. Which aren't worth a poot!

Junk. She passed by "Beware of Broadway B-Girls," and then closed the magazine. She got up and gathered the magazines in a neat pile, like Les kept them in, and then sneaked them back into the footlocker in the little room—dark as a grave! Tollie hurried out and shut the door. She went back to her room and got the radio.

In her mother's bedroom, she plugged in the radio and the iron and then opened the large plastic bag of sprinkled clothes. The inside of the bag smelled of mildew. Lately Janice would sprinkle down the clothes and roll them up, then let them stay in the bag until they mildewed or soured. From within the rolls of Les's khaki work pants and shirts and Janice's faded house-dresses, Tollie took out one of her

13

two bright white pleated skirts and sniffed it. It smelled like Purex. Her skirts didn't get a chance to sour. She wore one of them every night, washed one of them every day. She took out the skirt and spread it on the ironing board, then wet her finger and tested the iron. She turned on the radio and waited. "Thank Heaven for Little Girls," an oldie-and-baddie, "Tears on My Pillow" (half-goodie), a weather report, then "Broken-Hearted Melody," a definite goodie.

She thought about the dead migrants and her heat rash and Lily screwing herself silly, without a rubber. Something was going to happen. She could feel it in the air, though she didn't have a bit of patience with people who said they could feel things in the air. Maybe it *was* the heat. Everybody seemed in a fever. Trying to set themselves off from something, by howling and growling or whatever it took. Big Mack was always rhyming and calling attention to his own name, like he was now, breaking into the last bit of "Broken-Hearted Melody." "Settle back, Jack, cut Mack some slack, don't gimme no flak, Mack's putting on a stack. . . . "

It was awful. She turned the dial and found the Negro station. She listened a few seconds until she determined that they weren't playing music but preaching, and when the ad came on for the services of Madame Lucretia—"Palm-Reader, Advisor, The Future Foretold: she hope me, she'll hope you"—Tollie turned the dial back to Big Mack in defeat. She'd never waste a dime on somebody like Madame Lucretia. The Future Foretold! In Hope Mills, as any fool knew, you just had to put up with whatever came along. Big Mack. Crazy Mammas. Speeding trucks.

Tollie looked out the window at the stunted dusty trees. Why was it they were building Interstates for people to ride on when some people still *lived* on dirt streets? Lily was always saying, "Why don't y'all get somebody to pave that dirt road before I ruin every stitch of clothes I've got?" Who? Tollie wondered. Who and how? She wanted to live on a paved street more than Lily wanted her to. The sand-colored dirt rose in knee-high clouds each time a car passed, covering the shrubs and grass, and when the wind blew or a large truck went roaring by on its way to or from the Mill, the dust would find its way to the house itself, coming to rest in little drifts on the window-panes, like in drawings she'd seen of snow.

The new Lily was a case, in and unto herself, Tollie thought, testing the iron again and then beginning to work on her pleats. Dramatic. Melo-dramatic. Sometimes Lily wore a leather dog collar for a necklace, with a small metal heart-shaped tag engraved with "L & M," Lily & Mack.

"I feel like if I don't do something," Lily had said earlier in the week, lazing around on Tollie's bed while Tollie was powdering her rash—wrinkling the spread, which Tollie was going to have to re-iron herself—"If I don't do something real special, a big old wave of sameness is going to wash over the *land*."

From sea to shining sea, Tollie had thought, pulling out the elastic on her cotton underpants, and filling them up with cornstarch. That would suit her fine: a great bland wave rising up on one coast and rolling to a crest out where the radio stations switched from "W" to "K," and then crashing into the ocean on the other side. Washing the country cool and clean and leaving everything and everybody on an equal footing—comfortable, calm, and right as rain.

That would suit me finer than fine, she'd thought. But wasn't that just like Lily lately: "If *I* don't do something . . . a wave will wash over the *land*!"

"I feel like I got to do something real different or I'm going to get caught up in that old wave and lost," Lily had said, getting up, suddenly giving Tollie a look of pure venom. "Stop dusting that goddam stuff around. You're strangling me. And get yourself some grown-up panties, while you're at it!" Then she'd flounced out of the room, an inch of pink crinoline showing beneath her new low-cut sundress, her silvery page-boy bobbing in its crescent at her shoulders. She'd gone back into the living room to sit with Janice, who, Tollie knew, was the real reason for the new Lily's visits.

"You might at least straighten up the bed," Tollie had yelled after her. "You're not in this world by yourself."

Everybody was acting weird. Tollie sprinkled water on her skirt from a sprinkler screwed into the neck of a Coke bottle, set the iron in motion and let the hot smell of cotton blast her in the face, trying to pretend she was having a facial at one of the fancy beauty shops she'd read about in Lily's *Movie Star* and *Photoplay*. Acting like they were fighting for their lives. Everybody trying to be different, just like everybody else, and in all the same ways. If everybody weren't so caught up in that junk, she thought, half-drunk on cotton-vapors, half-blinded by sweat, maybe somebody would have had the sense to put first things first and remembered to put a caution light out at that intersection. You could fight for your life on the side.

15

Janice said everybody was just tired of President Eisenhower, though Janice called him General Eisenhower. "They're tired of toeing the line and minding their P's and Q's twenty-four hours a day," she'd say, without energy. "Three-hundred-and-sixty-five days a year, year in and year out, lest somebody thinks they're a Communist. Or a whore."

Tollie carefully pointed the iron's nose down a long stretch of pleat, accelerated, then sped toward the hem before the pleat got away from her. Yes, the summer was speeding by, and the decade, and even high school, and then what? She knew she was wasting time. You could waste time, but you couldn't save it. Time wasn't money, like Lily's father was always saying. Daylight Savings Time didn't even save time. It just got Management out of the Mill in time to get in some golf after work, like Les was always saying. She didn't believe much else Les said, but you could walk by the golf course if you were dumb enough to get out in the heat after supper and see the Managers knocking golf balls around, carrying big glasses of what she guessed was liquor and melted ice from hole to hole.

She wished she had a summer job, something more steady than babysitting. In her neighborhood, women couldn't afford to use a babysitter very often, even at fifty cents an hour. None of the stores were hiring girls her age. The weather was so dry there probably wouldn't be enough crops for anyone to hire extra pickers. Even Mr. Faircloth, who had the biggest produce farm in the county, probably wouldn't be hiring extra this year. Sometimes a person's prospects could look pretty dim, even when that person wanted to help herself.

Tollie tried hard to concentrate on her ironing, on the iron itself. She hoped she'd remember to unplug it after she turned it off. Janice worried all the time about unplugging things. She'd unplugged just about everything in the house before she'd gone to the Winn-Dixie, even. Once, not long after the baby had died, they'd gone to the beach for a week, the only time Les had ever taken them on a vacation. Before they left, Janice had been turning off and unplugging everything and she had reached for the toaster plug and unplugged the refrigerator by mistake. When they got back, the whole house had smelled like a cabbage that had rotted in the Hydrator and a black mold had been growing on everything inside the appliance. It had smelled like somebody had died in their kitchen.

"That just goes to show what happens when you go off," Les had said.

That was back when Janice still went out of the house. Now she almost never went anywhere except downtown on the bus to window shop, maybe once a week. She always came back looking exhausted. She let Les go to the Winn-Dixie on Friday nights, after he got paid. Les loved to spend the money himself, though he didn't have anything to show for it that Tollie could see. "Better spend it while I can," he always said, though he never gave her a dime, hardly gave Janice a dime either, especially now. Les said the Mill was going to start laying off. "Cotton's going out of style," he said. "Everything's going to be Easy-Care." Good, Tollie had thought. Maybe it'll stay pleated.

She thought the same thing now! She set the iron on end and tried to get better control of a pleat that kept slipping away from her. Ironing pleats was complicated, a science *and* an art. The bedroom was so hot she was beginning to feel weak. Between the heat and the pleats and the general atmosphere of 1959, she'd better watch out or she'd end up on a Prescription, like her mother.

She needed a rest. She left the skirt hanging on the ironing board and sat down on her mother's bed, fixing her eyes on the bottle of pills on the nightstand. The label on Janice's prescription said "Miltown." Tollie picked up the bottle and shook it. She thought "Miltown" said something about why Janice lay around the house taking pills all day and half the night, watching Les sleep on the couch, the tv going to snow—watching Les, even though, or maybe because, she'd taken off her wedding band and put it in the drawer with her underwear, like it was something porn-o-graphic! Miltown. . . .

That was one of the things Tollie had begun to notice: that names seemed to know more, on their own, than whatever people had in mind when they named things. There was Mil-town, and *Les* who was less, and *Jan*, like the month, + *ice*. And *Lily*, who worried all the time about who was white and who wasn't. There seemed to be an all-knowing Something behind it all, invisible but real and true. It was what she counted on, now that she'd given up Sunday school and revival. But it all moved in mysterious ways. There was, after all, *Hope* Mills. That didn't make any sense at all!

"Hot as . . . Haaaades," Big Mack said. "But that's allrrriiight! Look what's coming atcha now, ol' Mack's fave—"

Oh, no, Tollie thought, jumping up from the bed. She grabbed the iron and lit into a pleat, ironing faster. Already the guitar was rocking in the familiar sounds. All summer long, over and over, Big Mack had been playing "I Don't Wanna Hang Up My Rock 'n' Roll Shoes."

"I'm glad they weren't white," Lily said. She was sitting in Janice's living room, skimming the day's newspaper, waiting for 3:30 so she could get started for the radio station in her Daddy's new Oldsmobile. Her Daddy had made Foreman this year, after twenty years of being a grunt like Les, and the first thing he'd done was trade up his Plymouth for the Olds. She'd never have thought he would have let her drive it, but already he had his eye on a Cadillac. He said, "Wreck the son of a bitch if you can. Then I can use the insurance to trade up." He let her use the car every day, as long as she got to the Mill to pick him up no later than 5:05, which really cut into her time with Mack, but it was the best that she could do. She'd be glad when she was off in Hollywood or New York, with her own room in a studio, with a couch in it and pictures of herself all over the wall, her own schedule, and her own Cadillac, a pink one, like Jayne Mansfield's. Right now she'd just have to put up with things as they were, but not for long. Mack was her lucky break. He knew Dick Clark and a lot of people who were going to help her out.

Lily folded the newspaper so that the picture of the dead migrants showed, then propped it up against a vase on the coffee table so that Janice could see it from her day-bed. It seemed like the newspaper had been running the picture every few days all summer. Why?

"It'd make you feel worse," Lily said, "if they were white." She gave the picture one long look before settling back onto the worn cushions of the couch. She could smell the wet straw in the Water-Fan and the sweat from where Les's head had soured the couch's arm. God, she thought. How they live. I can't wait. I'm going to have Air Conditioning, and a couch without arms. I'm not going to marry anybody.

Janice didn't look at the picture. "If they were white," she said, "you can bet that picture wouldn't be in the paper. Tollie get me my prescription."

Tollie got up from the deep chair on the other side of the Water-Fan from her mother and dragged by Lily. She looks like she's half-dead herself, Lily thought, watching Tollie's thin body and brown Dutch-boy hair disappear down the hall. She'd better watch out or she's going to end up like Janice. Craaa-zeee, Mack would say.

A few minutes later, Tollie dragged back into the living room. "I think you take too many of these things," she said, handing the pills to Janice.

"How would *you* know," Lily said, picking up the newspaper and beginning to fan herself.

"I think you ought to go to a doctor and get some pills that work," Tollie said to Janice.

"These will work if I take them long enough," Janice said. She swallowed a pill with a few quick sips of water from a large glass on a plastic coaster on the floor. "What are you girls up to lately?" she asked.

Lily could tell she was just forcing herself to act interested.

"I'm making plans for the future," Lily said. "Meantime, I got a date every night of the week. Every afternoon, too. I'm getting so popular I can't hardly find a minute to myself."

"Tollie has a date every night too," Janice said listlessly. "Where are you going tonight, baby?"

"I think to see that new movie," Tollie said. "*On the Beach?*"

"That's a nice title," Janice said. "I bet it'll be good."

"It's with Ava Gardner," Tollie said.

Lily watched as Janice arranged her sundress around her legs. It was an old dress. She couldn't remember a summer when Janice hadn't worn it. It was green and yellow plaid, growing dimmer each year, with a bolero jacket that Janice had always put on when she went out of the house. The last time Lily had seen Tollie iron the dress, she'd noticed that the jacket was too bright now for the sundress. Why doesn't she make Les buy her a new one? Lily thought. Why doesn't she just take his goddam wallet out of his pocket while he's snoring on the couch and go buy herself five new dresses?

Tollie's real father wouldn't have acted like Les did. *Probably* wouldn't. You couldn't tell about men. Still, he ought to be different from regular Mortals. He was a dead War Hero. Not that it mattered anymore, dead being the main thing he was.

Lily watched the photographs of the bodies become a gray blur as she fanned the newspaper back and forth. She might as well fan herself. Janice wasn't even going to look at the picture. Lily looked at Tollie. Flopped in that old chair, hair in her eyes like a five-year-old. No makeup. Dungarees and tennis shoes. Teenie weenie tits.

She'd outgrown Tollie. All she came over here for now was to talk to Janice, when you could get her to talk. Janice was what people meant when they said Still waters run deep. She'd been the Southeast Cotton Queen in 1943. The *last* Cotton Queen. They'd stopped the contest out of respect for the War, then after the War, they'd never started it back up, almost like they could foretell the end of cotton, see Easy-Care coming down the pike like a Mack truck in your lane. Easy-Care! It was going to ruin all their lives. At least it would get her Daddy into another line of work, though. Then she wouldn't be a Mill Rat, suffering for the sins of her Daddy every day of the week. Unless he became a bum. Life sure was uncertain in Hope Mills. A place to get out of the minute you saw your chance, whatever it took!

Lily scrutinized Janice's pale face and flyaway hair. Queen Janice. . . . You'd never know it now. She still felt a little shock every time she remembered the rumor she'd just heard: that Janice was fooling around.

I don't believe it, Lily thought, squinting hard at Janice's face. That woman doesn't have the energy for it. She doesn't have the looks for it right now, either. Not to get somebody as good-looking as he is to be interested in her, even if he is a farmer. And he's a rich farmer, too.

Lily looked away. Looking at Janice just depressed her, even when she couldn't see the red X's on her wrists. You could lose your reputation in Hope Mills just by lying around in your living room all day, not even going out of the house.

Cotton Queen, Lily thought wryly. I wouldn't go out for something like Cotton Queen myself. Too local. I wouldn't even want to be Southeast Easy-Care Queen, if there was such a thing. I've had it with local.

Lily had been first runner-up in the Miss Hope Mills High School Contest in the spring, and she felt like she'd never live it down. She could have won if her mother had hemmed her dress right, not that winning would have meant a thing. She'd think about that till the day she died, that she'd lowered herself to enter a high school contest in the first place and that her mother hadn't even had the sense to hem her dress right. She'd stepped on it in front of everybody, including Mack, who'd promised 30-seconds on the radio if she was the winner. After it was over, he'd pretended to interview the winner and then he'd whipped out the door. He could have at least hung around to comfort her a little. They could have sneaked off somewhere out of sight. Well, never mind. She had her eye on the next State Junior Miss, then the American Junior Miss, and a couple of other things, and then Miss America. That was the way to get where you were going, not messing around with high school contests that were fixed so that the girls with important daddies won them anyway! Not representing a bunch of local cotton farmers. She already had a sponsor for the State, the Tastee-Freeze where she worked part-time, and Mack said he'd "see about" WMIL sponsoring her in the American. What was there to see about? He just didn't want to do anything public that was going to give his cute little wife ideas. She guessed she knew how that stuff worked.

Yeah, there was a lot you could learn from somebody like Janice, who'd wanted to do everything you wanted to do and had failed.

Lily especially liked to look at Janice's Portfolio, which Tollie had found when she was cleaning out the basement, trying to make a little spending money off of Les. It was a moldy old album full of yellow newspaper clippings of Janice when she was Cotton Queen, and a couple of photographs that looked to Lily like somebody had painted over them with watercolors. In the clippings, Janice had her hair piled up on her head, two shiny wings that ended in a funny-looking crown, with more shiny hair hanging down in the back. "Queen Janice— Whiteville Beauty Triumphs in Pageant." Janice was holding an armful of dry cotton plants with burst bolls, not a bouquet of roses. Lily thought her face seemed to be saying, "I can put up with anything. This is just the first dinky step on a long shining road."

That was how Lily thought about being first runner-up. By the time she got where she was going, nobody was going to remember that she'd stepped on the hem of her dress in front of 400 local-yokels in a high school beauty contest.

Lily looked at Tollie again. Like a limp chicken, that's how Tollie looked. Tollie irritated her, no end. With some work, that girl could look like Natalie Wood. Almost. But would she even try?

Lily turned the dead migrants away from herself and toward Tollie, beginning to wave the photo slowly . . . slowly. Just take a look at that, Tollie Ramsey. Dead niggers and dead Porta-Ricans, some covered, some not covered. It's probably the Porta-Ricans they covered up, but it doesn't make a whole lot of difference, does it?

Lily loved to remind Tollie, who hadn't even entered the beauty contest—no ambition, no future plans, just the pipe-dream that she might go to college: what for? And how in the world?—that Ramírez was a waste of time. A Porta-Rican and a soldier out at the Base. He was cute all right, sort of sulky like Elvis the Pelvis, but too dark to be white. The only time she'd lowered herself to talk to him was one night when her parents were at the movies and she'd let Tollie bring him over to their new ranch house to watch television. While Tollie was in the bathroom, leaving Ramírez brooding on the couch, she'd slipped loose the clasp on the Teardrop necklace Mack had given her and asked Ramírez to re-clasp it for her—*just* to make conversation. She'd sat on the floor and settled in between his knees and held her hair up to let him string the chain to either side of her neck. Looking down, she could see the cloudy Teardrop, what they called Opalesque at the store, jumping slightly on her chest as she breathed, and she'd begun to let her hair drop down on Ramírez's warm, dry hands, soft lock by soft lock, waiting. But he'd been so stupid he'd just clasped the necklace and moved his hands somewhere else, off her. After sitting there a minute, she'd got up and moved across the room to a chair. He'd given her a smirky look, which just about said I've got your number—from somebody who couldn't half speak English, couldn't count numbers for all she knew! Then he'd gone back to watching the tv, like she wasn't even alive.

"My daddy says a Porta-Rican is the next thing to a nigger," Lily said in a low voice, still waving the newspaper at Tollie, Janice already drifting like The Lost Missile, toward The Lost Lagoon, her eyes closed: still as death. "Yep, the next thing." This was what she usually said when Tollie got on her nerves, which was about every day of her life. She couldn't imagine what was going on in Tollie's mind. If she didn't watch out she was going to have about ten nigger babies hanging onto one of those pleated skirts she wore, and what would the War Hero have thought of something like that?

Actually, Lily was getting sick of the War Hero, though she sort of wished she had a real, dead other-daddy who was a Hero, something that proved she wasn't *really* a Mill Rat.

She waved her newspaper-fan faster, fuming. Why *was* that girl going out with somebody who was going to ruin her reputation and maybe knock her up too? Not that your reputation mattered in the long run if you had your eye on something bigger. But for Tollie Ramsey, who was never going to get out of Hope Mills, unless it was to Porta Rica, it was going to matter a lot.

She'd tried her best to fix Tollie up with one of Mack's friends. "Maybe he'd be somebody who could get you somewhere, at least," she'd tried to reason with her.

"I don't have anywhere I want to go," Tollie had said. "Yet."

Yet! Lily flexed her nose a little, remembering, and dug down in her pocket for the keys to the Oldsmobile. She had to get out of here. The whole room smelled like dead women.

"Well, I'm glad you stopped waving that thing in my face," Tollie said, turning toward the air from the Water-Fan as Lily stood up. Lily could see Tollie's own nose twitching slightly, her face relaxing into something like a smile.

"I'm going," Lily said in disgust. "That Water-Fan is stirring around a lot of hot air." She got up. Why don't they ever open the blinds? she thought. Why doesn't Janice get up off that damn thing and do something about her before it's too late? The chickens are going to come home to goddamn roost.

"Did you unplug that iron?" Janice asked Tollie, without opening her eyes.

After supper, pimento cheese-spread and lettuce on toast and Tru-ades, which Tollie and Janice had eaten on trays in the living room to take advantage of the Water-Fan, Tollie got ready for her date with Ramírez. She felt a little sick at her stomach: all that Miracle Whip, she guessed, plus the heat. It was early August now, and hotter than ever, drier than ever. What would September be like? It was always the hottest month.

Well, at least Janice had toasted the bread and put ice in the glasses, even put lettuce on the sandwiches. Tollie knew her mother was try-ing to make up to her for that afternoon. All through supper Janice had tried to talk with her, calling her by her old pet names, Baby and Tollie-lollipop, Cutie-Pie, but Tollie wished she hadn't tried. She could see how hard it was for Janice to will the energy alone to do it, and be-sides, there wasn't any way her mother could make this afternoon up to her. Everything was changed now, every single thing. But it was sweet of Janice to try, especially the lettuce, even if she had had to send Tollie down the street in the heat for it.

Before Janice had switched to another frequency, there had been good food on the table, day after day. Good Southern food like every-body had—fried chicken and fried oysters, shrimp panned in butter. Collards and pastry, corn pudding, country-style steak in onion gravy (Les's favorite, so they'd had that a lot). Sweet potatoes sliced and bob-bing in butter and sweet dark syrup, biscuits and tomato gravy. Butter beans, crowder peas, summer squash, crisp bread-and-butter pickles.

Cornbread, grits, hush puppies with little bits of onion inside. Sometimes Tollie would recite these foods to herself as if they had religious meaning. She didn't know how to fix any of these things, though she'd taught herself to iron after Janice had stopped taking good care of the clothes, so maybe she could learn. Sometimes when she had a little money from babysitting, or picking crops, when they'd hire white girls to do that work, she'd walk all the way to Parnell's Restaurant. Once while she was there, a crazy Negro man, babbling in tongues, had wandered in and sat down and tried to order a meal, before the sheriff came and carted him off, to jail or wherever the Dix Hill for Negroes was, Tollie never knew which. It was hard to resist Parnell's, whatever it cost you. There, she'd order herself a decent meal, and a trip down memory lane: chicken and pastry, ham biscuits, slaw, pickled peaches, lemon chess pie. It was good. You couldn't hardly get a bad meal at a restaurant in Hope Mills. But it was never as good as Janice's food had been, sitting at their own kitchen table, Les and Janice talking to each other, asking her what she'd done in school that day. All that was gone with the wind.

Janice had liked to try new things too, recipes she'd find in her magazines: drinks in coconut shells, a chicken breast beat flat with a mallet, then wrapped around a cube of frozen butter, battered and deep-fried. When you cut into it, the melted butter rolled out on your rice pilaf like gold. Cold shrimp in a salad. Thin slices of meat with a sauce of wine and little canned mushrooms. Janice said she didn't care if someone she knew did see her buy a bottle of wine at the Winn-Dixie, that all the best cooks used wine. Some school mornings Tollie had wakened to waffles with hot orange syrup, the orange sections looking like big happy grins as they tumbled from the syrup pitcher. Or pancakes wrapped around fresh strawberries, sprinkled with powdered sugar; French toast and blueberry syrup and a sweet pouf of Ready-Whip. Stuff the other kids would never have had. Their mothers wouldn't have had the imagination. The Good Old Days.

Tollie stepped into her skirt and zipped it, then selected a soft pink cotton blouse with a drawstring at the waist. She'd bought it, a size too big, at Kresge's for 89¢ during their end-of-summer sale the year before, and now it fit her just right. You had to iron it, but that's why she'd got such a good price, and the color was beautiful: like the Queen of Denmark roses that her grandmother had grown in her yard in Whiteville—what seemed like long, long ago. To Tollie the color seemed to seep into her face, giving her a little glow. Which was good, since she usually didn't have money to buy makeup.

Not that Ramírez would notice, she thought, losing a little of her pleasure in the blouse, feeling another twitch in her stomach.

They went out every night, even when there wasn't any place to go. Tollie wasn't old enough to get into the bars that Ramírez's friends went to, and there wasn't any place she could take Ramírez where he'd be welcome. Most of the time they went to a drive-in movie or they just got a six-pack and took it out to the lake, where they'd met, but in the daytime, a whole year ago. She'd been wading and had stepped in a hole in the lake's bottom, deep and cold. A feeling she'd never, ever forget. Ramírez had pulled her out. Maybe that was why, now, he took her life for granted.

Nights, they would drink beer while they listened to the radio and smoked cigarettes. Sometimes they'd slow-dance outside the car. She always remembered the music as "Chanson D'Amour," "The Long Hot Summer," "Volaré," "Tears on My Pillow," last summer's songs, as if their dating was already a thing of the past. Sometimes Ramírez would turn down the radio and sing songs of his own in Spanish. His soft breath would be against her ear as they slow-danced, but he would seem in a world of his own, lost to her in the sounds she couldn't interpret, sounds that kept her distant in a way that "Chanson D'Amour" didn't, though she didn't understand all of its words either. She didn't have the nerve to ask him what he was singing about. If he'd wanted her to know, wouldn't he have sung to her, in English? The same words came up, in song after song—*Isla*, which she could figure out meant island, and something that sounded a little like Coral Zone. She imagined an island, surrounded by coral that bloomed from the sea like bone-white flowers. But when she'd finally asked him what the word meant, he'd said Heart, it meant heart.

When they danced, she would take off her sandals and feel the powdery dirt against her soles. The dirt would be almost hot, even though it was night, and she would imagine herself swaying in Ramírez's brown arms under a palm tree a thousand miles away, secure in the implications of connection in their names—Ramírez, Ramsey—though Ramírez had never said a word about taking her to Puerto Rico. Other times, she was pretty sure Ramírez didn't even like her. He said he didn't like Gringos, and he always called her Gringa, like she didn't have a name. When he said it, there was something mean and indifferent in his voice at the same time. You had to wonder why he'd bothered to save her life.

Not that any of it mattered. Getting out of the house was what mattered.

Sometimes when they didn't go to the lake, they went to a drive-in restaurant where Big Mack played records most nights from a big glass room on top, The Kastle in the Air. You could call in your requests or put them in through notes you gave to the car-hops, though Tollie never had. Usually she sat in the car listening to the music, eating some of the Kastle's awful food—pizza-flavored chicken fingers or sweet and sour sea kabobs, just one of the terrible things they did to a catfish, trying to make it appeal to the soldiers who were from some place else. She would watch Ramírez outside the car, drinking beer with the other soldiers. Sometimes there were women with them, and sometimes the fast girls from school, and she could see Ramírez talking to them too. Sometimes the soldiers spoke in Spanish, to each other and to dark women—their wives, maybe, or girlfriends who had followed them here from Puerto Rico. Les said there were Puerto Rican women working in the Mill now, doing what he called "the dirty work." Some of the soldiers had Oriental wives, though these men were usually older than Ramírez.

Tollie sprayed an Avon cologne called "Here's My Heart"—a Christmas present from Janice two years ago, which she was trying to make last—behind her ears and then raised both wrists to her neck to catch any excess. It came in a blue heart-shaped bottle, and it smelled nice, mixed with the stolen bath powder that she'd dusted in her bra and underpants.

Out the window she could see Arlene, their next door neighbor, wearing pedal-pushers and a halter, pink, which redheads weren't supposed to wear, but Arlene looked good in everything. Healthy-looking, sweet and kind. She was watering her flowers with a hose, leaning forward in concentration. She looked sort of like Janice had looked before things went bad for her.

Tollie turned away. It was almost dark and it still must be 100 degrees. Already she felt her legs sticking together under her freshly ironed skirt and she knew the pleats were going to fall out before Ramírez even picked her up. She wished he'd hurry. If he didn't, Les would be home and she'd have to hear again about how going out with soldiers was going to ruin her reputation. How could someone like

Les, who spent so much time reading magazines full of soldiers' adventures, think like that? Even if it was true, which it was: going out with Ramírez was most likely going to ruin any reputation she had. Did she have a reputation? A reputation for what? That was one of the words that left out more than it said. She didn't think you could really have a reputation in Hope Mills, only lose one.

Every time Les started that, Janice always said What does it matter. "If I've taught her anything, it's to get on a bus out of here the day she graduates high school."

This always gave Tollie a chill. She knew if she didn't get on a bus she was just going to be one more girl with a bad reputation and a mother who was a pill addict and stepfather who was laid-off to take care of too. But she didn't know anywhere she wanted to go that she had a chance of going. The place she wanted to go probably wasn't even on the map.

She used to imagine herself and Ramírez living on a beach where cool breezes blew, in a house with a grass roof, coconuts falling off the trees and landing right by the door. Ramírez would be down by the water, wearing a shell-necklace and spearing a big happy-looking fish that had swum right up to him. She would be standing in the doorway, looking naturally beautiful in a sarong, one big pink flower behind her ear.

That was worse than the way Lily daydreamed and she didn't do it much. Still, there was something about going out with the-next-thing-to-a-Negro that was almost as good as getting on a bus. But there wasn't much pleasure in it.

So what? Ramírez was going to stop coming around any day now, she could feel it in the air. She was doing the best she could with what she had. She'd be glad when it turned into 1960. Maybe it would change her luck. Every now and then, she had hopes of going to college, working her way through, like actresses sometimes did in the movies. That would be a good plan for the 1960's.

1960. She wished it would hurry up and get here. Maybe everybody would calm down and things in general would change. Otherwise, why would Big Mack keep saying "We're going out . . . "?

Sometimes when Ramírez pushed her down in the backseat of his car, she blocked out all that she didn't want to know about it and imagined the warm heaving of the ocean some place faraway where the living was easy. The ocean, with no mind in it, just a warm salty cresting. What was the use of trying to figure everything out to a "T" anyway?

Right after, Ramírez, guilty of Statutory Rape, punishable by 5, 10, maybe 20 years in jail if you were a Puerto Rican in Hope Mills, always took her home and drove off, not even tooting the horn. It was never late and she always wondered where, exactly, he went. She could tell he was going somewhere, the bars, she guessed. It was like he was already wherever it was, even as he sat in the car in the driveway behind Les's old Ford, waiting for her to get out. His eyes wouldn't even focus on her.

But it was always late enough, her private time at last.

Janice has left the day-bed and gone to her bedroom and closed the door.

Les is snoring on the couch, and occasionally it's late enough so that the tv is going crazy with snow.

Tollie cuts it and the Water-Fan off, as if she'd save current.

Then she goes to her own room. Hot as Hades. She wishes Les would buy a Water-Fan for everybody. She turns on the radio and undresses in the dark, opening a heart-shaped cedar chest to hide her underpants till she can wash them without Janice getting suspicious. She holds them to her face and smells the ocean. A quick shiver and goosebumps, in spite of the heat. She buries the underpants in the chest with the Portfolio that Janice doesn't seem to want, knowing that when she takes the underpants out the next day they will smell not like the ocean but like another, better geography, the clean scent of cedar trees.

Her sheets are already clinging to her legs when she lies down and the curtains hang like they are painted against the dark windows. But she can listen to the Clear Channels, to the songs that are popular in Buffalo, New York, but haven't made it to Hope Mills yet, to the raunchy music you can pick up from Memphis. She listens to Big Mack sometimes too, reading his dedications: "To T. from J., who just can't wait till their dream comes true." Then he plays "All I Have To Do Is Dream," by the Everly Brothers. But it's not all roses.

"At the top of the hour" Big Mack gives the news: how neither the driver of the tractor-trailer nor the bus driver who didn't have a license is going to be charged with killing the nameless migrants because it's Nobody's Fault, how President Eisenhower is having trouble in the Dominican Republic and Lebanon and Indochina and other faraway places, how Caryl Chessman is going to be executed after 11 years on Death Row, how the Mill might shut down because of Easy-Care or if a certain Negro lawyer doesn't shut up about the Civil Rights Act, and a white one about something called Brown Lung, how some guy, somewhere, is starting up what he calls a chain of hamburger restaurants where you can get food in ten seconds, how the Food and Drug people think Miltown is addicting and should be taken off the market, how a woman's body has been found in a field of sweet corn right outside Hope Mills—then the temperature and the forecast.

All these interest her. She has saved, in the cedar chest, some clipped pictures of the dead migrants, she's not sure why; she's never sought them out like the pictures accompanying "South Pacific Cannibal-Women" and "I Survived the Death March on Bataan." Still: she thinks about the migratory men, in their fateful bus. She thinks about their lives and deaths, about the ones who were born in a foreign place, who also died in a foreign place. Said this way, it seems as true of the Negroes as of the Puerto Ricans. She's interested in the President's problems, because Ramírez says if they send him to Lebanon, okay, but if they try to send him to the Dominican Republic, he's going AWOL. She's heard him telling the others at the drive-in that they never should have been able to draft him in the first place, since he can't vote in the States. He swears they're training soldiers from Indochina right out at the Base, in a secret operation that nobody can find out about, not even the soldiers themselves. He seems to worry about that stuff all the time, like Les worries about getting laid off or losing his job to a Negro. She hopes they won't execute Caryl Chessman, who seems to have some redeeming features, in spite of being a rapist and robber. The idea of getting your food in ten seconds seems as good as a fish that swims right up and lets you spear it, and Miltown ought to be off the market. She doesn't know exactly what to think of the dead woman, though the fact of her sends a chill clear down to a person's toes. She'll have to wait for more news. The temperature is only a few degrees lower than it was at high noon. The forecast is more of the same, and Big Mack sounds delirious when he reads it.

All of these things seem connected, she's not sure how. It's like the names of things, very mysterious.

When she cuts off the radio and gets ready to sleep, she can hear the faint dialogue of an old movie on tv, then the station signing off with "Dixie." Les always gets up and turns the tv and Water-Fan back on and finds a channel that hasn't turned to snow, but at some point Janice always gets up and pulls the tv's plug, though never the Water-Fan's. Tollie hears Les snoring again, his breath seeming to scrape up

31

through him and out into the room, as if to escape him altogether, but he catches it just in time and scrapes it back inside. Even his snoring is punctuated by little coughs. Then, over the tv racket and the terrible sounds of Les's breathing, she isolates the soothing, persistent hum of the Water-Fan, listens, and falls asleep.

It was dark and Les was pulling into the driveway before Tollie realized that Ramírez wasn't coming. She'd been waiting for it for several weeks, but now that it was happening she felt a panic. She left the window where she had been sitting on the edge of her bed in the dark, watching the street, and she sat at the vanity dresser and lit one of her secret L & M's, blowing the smoke toward the windowscreen. She'd known that this was how he would do it. One night he just wouldn't come, and that would be it.

She listened to Les move across the living room floor, to his cough, always there, winter and summer. Then there were the clicks of the light and of the refrigerator door opening. She imagined the puff of cold air and shivered. She already felt like ice. She heard him go back into the living room and turn on the tv, nobody saying a word, him or Janice. She knew he would be eating a cold hot dog, right out of the package, or slices of processed cheese and saltines. Then she could hear the music from "Have Gun Will Travel" drifting down the hall. Les watched all the westerns: "The Lawman," "The Life and Legend of Wyatt Earp," "Wanted: Dead or Alive." "The Zane Grey Theatre," "Rawhide," "The Rifleman," "Tales of Wells Fargo." "Laramie," "Cheyenne," and "Sugarfoot." He said he wished he had lived in the Old West and had a little jap to wait on him like Hey Boy waited on Paladin. She thought he was crazy. Everybody knew that in the Old West anybody could ride into town and take everything you had, rape and murder you and ride on, any day of the year.

She didn't need Ramírez, she thought, moving back to the window and looking out into the empty street. Somebody's dog was barking and she could hear thunder in the distance. The little houses were low and dimly lit. The old sidewalks that someone had thought to build years ago, as if to encourage a neighborhood, lay cracked and useless beneath the weeds that flourished without rain. The Mill, blacker than the sky, loomed above everything, shut down for the night. It had already cut production by a third, she'd heard on the radio.

That afternoon, after she'd finished ironing her skirt, the pressure of her mother's sadness had built up in Tollie, like it did sometimes: like it was more her own than her own. Your own you could handle, some way, because you knew exactly how bad it was and you knew you were going to be able to take it, even if you'd thought beforehand that you'd never be able to. But with other people, you didn't know how bad it was. No matter how much you could see and surmise about a person from the outside, the inside was different. The "I" of them would always be a mystery. You didn't know how bad a thing was for them or how much they were trying to take, didn't know if they could take it or if it would kill them, as sure as a speeding truck would. The mystery of their sadness built up in your heart, like pressure from a storm. But it was like there were chains around your heart too, pushing back. Every time you looked and saw their blank faces and dead hair, their old faded sundresses and old faded newspaper clippings, your heart would turn soft and swell up. But when you saw them sucking down pills and clammed up in a house unplugged from the world outside, the chains would squeeze back, rubbing your heart raw until the chains won, and your heart shrank to a little mossy stone, cold and slimy within you. Then you'd say the things you'd hate yourself for later.

"Why didn't you take your old Portfolio and go to New York?" she'd burst out at Janice that afternoon. "It's not my fault you never got what you wanted." She wasn't going to mention the baby, or the x-marks on her mother's wrists.

Janice had looked up from the day-bed, her face pale and beginning to crimp up near her eyes, like they were trying to protect themselves. That's just like her, Tollie had thought. Somebody's getting ready to beat the junk out of her and she can't even raise her hands and arms to protect herself—she just squints about a millionth of an inch.

"I did go to New York," Janice said finally.

Tollie felt the chains snap. She was on alert. "What do you mean?" How could a woman have gone to New York, who, by the time she was thirty-five years old, wouldn't even be able to go to the grocery store?

"I went," Janice said, sitting up and reaching for the Miltowns. Tollie could see her hair flattened against the back of her head and spread out to the sides, like a dying moth spread flat against a wall. "I went, but it wasn't any different from here. Just bigger, with snow."

"It's got to be different from Hope Mills," Tollie said, carefully now.

"Well, it's not. It's all the same."

33

"Then why are you always saying I've got to get on a bus?"

Janice put the pill in her mouth and lay back and swallowed it dry. "I don't know," she said.

"I don't believe you went to New York," Tollie said, hardening. "You're breaking my heart. Or trying to."

Janice looked at her. "You're so impressionable."

"I don't believe you went." Tollie watched her mother's face turn strange, like it sometimes could. Sharp-featured, Jekyll to Hyde.

"You don't?" Janice asked coolly, seeming to slither into another voice. "You're *so* impressionable. Where do you think you came from?"

"What do you mean?" Tollie said, her arms suddenly cold from the fan.

"What does it sound like?"

"I came from Whiteville," Tollie said defensively. "I was born in Whiteville while Daddy was in the South Pacific. I don't even know what you're trying to say."

"You came from Manhattan Island," Janice said. "Your Daddy came from Fairfield, Connecticut. And he went back there every night." She closed her eyes and turned back to the fan.

Tollie watched her, her insides cold.

"You didn't have to make me say that," Janice said after a moment. "You're worrying me to death."

Who needs them? Tollie thought, pulling down the shade.

It was the 6th of August, the anniversary of the day they dropped The Bomb on Japan. The newspaper had printed a picture of the bomb's cloud on the front page that afternoon. The caption called it a mushroom cloud, but when she'd seen it on the tv news at suppertime, it had looked like a monster tropical flower, growing bigger and bigger before your eyes, like something you'd see in a horror movie.

They're dropping bombs on me, Tollie thought. They're trying to . . . obliterate me. That was the word the tv news had used: obliterate.

I don't need her, or the idea of Daddy, *or* Ramírez, not even a little bit!

It did make her feel good, a little, she thought a few minutes later, that Ramírez trusted her not to tell about the Statutory Rape, now that he and his car had disappeared from her life in a cloud of dust. She guessed she wouldn't tell. I don't need to get on a bus, she thought. I need to get on a Sputnik.

She walked over and turned on the light. Near the door she was aware of voices that were not on tv, a rare sound. She eased open the door.

"Not for me, I hope," Janice was saying.

"I don't know," Les said.

"I wouldn't want you to sell those guns for me, Les. There isn't anything I want."

"I never shoot them anyway. Anyway, it's done. Buy the kid some school clothes out of the catalog, get yourself something too. You might as well, while we can."

"This isn't like you," Janice said.

"I'm a changed man, Janice," he said. "It's going to be a new day."

"You'll find something else," Janice said. "*If* it even closes down."

Tollie closed the door and turned on the radio to drown out their voices, which were worse than their silence. She could smell the promise of rain in the air even with the shade down, and she could hear the thunder not too far away. Maybe they were going to get a storm tonight at last.

"Hot enough for you folks out there tonight?" Big Mack asked. "It's hot as Hell-O up here in The Kastle in the Air. And ol' Mackie is up here all aloooooooooone." He howled the last word like a wolf, imitating the famous deejays, then growled down low in his throat like he was going to pounce on Little Red Riding Hood and drag her into the weeds: "Time for a Big Mack Attack. . . . " His voice suddenly cracked and he missed a beat. "Now don't let a little lightning scare you off. We got music coming atcha for four more hours. Here's Jackie Wilson with Looonely Teardrops."

Tollie imagined Big Mack sweating in The Kastle, like he was being attacked by Sex-Starved SS Women on the Isle of Hate. Like there were lightning bolts coming at the glass dome in great Z's, lighting him up like one of those mad-scientist villains you saw on the tv cartoons, getting his.

"Now, don't you worry about ol' Mack," Big Mack said when he came back on. His voice was recovered, phoney again. "He's living riiiight! Here's one for L. from M."

That would be Lily's song. He always played one for her at the same time every night, the shithead.

It was "I Don't Wanna Hang Up My Rock 'n' Roll Shoes," which it was nine times out of ten. Tollie groaned and turned down the volume. She slipped out of her skirt and started to hang it up, but she saw a little sweep of black dots across the back of it, where it was wrinkled from sitting: her skirt had got mildewed after all! She sank down onto the floor. She felt defeated.

She studied the mildew. Was that another one of those words that said something: Mill Dew? A joke, maybe, like Mountain Oysters, or Hope Mills itself? She could almost imagine the Managers calling something that was run-off from the Mill, or even Les's sweat, "Mill Dew," and laughing about it. She looked at the spot on her skirt again, squinting. It looked like connect-the-dots, like it could hold a sign or a message. That it was where she sat made her stomach feel sick again: Was that a way to think of the inside of herself, her own juices: Mill Dew?

She balled up the skirt and tossed it under her bed. Maybe that was what she and Lily both had in them, sure to seep out sooner or later and leave its tattletale mark. They were Mill Rats, even if Lily's daddy was a Foreman now. Lily was going to go some place and come back with a baby and marry somebody like Les, except the Mill would be shut down, so they'd probably lie around on two day-beds not even speaking to each other until they couldn't take care of themselves and the baby would be waiting on them hand and foot for the rest of their normal lives. Something like that was the Future Foretold.

Suddenly she wanted to talk to Lily. It was a dangerous world, inside and outside of Hope Mills.

She took her bathrobe out of the closet, thinking that if you could get inside a person like Lily, you'd probably find some better qualities. Everybody ought to have a chance to show their "I" to the world some time or other in life. Besides, the new Lily had only burst into bloom after she'd seen the Portfolio. That made her, Tollie, sort of responsible, having unearthed the Portfolio in the first place.

Tollie left her room. Down the hall one way she could see Janice's closed door, down the other the silvery light of the television. She slipped down the hall toward the living room, then veered into the kitchen, closing its swinging door. She dialed Lily's number in the dark, counting the holes in the dial with her fingers.

"Hello?" Lily said, sounding expectant.

"It's only me," Tollie said.

"Tollie? You sound funny."

"So do you."

"I'm listening to the radio. What is it? I thought you'd be out with The Cisco Kid."

"He didn't come."

Lily hesitated. "Well," she said, "Don't sweat it. There's plenty more fish in the sea."

"I hope so." Tollie saw now that she hadn't called Lily to warn her. She hadn't even called her to talk about Ramírez, exactly. But she was grateful that the old Lily was back for a minute, even if they didn't talk about much.

"Look," Lily said. "I'll come by Sunday. When I don't have to work or go to the radio station. We'll go riding in Daddy's car, if he'll let me take it. Maybe we can wreck it."

Tollie laughed in spite of how she felt.

"There's a new picture at the Miracle, too. *The Best of Everything*. It's about four girls who go off to New York to take it over? I *got* to see that."

Tollie didn't say anything.

"My treat," Lily said wearily. "I'll be glad when you get some income."

"Not as glad as I'll be."

"I'll come over Sunday as soon as Daddy gets back from Holy-Rolling."

"Okay. I'll let you get back to the radio."

"I'm listening to Memphis."

"Me too," Tollie lied.

Back in her bedroom, the door locked, Tollie knew she'd be able to take it, but it made her mad that you couldn't see your way out of the junk, ever. She tuned in a Clear Channel in the dark and heard the loamy voice of Dinah Washington, singing her new hit song, about sunshine and flowers where there used to be rain. The lightning was very close now, and even the Clear Channel had static. The thunder was crashing right over the roof, but she still didn't hear any rain. Between crashes she could hear Janice moving frantically through the house unplugging things, and the dead silence from the living room. Tollie put her hand on her stomach: she felt sick.

Then Janice was rattling her doorknob. "Shut off that radio, Baby," she was saying. "Baby?" Tollie could hear the rising panic in her mother's voice. "Tollie?" Janice pleaded. "Cut off the radio? And unplug it! Do you want to burn this house down, and maybe the whole town with it?"

In the sun, waiting for the bus, Janice wondered again if she should have unplugged the radio in the bathroom. She'd unplugged the Water-Fan, cut off the coffee on the stove, checked the iron twice to make sure it was unplugged. She'd left a note for Tollie reminding her not to move the radio or to touch it while she was wet and to unplug the stove and the refrigerator and the lamps if a storm came up. But she couldn't get the radio off her mind. If she had unplugged it, Tollie would have just set it somewhere less safe. Would her daughter survive in this world?

She could feel the worry scattering her. She reached into her pocketbook, briefly touched the money that she'd taken from its secret place under the protective fireproof aluminum-coated cloth of the ironing board cover. She was going to use her own money. She had to, since they'd had to spend the money Les got from his guns at the Winn-Dixie. So much for school clothes. But he'd meant well. She wanted to spend her own money today anyway, or her daddy's money, more *directly* hers—wasn't it?—than her husband's money?

She located one of the Miltowns. She worked up a little saliva in her mouth and swallowed the pill, which stuck in her throat a second and left her with a small wound after it passed on. She already had her dime in her other fist. She could feel it slick with sweat. A layer of dust had settled on her arms and feet, on her sundress and sandals, from passing cars. She didn't mind the dress too much, since it was old and light-colored, though she hated that Tollie's careful ironing was for nothing, no match for the damage ten minutes out of the house could do. Her sandals were old too, black patent-leather. They looked awful covered with dust. Inside, her feet looked dirty, though she'd bathed them a half an hour ago. They looked swollen, knotted and flat. How long would she have to stand here? And when would they ever pave these streets? With the Mill cutting down, never. Was the radio set securely on the back of the toilet or was it at some dangerous angle, easy to topple? Had she closed the toilet's lid?

The air prickled with a sharp weed-smell, brought out by the heat. She could hear a dog barking somewhere down the street, but not a soul was visible anywhere, not even a car now. She surveyed Arlene's house, the last one you could see from the bus stop. Beyond it, Tollie slept or was getting up and getting ready for her shower. Would she see the note slipped under her door, aimed exactly at a clearing where it would stand out like a footprint in the sand of a desert island? Would she eat the strawberry jam and margarine sandwich wrapped in waxed paper and left for her on the kitchen table, cut into four neat pieces with just a butter knife? Read the I've gone window-shopping, I'll bring you something, Love?

At last. The bus was just coming into sight.

"Hey, Girl," Warren said as he opened the door with his lever. He moved the lever a little, making the door flutter dangerously near Janice's face.

"Don't mess with me this morning, Warren," Janice said, pulling herself up onto the step by the chrome bar. "I'm not in the mood."

"I'm in the mood for love," Warren said, winking at her and chewing his gum a little faster as he smiled.

Janice could see a dozen colored people sitting silently at the back of the bus. There weren't any white people.

"I don't know what makes you think you can talk to me any way you want to," she said, dropping her dime in the slot. "I wouldn't know you on the street. I have to see you behind the wheel of this bus, grinning like a jackass, or you're nobody I know at all." She could feel the negroes looking away.

"I don't mean nothing by it," Warren said, still grinning but looking mean anyway. He steered the bus away from the side of the road, sending up a flurry of dust that obscured Arlene's house as Janice looked down the aisle and out the back window.

"Then keep it to yourself," she said.

40

"You sure? You look like you could use a little attention, to me."

"I'm not that hard up." Janice grabbed the bar across a seatback as Warren sped up and the bus hit a hole in the road.

"Take a seat *Mis-ris* Ramsey, before you hurt yourself. You got a lot of seats to choose from this morning."

Out of weariness, Janice sat a couple of seats behind Warren, but she really wanted to go to the back of the bus, far away from his stupid dog-face. Why did women have to put up with every man they met?

She adjusted her skirt over her knees, aware of her hand, the whole palm still raw from dish detergent's collecting under her wedding band and starting a rash that spread. She'd been glad to take the ring off. Too-thin and dull in its few karats, it depressed her. Warren's sarcasm was to the point, she guessed. Being married wasn't necessarily any help. Unless you had the protection of the nice things to wear or carry or display that said your husband could take good care of you. Her cheap wedding band was nothing next to the fact that she had to ride the bus to town in an old faded sundress that didn't match its out-of-style bolero any more. Getting skinny and tired-looking wasn't much help either. It all just made her want to stay in the house the rest of her days.

The weeds along the road were straw-colored. The air coming in the window was hot and gritty. There were almost no cars on the road as the bus wound through the neighborhoods of small, old houses, then across a section of the old four-lane that had been by-passed. Huge turned-off neon signs, most of them broken in some way, rose from plots of weeds: Tropical Motel, Shangri-La Cottages-with-Kitchenette, Jim's Mobil Station, Florida Motor Inn, The Paradise Café, places that had once existed for tourists on their way to Florida, the names calculated to profit a little off of Florida in advance. Almost all the original businesses on the highway had closed after the Interstate had opened, but here and there, in the weeds, were occasional signs of activity: Sue Ling's Oriental Massage, Dixie Rooms for Rent, Scully's Pawn Shop, Mary's Adult Books and Entertainment. A few cars with stickers from the Base were parked on the cracked concrete in front of the Dixie Rooms, but the rest of the businesses looked woeful, set apart from their dead neighbors only by flashing arrows and "Open" signs propped in the windows. They probably do more at night, Janice concluded.

On the other side of the highway, the bus passed a dusty, treeless trailer park, its bus stop empty, then ran the length of a low-lying road lined with unpainted shacks up on brick and concrete supports, where Warren picked up more negroes, stopping the bus with the back door in front of them. Then he drove back to the highway and started downtown. They passed a tall white sign painted with a big red hand: "Madame Lucretia • Palmist • Advisor • The Future Foretold." It gave an address on B Street.

"Yep, plenty seats. Ain't nobody out today," Warren said, looking at Janice in the rearview. His face was white and shiny with sweat. The dark carets of his eyebrows shot up into the wide blank of his forehead, but the rest of his features were flat, without color.

"I see a bus half full of people myself," Janice said.

"I'd like to aim the damn thing off a bridge and jump out the door," Warren said viciously, not lowering his voice. "You know what I have to do every night when I take this bus back? I have to go around, seat by seat back there, and wipe the goddam promade off the seatcovers. Any day, if things keep on like they're going, I'm going to have to wipe every seat, back and front. I'll quit. They can have it. It smells like somebody took a shit in a seat back there, all day long. I'd just like to head the damn thing off a bridge."

"I don't smell anything," Janice said, reaching for the bell cord that sagged along the window. "Except maybe your breath. Let me off at the corner before The Dome."

"The Dome?" Warren said, grinning meanly again. "You must have sold something to be able to go shopping at The Dome, with the ladies. You want to sell me some? What you want, five dollars?"

"I'm going to report you to the bus company," Janice said, standing, holding on to the chrome rod near the bus's front door.

"Ten?"

"I swear it," Janice said. She felt like she was going to faint if she didn't get off the bus.

"Aw-ight," Warren said, pulling over but not opening the door. "And I'll just tell them you're crazy. They'd believe that, wouldn't they?" Warren opened the door with his lever, then slammed it shut in her face before she could get off. At the back of the bus, she could see a negro woman standing still and staring straight ahead near the door that had just shut in her face too.

"Stop it," Janice said.

"Look at that," Warren said, nodding his head toward the almost empty street. Only a few shoppers moved along the sidewalks in front of Belk's and The Jewel Box. A young couple turned into The Palm Court Restaurant and closed the door. The restaurant had an ice-covered Air Conditioned sign painted on its window. In the shade of the bank, as private-looking as a tomb, two negro men stood near their shoe-shine boxes. Others gathered in clumps across the Square, where the negro section of downtown began. Janice could see them talking with their hands in their pockets in front of a billiards room, an X of cuesticks painted on a sign over their heads, the sign of another Scully's pawn shop looming in the background. Negro men were also sitting on concrete ledges and moving slowly along the streets. Negro women were moving along the streets too, some holding children in their arms or by the hand. Right outside the door of the bus, Janice could see an older white man down on his knees with a spatula, frying an egg on the sidewalk, another man standing back in the shade with a camera, taking a picture.

"They say just mad dogs and niggers come out in the noon sun," Warren said, opening the door. Janice hurried down the steps and toward the streetcrossing. "You some kind of mad dog, ain't you, *Mis-ris* Ramsey?" he called after her. "Some kind of crazy bitch?"

Inside The Dome, Janice moved slowly down the tiled floor of The Promenade, which led to the main part of the store. The Promenade was a fragrant aisle of cosmetics, almost half a block long. There were islands of perfume and toiletries, tables covered with the newest no-iron fabrics or with layers of silk scarves, then laid with dresser sets, or soap and powder dishes arranged around vases of cloth flowers or around the china pedestals of two-sided makeup mirrors suspended in hoops, the mirrors twirling from normal reflection to magnified close-up at a touch. Straw baskets were tilted in studied overflowing: wrapped soaps from Europe, bath sponges from the Mediterranean Sea, an array of skin products made with seaweed and sea-algae, a sampling of citrus toiletries from a single manufacturer. Small footed dishes held amber beads of dissolvable bath oil, tiny soaps shaped like shells, the dried leaves and blooms of lavender and roses.

Along a counter that ran the whole length of the aisle, urn-shaped glass jars of cotton balls were spaced out every few feet. The counter was lined with leather stools, like a soda fountain made of glass. Here, a woman could have powders mixed just for her complexion, perfume mixed to exploit her own special chemistry, or she could sample the most expensive ready-made perfumes and powders from Paris. The saleswomen behind the counter wore pink smocks with "The Dome" embroidered in a silver cursive to the side of one lapel. They were themselves made up in great subtlety, their hair colored and combed in sophisticated ways.

The air-conditioning that had re-energized Janice a little when she'd come through The Dome's arched glass doors couldn't combat the sag of spirit she felt in looking at the counter. In all the years she'd been coming to the store, "just-looking," she had never even approached the counter, much less taken a seat. Not just because she couldn't afford any of the products; there were plenty of free samples set out. It was more that she felt she would have to purchase an enormous amount of merchandise—dress, hosiery, shoes, bag, a tasteful set of jewelry, even makeup—just to get to the place where someone could try to sell her something else.

At such times, the gap between her life and the lives of women who'd planned better than she had seemed dark and bottomless. She turned away from the counter in a vague shame, toward the more democratic islands and tables.

Though she had nothing in mind to buy from The Promenade, she couldn't hurry past these inviting displays, where no human assessments stood between women and hope. She moved slowly, taking her time, occasionally touching something or bending to put her nose to it. Her dress and dusty feet and dead hair didn't make her feel especially conspicuous, now that the counter was out of sight. By now, instinctively, expertly, she could evade saleswomen and other browsers by circling the displays away from their approaches. The store reminded her of New York City, of an endless selection of improvements and enhancers and possibilities. The smells alone made her linger. She paused to pick up a set of bath powder, spray perfume, and perfumed bath soap, packaged together in cellophane. The three products were arranged on straw-colored shredded paper, in an open straw basket with its lid underneath. The fragrance was called "Straw Hat." The display was decorated with a large straw hat tied with a ribbon whose bow was pinned with a nosegay of summery paper flowers. A discreet sign reminded the customer that the fragrance could be bought only in the summertime.

Janice put the set back on its shelf and picked up the sample atomizer and sniffed it. The perfume had a clean, new smell. She looked over her shoulder, then craned out and checked the counter. The saleswomen were busy with women seated on its stools in pastel linen dresses—managers' wives, she guessed, or officers' wives from the Base—wearing the new seamless stockings and pumps of straw or leather woven to look like straw. For a moment Janice felt frozen, as these women always made her feel, the atomizer suspended near her heart. Even their hair looked like it had been trimmed that morning, every single hair. They wore versions of Mrs. Eisenhower's short cut with bangs, some shorter, some curlier than others. On their laps, their straw clutch purses rested like large stuffed envelopes.

I wouldn't have wanted that, Janice thought. I didn't want that.

She wet her scarred wrist with a furtive squirt of the perfume, put the atomizer back where she'd found it, and moved casually to the next display. The scent of the perfume rose up like fresh air. Would I want it now, she wondered. Instead of what I have? Wouldn't I be a fool not to?

At the end of The Promenade, the tile turned into deep wall-to-wall carpet and the main part of the store opened up under a huge glass dome. Here were women's suits, dressy dresses and cocktail dresses, casual dresses and sportswear, fur stoles and fur coats, shoes, lingerie—each section separated by French settees and chairs decorated with gold-leaf and arranged around glass tables with copies of *Vogue* and *Town and Country* spread out like the pleats of a fan. There were strategic painted screens, potted palms, brass carts displaying reminders from The Promenade. Rich burgundy drapes with gold fringe and tassels opened into short hallways that led to dressing rooms, and just as the dome gave way to ceiling plaster, staircases led to The Mezzanine, where young women could buy formals and wedding gowns, to The Balcony, with its maternity fashions and baby clothes, and to The Aerie, a restaurant that served lunch and a 4 o'clock ladies' tea.

Janice was less comfortable under the dome's glass. In the generous spaces among the merchandise, there were few places to avoid the other women. She also wasn't sure what she was looking for, and so she had come to a stop out in the middle of an empty space. She felt the glances of passing shoppers, the more frank look of a saleswoman dressed in black, wearing gold-rimmed glasses that trailed two gold loops of chain, over whose lenses the woman peered like a raptor.

To avoid the woman's certain advance, Janice headed for the stairs to The Aerie.

Inside, seated at a table that overlooked the shoppers below from behind a wall of glass, Janice ordered a cup of coffee, and since it was lunchtime and the tables in demand, a cottage cheese and fruit plate. It was served with two pieces of melba toast.

I can't get away from it, Janice thought. The baby had begun his aborted teething on melba toast. Across the canyon of the main part of the store a large plaster stork on The Balcony dangled in its sling a plaster baby wearing a pretty yellow play suit.

Janice pushed the plate away and drank her coffee. *I loved that baby,* she thought, feeling herself listing toward one of the dangerous conversations she had with herself. *I loved him more than my own heart. You could see his veins through his skin like lines on a road map. He was perfect. When you bounced him up and down on your knee, he'd smile and go Ah, Ah, Ah. When he went "walking" on his tiptoes with his fists wrapped around my two fingers, he'd go Ah, Ah, Ah, smiling like his life-line was going to be long and deep and perfectly drawn. Diaper dipping down. Little Droopy Drawers. . . .*

"Is something wrong with that?" the young waitress asked, pointing to the fruit plate. She was dressed in a pink uniform with "The Dome" stitched in silver, too.

"I'm not as hungry as I thought I was," Janice said. The girl looked about Tollie's age, maybe a little older. *I can't get away from it long enough to take care of the baby I've got left.*

"Then I guess you won't want dessert? We've got something new, New York Cheesecake. I hear it's real good." The girl leaned in as she lifted Janice's plate from the table and grinned, whispering, "I haven't been able to slip a piece for myself yet."

"Did it really come from New York?" Janice said.

"Naw," the girl scoffed. "Henry, the cook, made it. But somebody from New York told him how to do it. I bet it *is* real good."

Janice hesitated. "Do you think I could buy a whole one? How big is it?"

"A whole *cake?* It's supposed to be real rich."

"I was thinking I could take it home," Janice said.

The girl looked doubtful. "It's a refrigerated cake. I don't know how far you have to go in this heat."

"Not too far," Janice said. "Could you ask?"

"I'll ask," the girl said, still looking skeptical.

46

Janice finished her coffee, mentally tallying what she might need to buy against the money in her pocketbook. Money her mother had slipped her on her wedding day, leftovers from what Daddy had left her mother. Secret money, emergency money. She'd never spent a dime of it until now.

On the way to town she had thought of getting herself a pair of the new seamless nylons. If she were wearing hose, then the dust on her feet wouldn't look so bad. She'd wait on them. She wouldn't be able to wear them with her sandals anyway; the dark reinforced toes and heels of the stockings would look awful with sandals, as bad as seams up the back of your legs. The nylons were $3.50, a shocking price. A cake couldn't cost any more than that.

"Four dollars!" the girl breathed, scandalized, coming back to Janice's table. "It's not even as big as a regular cake either."

"Can they wrap it for me?"

"Well, sure." The girl seemed insulted.

"Do you have any birthday candles?"

The girl hesitated. "I'll check. But I have to take care of my other customers first."

"Take all the time in the world," Janice said, her heart pounding with the extravagance of the cheesecake. She would hide it in the freezing compartment of the frigidaire until Tollie's birthday. If she could get candles, and if she could save up just a little energy to make a sugar icing to decorate the cake, it would be as good as having baked a birthday cake. Better: a New York Cheesecake. Someone who liked the outside world like Tollie did would be happier with that than with a homebaked cake.

"It'll be a dime more for the candles," the girl said. "Is that all?" She scribbled out the check before Janice could answer.

"A little more coffee," Janice said. She needed a minute to calm down from the unexpected, impetuous purchase.

"That's free," the girl said.

"That's good," Janice said.

Back on the bus Janice sat as far from Warren as she could, just in front of the silent negroes, most of them maids going home from other women's houses. The negroes rode the bus apologetically, she thought, rarely talking among themselves and never to a white person. They sat up straight, with their feet flat on the floor and their hands always visible. Usually the fingers were laced together, as if they wanted everyone to know, every minute, what their hands were doing.

Warren's baby-blue battery-powered radio was turned up loud on the floor near his seat. For once, Warren seemed transported, tapping his white fingers energetically on the steering wheel. The song seemed familiar to Janice, and also unfamiliar, a snappier arrangement than what she almost remembered . . . a shark's bite, scarlet billows. . . .

She hugged her shopping bag in her lap, the cheesecake cool against her legs through box, bag, dress and slip. She was exhausted. She didn't know whether she'd be able to make icing decorations or not. She'd had to rest almost a half an hour on a lounger in the restroom of The Dome, but finally she'd got the shopping part of it done. She'd found a plaid sundress in Tollie's size, made of very soft cotton, its weave so fine the material felt like air against your hand. She hadn't known that there was a grade of cotton that could produce a fabric like that, and wondered if even her Daddy, a cotton broker, would have known it, if he had been alive to pinch and pull apart its boll, or whether it was some kind of advanced species. It seemed like something new, as if cotton, in its last hours, had surpassed its ordinary self and was fighting for its life. It was a well-made dress, she felt good about that. After all, she'd been a seamstress on 7th Avenue in another life. She had standards. The dress had good-sized seams, fine stitching, attention to detail, style. Double spaghetti straps, the top edged with a trace of red rickrack, the color muted to blend in with the other muted colors. It was all so subtle, that's what you paid for.

Janice felt a cool bolt of nervousness shoot through her stomach, remembering that the dress had cost $24.00. She hadn't brought enough money with her and had had to put it on lay-away. She felt another nervous bolt. She was saving her money for something more important than Tollie's having one of the last, best cotton dresses before they became extinct. Though that was important too. Especially since it was Daddy's money, fitting that some of it was going for an exceptional grade of cotton. But the money had always been for some unknown but certain to come emergency. Without money in an emergency, things could get worse than you ever dreamed . . . Someone could be sneaking round the corner. . . .

Now Janice remembered the song. She'd heard it in New York with Tollie's father. They'd gone to see a play, "One Touch of Venus," and afterward he'd been disappointed.

"It was just something for entertainment," he'd said.

Janice had been puzzled. The play *had* been entertaining. Wasn't it supposed to be?

The next week he had brought her a record player and a record, the real stuff, he'd said. This was one of the record's songs, "Mack the Knife," but by a different singer. The album had been witty, insinuating. Tollie's father had sung part of it in German, which he had studied at college. He thought it was silly not to keep up his German, just because of the War. He made a point of speaking German on the street and in taxis, taking her to German restaurants. He said the other attitude was smalltown, petty.

. . . immoral, she was thinking now, listening to the new singer's version. Could it be our boy's done something rash? Our boy . . . for a murderer?

Janice wanted the song to be over. It was threatening, too close to home.

It ended in a flourish. The disk jockey picked up on it.

"Ol' Mackie'll be right back after this message from The Dome Ladies Department Store, a little bit of New York City and Paris, France, right here in Hope Mills—"

This reminded Janice of the other extravagance in her shopping bag, the "Straw Hat" trio, the "something" she'd promised to bring Tollie. She felt herself smiling, trying to forget the money she'd spent: on Tollie, on bus fare, on lunch, on the cake, which they would all eat.

She caught her reflection in the window as they passed in the shadow of a warehouse and she resumed a straight face. But she could feel herself smiling inside, an almost foreign feeling. It would be a rare good day for Tollie. She deserved something better than 16-year-old bath powder. It was only money.

The bus passed along the littered edge of downtown, moving slowly in the mid-afternoon traffic. The heat coming in the window hit Janice's face like exhaust. Warren's loud radio and the obnoxious disk jockey were getting on her nerves. Had Tollie remembered to unplug the radio? Was she ironing right now? Would she remember to unplug the iron?

The bus stopped for a red light and the air stopped dead-still. At the Mobil pump outside the window, a boy was filling the tank of a

49

long, new car. From her high vantage in the bus, Janice could only see a woman's long white arms and covered legs inside the car, arranged in the driver's seat, her blue sheath that seemed to match the car's paint. The car looked like something Janice had seen on a television show about the Future. Was the Future already here? It seemed impossible.

The boy finished polishing the woman's windshield, then began to wipe at the chrome. In the backseat, the brown forearms of the woman's housekeeper ended in hands folded on a purse in her lap. *You could get off at the house,* Janice argued with herself. *You could get off at the house and check on her.*

When the light changed and the bus took off in a hot diesel-scented rumble, Janice found herself looking back, catching a glimpse of the white woman's face. It was edged with a blond pageboy tucked behind her ears and half-hidden by sunglasses whose dark green lenses were aimed straight ahead. The woman was holding the car's cigarette lighter to her cigarette and puffing, defying the gas pump's fumes. The negro woman in the backseat was invisible now and the boy too, perhaps down on the ground checking the tires. Next to the station was a row of shiny red rental trailers, something new in town.

Janice tried to relax. If a woman could light a cigarette next to that much gas and not blow herself up, things weren't as dangerous as they seemed.

But she couldn't relax. She could feel things tilting in her mind, a 45-degree angle instead of straight ahead. *I should get off at the house and check on her. Rowen Faircloth isn't going anywhere.*

The bus drove past a group of men putting up a pumpkin-colored revival tent, past an ugly drive-in restaurant with a glass box of a tower, "Kastle in the Air" barely readable without its neon lit, past a man sitting on the tailgate of his old pickup, its bed full of watermelons. There couldn't be water in the watermelons in a dry summer like this. Who'd be stupid enough to buy one? *Swallowed a watermelon seed. Never, never a trace of red.*

Janice felt inside her purse for a Miltown and slipped it into her mouth. They were driving along the Cape Fear River, its water low, not moving. The street was unpaved, full of ruts.

The bus passed Madame Lucretia's low, peeling house, her sign with its large red hand, its palm crisscrossed with black lines.

"I wish they close her down," one of the negro woman behind Janice said to her companion in a low voice. "Voodoo, you ask me. Folks call her The Creature."

"Woman got to make a living somehow. They's worst ways," the other woman said.

"Jesus forgive most of *them.*"

The women fell silent again. Janice rested her head against the seat-back and closed her eyes. She could no longer feel the refreshing coolness of the cheesecake against her lap. Her nylon slip was clinging to her like a repulsive skin.

After Warren had left downtown, crossed the highway and crossed back, he made his circle through the neighborhoods near the Mill. He stopped at Janice's stop and opened the door, grinning, trying to catch her eye in the large mirror above his head. She kept her eyes down.

After a minute, he closed the door and drove on out in the country, re-absorbed in the music, but never missing the bell cord's sound. Ears like a jackass too, Janice thought. He always stopped at her stop and opened the door, grinned his jackass grin.

She stood up and pulled the bell cord, gathered her packages and pocketbook.

"Don't do nothing I wouldn't do," Warren called to her as she left by the back door. "And if you do, name it after me."

Tollie and Lily were lined up with the sun's rays on a blue blanket that was one of the Mill's mistakes. Lily's father took these home as secret bonuses. Though it was still August, and the temperature almost a hundred degrees, it was beginning to look like fall, Tollie observed. Most of the shriveled foliage had fallen off the deciduous trees, leaving the tall longleaf and loblolly pines all around Rolando's Beach the only green in sight. The Beach was packed with people, the water of the manmade lake bobbing with plastic rafts and rubber tires. High above, a blimp lettered in red, "Rolando's Beach and Dance Pavilion," drifted lazily, its message cloudy in the humidity. Rolando himself— sunburnt, middle-aged, his beer-belly ballooning out the oxford cloth shirt above his madras bermudas—presided up on the lifeguard's bench, sipping from a paper cup. A large thermos of whatever it was rested at his feet—something boozy, Tollie felt sure. Rolando's face was shiny as a beacon, and when he talked to the lifeguard, little spumes of something gathered in the corners of his mouth, visible to Tollie from the slits of her eyes forty feet away.

All around the beach portable radios cracked with static, unless they were tuned to WMIL, whose familiar music and half intelligible Mack-talk reached the blanket from several directions, like a new kind of electronic sound Tollie had read would be on the market soon. Lily seemed tuned out, but Tollie sang along in her mind to the best Oldies from 1957 and 1958—"Blueberry Hill," "Lucille," "Twilight Time."

She tuned out the worst: "You Are My Destiny" (Paul Anka, whining through his nose), "Love Me Tender" (old Elvis Presley, sounding like he was about to go to sleep with cotton in his mouth), "All the Way" (Frank Sinatra—!). She had too much trouble in the back of her mind to listen to that junk. It was so boring it let the trouble get to the front of your mind.

Tonight the beach would be empty, except for blankets spread far apart in the dark for couples making out, but the pavilion would be packed with dancing fools, as Lily kept remarking. Then the fun would start: rock 'n' roll.

Tollie had never been to the dances at Rolando's Beach, but Lily insisted that she was going to drag her to one before the summer was over: "So you can *meet somebody,* for Jesus sake!" Tollie didn't know if she could rock 'n' roll or not, though she'd practiced a lot in her bedroom, holding onto the doorknob like it was a boy's hand, following the steps she'd observed on Teen Tyme, a local dance show on WMIL-TV that imitated American Bandstand, all the popular girls from school wearing their angora sweater sets and soft pleated skirts from Scotland, all the popular boys in crewnecks, also from Scotland, or bleeding madras shirts and neat khaki pants—nothing as interesting as the clothes Bill and Justine wore on the real American Bandstand in faraway Philadelphia.

Tollie looked up at the edges of the pines and blurred her vision by half-closing her eyes, trying to imagine the pines were palm trees, that she was on a real beach, on the Mediterranean Sea or the Caribbean Sea. That the pinecones were coconuts.

The pinecones looked like pinecones. Or stunted pineapples, but she didn't think pineapples grew on palm trees. Pine apples. She'd never though of them that way before.

She squinted her eyelashes toward each other, cross-hatching the pines, trying harder to transport herself to the land of palms. She closed her eyes in defeat.

"Is my hair getting any lighter?" Lily asked.

"I can't see it," Tollie said.

"Well, *look,*" Lily said.

"I'm resting my eyes," Tollie said.

Lily grabbed Tollie's forearm and gave it a yank.

"Okay!" Tollie said. She sat up and looked at Lily, whose neck was resting on a fuchsia tube of rolled towel, another of the Mill's mistakes.

Their beach towels, spread out beside the blanket for when the blanket got too hot or wet, were mistakes too, dark blue and bright green, one printed with the moon and stars above a nighttime ocean swimming with silvery fish, the other with a tropical beach scene, a large palm arching across the foreground.

Lily had pulled down the straps on her bathing suit and tucked them into the top so she wouldn't have lines on her shoulders. Tollie's suit was Lily's last year's suit, but she didn't mind; it was new to her.

Other people were looking at Lily too, Tollie noticed: at the eight-inch-wide band in the middle of the new black bathing suit Lily had ordered from the back of a romance magazine. The band of material had checkerboard cut-outs and Lily's bare belly showed through in square-inches, her navel framed like a picture. She was greased with her special tanning formula, cottonseed oil mixed with iodine. The iodine gave her skin a purplish-yellow cast, like a piece of copper that needed polishing.

"Well?" Lily demanded.

Tollie couldn't tell if she was being observed from behind Lily's "sunglasses" or not. Lily had broken her real sunglasses a few days before and now she was wearing a pair of 3-D glasses she'd got at the movies. "I can't splurge on a pair of sunglasses this late in the summer," she'd said impatiently when Tollie had stared at her putting them on. "Not for a few last days at Rolando's Beach. Nobody I care about will get here till after dark anyway."

By now, Tollie was wishing she had a pair of 3-D glasses. If she kept having to sit up and squint at Lily's hair every five minutes, she'd have white lines in her tan, like crowsfeet before her time.

"I can't tell," she said. "Your hair's got oil in it."

"Maybe I better go in the water, then re-do it." Lily sat up, holding onto each side of the bathing suit's top. "Do you think I can get down to the water like this or is it going to slip down and give everybody a peek of Heaven?"

"It's going to slip and show a boob," Tollie said emphatically. "Before you even get yourself up off the blanket, like it did when you put your straps down."

"So what?" Lily said. "Nobody saw but you anyway. And don't sound like I did it on purpose."

Tollie had seen. She was surprised to see that Lily's breast was so mature. It swelled against her skin so firmly that the skin almost looked strained, and it had a much more graceful shape than it did in the pointy bras Lily liked to wear. The nipple was tiny and brown. It looked like a hard little acorn, but smooth where a real acorn was rough.

"I'm going to go like this," Lily said, throwing the 3-D glasses on the blanket and scooting away from Tollie. She grabbed the suit's top firmly in the middle, pushing herself up quickly with her other hand. Tollie couldn't tell if anyone had got a peek of Heaven or not. "Get my hair stuff out," Lily said over her shoulder as she started toward the lake. "And rub some of that lemon juice on your own hair. You look like a mouse."

Tollie hated the way Lily bossed her around, and instructed. Just because it was her daddy's car, her last year's bathing suit . . . because her father was a Foreman now? They'd become friends again, after Ramírez was out of the picture, though Tollie wasn't sure what the connection was. Misery loved company, she guessed. Lily and Big Mack were what Lily's movie magazines called P-f-f-f-t! But Lily was still the new Lily. They'd never be little girls together again. That struck Tollie as sad, though she didn't know what she'd expected. They couldn't be little girls forever. Boy, was that ever true! They were grown up, whether they were ready for it or not.

She watched Lily walk to the water, swaying her hips a little like Marilyn Monroe did, but not as extreme. Not even Lily would walk like that in public, looking like a cartoon.

Tollie heard a wolf whistle and tried to follow its sounds among the Mack-sounds. Rolando. She could see him watching Lily behind his sunglasses, the shirt opened now, his beer-belly poufed up like a large beach ball. The sight of it made Tolly automatically run her hand down over her own stomach. When Lily disappeared into the water, Tollie saw Rolando turn back to the lifeguard and say something. The two of them laughed a little, like men and boys always seemed to do when they watched a girl or a woman together.

Tollie had heard about Rolando. Everybody in Hope Mills had. The beach was just one of the properties he was involved in—"my toy," he told the Living section of the newspaper. "'You could say it's where I got my feet wet,' Roland W. McLaurin laughed," the reporter reported.

Ho ho. His toy! His place to sniff out fresh meat, Tollie thought, watching Rolando drinking his drink, casting his eyes about.

In the article's photograph, Rolando had been leaning up against his shark-like Cadillac convertible, which—right now—was parked in the parking lot next to the beach's admission booth. In the photo's background were the skinny, stunted palms Tollie had seen down at the real beach, the time Les had taken her and Janice. "Somebody is always trying to get those darn things to grow," Janice had said at the time. "It's hopeless." But Tollie had liked them. She'd liked them a lot, until she saw how puny they looked in the photographs of Rolando.

Everybody said that Rolando had bought up a lot of land around Hope Mills for nothing years ago, and that he'd made a million dollars already just selling business lots along the Interstate. They said he was in business with people in Florida and New York and California. Nobody knew what kind of business, though they assumed it had something to do with real estate. "I've got a lot of interests," he'd conceded when the reporter had mentioned it. "But I'm a home-town boy. Basically, I'm a hometown boy, and I do most of what I do right around here, where it'll benefit Hope Mills."

In the Hope Mills *Observer,* the hometown boy advertised "Coastal Property on the Installment Plan," $10 down and $10 a week for twenty years, for a half acre. Janice said it was junk ground south of Whiteville, miles from the beach, sandy and full of scrub pines, flat as a sheet of paper and close to a dump that the Army used for something. But people were clipping the coupons out of the newspaper, sending in their $10 and buying the lots sight unseen. Lily's father had bought two of them, side by side, though Tollie had tried to warn him. He said he was gong to build a dream house there and retire.

Rolando refilled his paper cup from the thermos, stood up on the lifeguard's bench and turned his back to the water, surveying the blankets laid at his feet. Young girls were what he liked, people said. He rested his drink on his belly, the wristwatch shining like a band of stars. His name fits him, Tollie thought—Rol, like roly-poly; ol, like oily; land, he had it; do(ugh), he had that too.

Rolando's eyes skimmed across Tollie, backed up for about an eighth of a second and moved on. So what? Tollie thought. If a creep like that got interested in me, I'd wonder if I didn't have a disease.

She looked away, her eyes lighting on a nice-looking boy in red swimming trunks making his way onto the beach from the parking lot. He had a white towel around his neck, and he was carrying a paperback book. He was walking right toward her, like someone coming to her in a dream. Tanned, sand-colored hair. Nice medium size. Sunglasses. Who was he?

57

"Hi," he said when he was a few feet away. He smiled at her.

"Hi," she said. She smiled back, but she felt shy; she had to look down.

When she looked back up he had already passed her blanket and was heading toward Rolando, who had stood up and was motioning him over. Well, if he was a friend of that creep, forget it—!

Tollie picked up the straw-colored tote bag that was full of things Lily thought she might need before the day was over. She began to look for the peroxide with a few drops of Clorox that must be in there somewhere, Lily's Beauty Shoppe in a Bottle. She fished out a baby-blue transistor radio, cut it on, found nothing but static, cut it off and set it aside. Lily didn't like listening to the radio much anymore, now that she and Big Mack were finished. Tollie didn't care to listen to it either, out here on the beach where you could listen to human voices having a good time in the water. All you heard on the radio now, anyway, was Khrushchev's visit. How some people were glad about it and others thought it was a dangerous mistake. A Negro woman in Hope Mills had named her baby Nikita Khrushchev and it was in the *Observer.* Tollie didn't know what she thought of Khrushchev. He looked a lot like Ike to her, two old farts farting around on tv while mills were closing and soldiers were being shipped out to parts unknown. She wondered if Ramírez had been sent any of those places in the news. She hadn't seen him since Bomb Day, nor heard a word about him, though she and Lily had sometimes circled the Kastle in the Air at night in the Oldsmobile so that Lily could give the finger to Big Mack up in the tower, even if he probably couldn't see it. Once, after she'd cooled off about being dumped, Tollie had sent a request up to the tower by a carhop, "From T. R. to T. R." Ramírez' first name was Tomás, but he had liked to call himself *No más,* saying he didn't take *no more* shit. She'd dedicated "Think It Over" by Buddy Holly (Old Mackie always said, By the Late, Great Buddy Holly), but she'd never heard another word from Ramírez. Maybe he hadn't heard the song. Maybe he was on his way to Indochina or Lebanon or the Suez Canal or one of a hundred other places the two old farts kept sending soldiers off to. She liked Fidel Castro herself. She'd like to go live on a beach in Cuba. Marry Fidel Castro, make him shave his beard and get some decent clothes—they could be King and Queen of an Island. She didn't mind the Russians, particularly—not like most people, who said they'd rather be dead than Red and all that junk. For all she knew, she might be a Russian herself. She had a Russian name, Tanya, even if nobody would call her by it. The only thing she held against the Russians was sending a rabbit up into space. She'd seen its picture in the paper: it had looked scared to death. She didn't understand how they could do that, or send up dogs and monkeys and everything else they were planning to send up there. Why didn't they send cameras or robots?

Tollie looked back at the lifeguard's bench. Rolando was sitting down again, the cute boy gone. She looked around but didn't see him anywhere. She looked up at the blimp, which had receded from the beach and was drifting high up, out beyond where the water gave way to the sandy ground that was the part of the army base used for maneuvers, off limits. It would probably take ten years off her life just to go up that high. She'd probably die if somebody shot her into outer space.

She turned away from the water and the sun and tackled Lily's tote bag. She pulled out Lily's lipstick, her mascara, eyelash curler, a plastic lemon full of juice, and an old greasy, dog-eared copy of *Peyton Place* that had probably been passed around to every woman Lily's mother knew, a spray bottle of Avon's Persian Wood, a toothbrush, another lipstick, Nos-kote, Ipana, a plastic bottle of the purplish-yellow tanning oil, a rubber—A rubber? Jesus. Tollie looked at it thoughtfully and slipped it back into the bag. How in the world was Lily going to give a boy a rubber? Some remark about being a good Girl Scout, always prepared? That sounded like her. Billfold. Tweezers, a glass jar of deodorant pads. A few cotton balls that had picked up bits of this and that from being loose in the tote bag, making them look like real cotton out in the field. On WMIL-TV's "Viewpoint," some politician had said getting out of the cotton business was a good thing, that it was cotton that had enslaved the Negroes and still enslaved them as cotton pickers, that cotton was a symbol of evil. Tollie stuffed the cotton balls back in the tote before they got any more dirt on them. That was junk. Getting rid of cotton wouldn't free the Negroes from hard work. It would just get rid of a good material and the Negroes would be working their butts off doing something else, like handling dangerous substances to make Easy-Care. She felt sure it was made of some dangerous substance. By now she'd felt Easy-Care. It felt like something crawling on your skin. It did crawl on your skin: she and Lily had tried on dresses made out of it at Belk's.

Ice-o-Derm—that would be good for your tan! A pack of Winstons. *Datebook* magazine. A handmirror about the size of the cigarette pack. An over-blouse. Clorets. Noxema. A tampax *and* a Kotex, hiding together in a little crumbled paper sack. White Rain shampoo. A large

59

glass jar that must be the peroxide and Clorox, but why stop now? A pair of rubber flip-flops, a necklace, a change-purse full of change, a scarf, a hot pink swimming cap that ruffled up like a rubber flower.

"Haven't you found it yet?" Lily said, standing in front of Tollie with her fists ground into her checkered waist. "You're just using this as an excuse to go through my things, Tollie Ramsey."

"Well?" Tollie said. "I got interested. Here's your old hair stuff." She held out the glass jar toward Lily.

"It is *not!*" Lily reached down and jerked the jar out of Tollie's hand and put it back in the tote bag. "That's something else. Give me that bag."

Lily found the peroxide and started to put her things away. "I swear," she said.

"That's what you get for treating me like your lady-in-waiting." Tollie picked up *Peyton Place* and looked at the author's picture on the back, a sickly looking woman at her typewriter, wearing a plaid shirt and jeans. That woman didn't look like she could know much about the things that were in the novel—"the steamy novel," someone always said when they referred to it in print or on the radio, which they used to do a lot, especially when it was being made into a movie. Tollie had read it. It was steamy—things she'd never read about before. Tollie squinted at the woman. Did she know about those things? Pregnancy, abortion, virgins de-virgined in sinister or brutal ways? Maybe so. She looked as beaten down as Janice did.

Thinking of her mother depressed Tollie. Janice, sad and tired, moving between bed and daybed. Except for an afternoon every week or so when she'd fix herself up and go to town on the bus to window-shop, then drag home and lie down. Tollie didn't understand why her mother put herself through a wringer just to window-shop. If that was all it was. . . . Even when Janice bought something, like the "Straw Hat" stuff, you couldn't enjoy it, knowing it had worn her out to go get it. Not to mention, worry about where she'd got the money. Not to mention, you had to hide anything new from Les. Tollie felt her mood sink lower.

Lily gripped both sides of the bathing suit's top between her thumbs and fists and plopped back down on the blanket. She began to survey her face in the little handmirror. "I better leave these glasses off or I'm going to have white circles."

"Can I wear them?" Suddenly Tollie wanted to see a different world.

Lily shrugged. "It's a free country and they were also free. You probably do want to take care of your eyes. So you can see what's right under your nose."

"What does that mean?"

"Janice and Rowen, sitting in a tree."

"Shut up! It's not true." Tollie put on the glasses. God. They hurt her eyes, but she didn't care. Penance, just for being alive and at the beach!

"Aw-right. *You* should know, I guess. I think I'd better let my hair dry out before I re-do it. I can't tell what color it's getting to be. Besides, if my hair's wet, the peroxide might run. It could drip down on my bathing suit and ruin it too. I was thinking that if I just bleached one streak—following the wave that comes across like this?—it'd be a nice effect."

"Have you been thinking about that all this time?" Tollie said irritably. Sometimes she couldn't believe the way Lily's mind could stay on the subject of herself and her looks.

"No," Lily said sarcastically, shaking the fuchsia towel from its roll and beginning to dry her hair. "I been laying out there in the water thinking about the Suez Canal and old Khrushchev and World War Three and what it's going to be like for all those monkeys and dogs circling around the moon, what do you think?"

"I think I'd like to get together with you a little later for a game of checkers." A man had suddenly materialized at the edge of the blanket. Tollie and Lily looked up at him. He was old, thirty or forty, Tollie thought, not good-looking but cocky anyway. He wasn't wearing a bathing suit but a pair of nice-looking bermuda shorts and an open pinstriped shirt with its sleeves rolled up. Nice loafers, no socks. A gold watch on a leather band and some sort of special-looking ring.

"When Hell freezes over," Lily said. She began to comb peroxide through a segregated section of her hair.

"How about chess, then? You be the Queen and I'll be the King and we'll Mate."

"If you don't leave me alone, I'm going to tell the lifeguard." Lily scowled at the man.

He grinned at her.

"You're really provoking me, shithead," Lily said.

"I'm scared, Mill Rat. If you don't want people messing with you, why you showing off your belly to the whole world?"

"I show it off to remind creeps like you of everything they're not going to get in life," Lily said. She picked up the open bottle of peroxide. "And if that don't sit well with them and they start acting mean, like you are, I think of my naked belly as the one last beautiful sight they're going to see before I put their eyes out with this bleach." She leapt up and aimed the bottle toward his chest. A little of the liquid slogged out onto his nice loafer.

The man jumped back. "You little whore, watch what the hell you're doing!"

"Lily—" Tollie said.

"Hey, Wiggins," another man who looked a lot like this man yelled from the food stand. "What you want to drink?"

The first man looked at his friend, then abruptly put his hands in the pockets of his shorts and started toward him.

"*Lily*—" Tollie said again.

"I guess my aim's not as good as it was," Lily called after the man. "I usually get the eyes the first time."

"Screw you," the man said over his shoulder. He kept on going for several feet, then turned around and started walking backwards, grinning again. "Hey Mill Rat," he called to Lily. "Better pull up that bathing suit or somebody's going to want to play push-ups with you."

"Shit," Lily whispered, yanking up her bathing suit top to cover her exposed nipple and sitting down hard.

"I tried to tell you," Tollie said, glancing at Rolando smiling from the lifeguard's bench, his sunglasses pointed toward Lily. She was glad the cute boy was gone, that he hadn't seen *this* spectacle.

"Well I wished you'd tried harder!" Lily said, glaring at the people on the nearby blankets. "I hope they get their goddam eyes full."

She yanked a plastic bag of bronze-colored cyclinders out of the tote bag and began to section off her hair and roll it. Rolando had turned away and was talking to a tall redhead in a white one-piece bathing suit with a halter-strap and a low top. She looked like the actress in "God's Little Acre," Tina Louise. She looked too sophisticated to be from Hope Mills. Probably a soldier's wife or girlfriend or sister, Tollie thought. The beach was full of people from somewhere else, their accents buzzing in the air like bee-sounds. Oriental women, Oriental kids. Or half-Oriental, she guessed. Soldiers' families—maybe the soldiers from Indochina they were rumored to be training out at the Base. Though probably not. Those soldiers probably came alone, like the dark men in odd uniforms from Guatemala, El Salvador, Honduras, that Ramírez *hadn't* introduced her to in the parking lot of The Kastle in the Air—!—though he'd, grudgingly, answered some of her questions about them, like, Did they bring their wives and children: answered with a look alone.

Tollie watched Rolando climb down from the stand, reach up for his thermos, and walk off with his arm around the woman's waist.

"I just wish the jerk hadn't made that Mill Rat remark," Lily said after a while. Tollie was surprised to see that a thin wash of tears lay across Lily's eyes.

"Forget it," Tollie said. "He's just some old Wiggins. It's junk." Of course it wasn't junk, and about a hundred Wiggins people owned half the county. Not junk at all. It was the truth, the truth that hurt. The truth that leapt out and jabbed you just when you thought everything was going all right: somebody suddenly drew the line and made you feel like you weren't made of flesh and blood, or maybe that you were, she didn't know. Just that they made you feel like you were low quality, goods made out of inferior material—maybe flesh and blood, while they felt like they were made out of gold and silver, or air.

That spring, at school, Tollie had had a moment of hope when her class had read Shakespeare's play *The Merchant of Venice*. Mr. Thornton recited, in his dramatic, beautiful voice, "Hath not a Jew eyes . . . hands . . . organs . . . dimensions . . . ," measuring it out without even looking at his book, pacing slowly across the front of the classroom with the book resting on his heart. " . . . senses . . . affections . . . passions?" She'd thought the kids would laugh, but they hadn't. They'd sat still and listened, hypnotized by Shakespeare and Mr. Thornton. Tollie had thought: At last. They'll see.

But they hadn't seen. Nothing changed. "Mill Rat" and the attitude that went with it were as common as the mockingbirds in the trees. Before the week was out, she'd heard Mr. Thornton himself say "Mill Rat," joking with one of the Managers' kids, and she'd lost all respect for him, and for Shakespeare too. What was the good of a play like that if people could listen and believe and then forget so fast, or just not be able to transport an idea from one place to another? Not one bit of good. And people like old Thornton were too stupid to have the fate of a whole town of kids in their hands, Mill Rats and tormentors of Mill Rats alike. In her own private gradebook—which naturally counted for nothing in the world that was not-Tollie, but still, everybody ought

63

to have one or what were you?—she gave Thornton an F, with "comments": Showed promise, but fell asleep during the test.

"They act like if your daddy works down *in* the Mill you haven't got feelings," Lily said, clipping some hair around a curler with a long aluminum clip that looked like the beak of a stork. "They act like we're another brand of animal!"

Tollie watched the beak half disappear inside the roller and clamp shut. "Oh, come on," she said, impatient with Lily. She had bigger problems than Lily's crocodile tears, and besides—! "You've been lording it over me, in *little* ways, ever since your daddy got to be Foreman."

Lily paused and gave her a look, her curlers bobbing. "You're crazy."

"No I'm not," Tollie said. "Think about what you just said, too. That's how you think about the Negroes, not to mention Puerto Ricans. You won't even go to the trouble of saying 'Negro' or 'colored,' you just throw around 'nigger' like these shitheads throw around 'Mill Rat.' Don't you think Negroes have eyes? Hands? Organs? Dimensions, senses, affections? Passions?"

"What in the world are you rambling on about?" Lily said, losing her hold on a clump of hair that she'd almost completed wrapping around a roller. Her irises shifted slightly as she looked from one lens of the 3-D glasses on Tollie's eyes to the other.

She's probably checking the pattern of her rollers, Tollie thought, guardedly, behind the glasses. And yet she could almost swear she had seen something like surprise in Lily's eyes, and for one amazing moment, recognition.

Lily placed her order at the food stand and went into the restroom. In the stall, she squatted above the commode, eased the leg of her bathing suit over and took a leak. Her eyes were fixed on the green concrete floor, her feet planted at the blurry borders of her vision. They didn't seem like feet when she looked at them like this, without focusing. They seemed to be something else. The bright blue rubber of her flipflops cut across the tan color of her skin and curved out of sight against the green floor, like a leaf-shape or two skinny blue paths that ran together out in the distance of a landscape she was viewing from way on high. The ten pink spots of her toes could be pink houses, or a garden of hew-mong-us flowers out where the paths met up. Or it could all just be geometry. Pink squares, most of a blue triangle, ten tan-pink rectangles, big old green square underneath.

It was a kind of game she played with herself. Slipping into a special kind of vision that could take the most ordinary thing and make it like something out of a movie, or a cartoon. It was refreshing to make up a different world and then to look down on it. It was refreshing to transport yourself to some other place *on* the earth, not above it— mind over matter, like her mother, Marie, was always saying anybody with half a brain could do, and if you had a *whole* brain and your wits about you, like Lily Jones most certainly did, no matter what they thought at school when they'd herded her into the secretarial course with all the other Mill Rats, you could look around any old ordinary place in Hope Mills, like this bathroom or the inside of a grocery store, and say, I'm inside a bathroom or grocery store in New York City or Paris, France, or Hollywood, California, and right outside that door there's everything I need to become everything I ever dreamed I could. They're waiting for me out there, breathing hard and tapping their feet!

She patted herself as dry as she could with the skimpy sheets of non-absorbent paper that always collapsed out of the dispenser all at once, most of them ending up on the wet floor where they stuck to your shoes and then trailed you for half a mile. Who'd invented a thing like that? She kept holding the leg of her suit over and pinched up into the dispenser for the last of the paper. It excited her to pull the leg of her suit over. She could imagine some cute boy doing the same, or some rich helpful older man, whether he was cute or not, as long as he wasn't too disgusting, like that jerk who wanted to play checkers on her belly, or Rolando McLaurin, pig of pigs. She'd seen him watching her on the beach. Well, just let him fry in his own grease. Someone like Rolando wouldn't be helpful at all, he'd set you back.

Mack had pulled the leg of her panties over a few times, a quickie. She didn't know why it was so exciting, but it was. Maybe because it was so . . . direct. Getting right down to business. She liked the idea of the man and the woman all dressed in their clothes, just baring the essentials. Why should you have to go through all that I-love-you-honey-sugar-molasses pie? Take off this, take off that, take up the whole night out in the boonies when you could be at a dance or the show or some place where people could see you? She liked to be direct, at least where men and boys were concerned. Wham-bam-thank-you-Sam. As long as the bam wasn't *too* quickie. That was sort of insulting.

Not that she'd even done it at all anytime lately, she thought, releasing her bathing suit's leg and standing up. That seemed unnatural, a healthy girl in the prime of life drying up like an old prune for lack of anybody suitable. Somebody really suitable you could be more or less direct with, some of the time. She saved the undirect stuff, blue paths leading to pink gardens, for herself alone, whenever she needed to refresh herself or had to kill a couple of minutes squatting over a john.

She flushed the toilet with her foot and went out to the line of sinks. She worked soap around the getting-tighter-every-day Sweetheart ring—two silver hearts entwined with a real diamond chip in the middle. Maybe she ought to stop wearing it. She and Mack were as dead as some old stray cat on the Interstate. She'd already stopped wearing

66

his old Teardrop necklace, mainly because Teardrop necklaces weren't a fad anymore. She'd hold onto it though. It was a pretty thing. As soon as people forgot it had ever been a fad and everybody had thrown theirs away, she'd have herself a decent piece of jewelry on a real-gold-plated chain. By then, she'd have forgot it was ever attached to a local-nobody deejay.

Mack had dumped her like garbage, once another little cutie had started coming around the station, pulling over the leg of her underpants and lying down on his old puke-green plastic couch and opening her peanut butter legs, creamy-smooth-and-easy-to-spread, saying Oh, Big Mack, you can do *anything* you want. . . . That was what excited men, the idea that they could do *anything*. She didn't think women and girls were that way. They were used to having something particular in mind to guide them. When she thought about somebody offering her "anything," her mind went into a big gray blank. Not that she didn't want a *lot*. But "anything" was so confusing it just about put her to sleep to think about it.

She peered at her face in the mirror's fluorescence. Not pimple one. Not freckle one. Not mole one. Though sometimes she drew herself a mole with her eyebrow pencil, near her mouth, like Marilyn Monroe's. Sometimes up near her eye, like about a dozen famous movie stars. But if she ever got a real mole, anywhere on her body, she'd cut it off with a knife, she swore it.

The ring came off and she laid it on the edge of the sink and let it go out of focus, just a little twinkle of light. From the silver. The diamond chip was so small you hardly knew it was there, the cheap shit. You could get the very same ring with an eighth of a carat, a fourth of carat, a half-carat and a whole carat diamond in it, and he'd got the one with the chip, bottom of the line. He probably kept a supply of them in the drawer of that old steel desk at the studio. Well, she was tired of stewing about that. It was scary to think she'd been stupid enough to take up with him. He never had intended to help her out, he'd just taken advantage of her. Or he would have, if she thought that way, which she didn't. Nobody could take advantage of you if you could keep yourself thinking that there was nobody in the world who could. Mind over matter.

Of course, if you thought about it a certain way, telling a man or a boy he could do anything he wanted was opening yourself up to somebody taking advantage. A little scary too. He could be a pervert and

67

come up with something you'd never heard of. Or you could end up dead or worse, your face cut up. A broomstick stuck all the way up to your throat, like those men had done to that waitress from downtown. Those guys were out of jail already. They said they'd just got carried away. Around town, men said they could understand how a thing like that could happen, getting carried away, and women said the woman ought to have been home that late at night with her kids. Every time Lily thought about that woman bleeding to death all night out there in a cornfield, her insides ripped up the middle, it gave her the creepiest feeling she'd ever had in her life.

She washed her hands thoughtfully, watching the rainbow-color in the lather. She could just as easily be washing her hands in a bathroom in Grand Central Station, getting ready to pick up her suitcase and go out into a city just waiting to welcome her with open arms and open doors. If there were perverts out there, she didn't intend to run into them. How many could there be? On second thought, it probably wasn't taking much of a chance to tell any man that he could do anything. If you wanted to get their full attention, promising them anything would do it, even if they didn't want to do much out of the ordinary, which she'd bet they didn't. You'd tell them, You can do *anything* you want, and they'd all do the very same thing, she'd bet her life.

She shook the water off her hands and walked over to the paper towel dispenser, which worked more or less like the toilet paper dispenser, raining brown paper down to the floor where it would stick to your shoes and cause you to trip-up and almost bust your tail before you got out of the restroom. She dried her hands, rubbing the towel into the webs bordering her ring finger so that cheap old ring wouldn't give her a rash. Men and boys weren't too complicated at all, she'd been glad to discover. They liked the idea that you'd do anything, but they liked it better when you told them they were so irresistible you'd do anything just for them and them alone. Help yourself, *anything*, but just for *you*, honey. And it helped a lot if you told them you'd never done anything they were doing to you before. But then you had to know how to do it *and* say you'd never done it at the same time. Some believed you, and some—the real pain in the asses—got suspicious and said things like, How did you know where to put your legs? Jesus H. Christ! Sometimes it wore you out. Sometimes it seemed like you ought to say what the hell from the first, just let them go on and think you were a whore. Which they liked to do anyway, once they started losing interest.

Janice had better watch out. How long could someone who looked like Rowen Faircloth stay interested in somebody who looked like her?

Lily stood over the wastepaper can and wondered—again—whether she ought to force the truth on Tollie about Janice and Mr. Faircloth. No, she decided—again. I don't believe it myself yet. Janice—!

She dropped the paper towel in the can. Janice wouldn't appeal to any men she knew, these days. She'd bet old Les had moved on to greener pastures, even. Men—!

Of course if they ever suspected you'd done it with just one other person, they thought they had a right to do it too. Once you said yes, you couldn't say no, that's how they acted. She said no a lot, but nine times out of ten she had to have a fight to get away with it, drag home with her clothes torn, *walk* home sometimes. It was a jungle out there, like Daddy always said when he came in from work, grinning and swooping up Marie like he was Tarzan, survival of the fittest—that was a joke.

She went to the mirror and unclipped one of her rollers. She let fall the one section of hair she had bleached more than the rest. She stood considering it. If you had ever once said yes, they could use that against you in a court of law. Say, if you did meet some pervert and he did something awful to you, or even if you said no to some old regular unimaginative boy who just wanted a quickie, if it came out that you'd said yes *one* time, you didn't have a leg to stand on. That must be what happened in the case of the dead waitress. The judge must have decided that if she'd had one thing stuck up her, another thing didn't make that much difference, even if it was a broomstick.

She could hardly believe that you got punished so much for just showing a little natural healthy interest in a naturally good thing. Or at least you got punished in Hope Mills. She'd be lucky if this town didn't pervert her natural instinct for life itself before she could get out.

Boys used that "one time" to threaten you too. "Go on and walk home, you little whore. Go on and tell somebody I tore your best dress, see how far it gets a little whoring Mill Rat like you."

Lily felt tears biting at her eyes again. It hadn't made one bit of difference that Daddy was a Foreman. He'd gone around crowing about how he was a Foreman before he was thirty-five. Bought a new car, set his eye on a bigger car for the future. Bought two lots of beach property at Palmetto Plantations, on time, sight unseen. A ranch house out on a new paved street of ranch houses, every one just like the other, except the door might be on the left side of one, the right side of the other, everybody with the same thing as everybody else—it had given her hope. But now she could tell that things weren't going to be different until she got to some place so big they never knew where your daddy worked, or that you'd ever said yes in your life, or that your family lived in a ranch house that old Ricky Tuddle, whose daddy was in real estate, said—right to your face and in front of some other kids— was made so cheap it was going to blow away in the next strong wind. Well? *She* hadn't built the damn thing!

They were probably going to lose it all anyway. Daddy got to be a Foreman before he was thirty-five, all right—after twenty years of grunt work and just in time for the Mill to close. She didn't see why they'd promoted him if they knew they were going to shut down, which anybody knew they did know. It seemed cruel. Her family could just have toughed it out in their old neighborhood and waited for whatever it was that was going to happen to them.

And Marie—! What in the world was her mother going to do when everything blew away in the wind? That woman lived in another world. Always reading, couldn't sew you a decent dress or cook a decent meal. They had tv dinners and frozen pot pies just about every night, which had been good at first, but then they all tasted the same. You had to start eating most of what you ate at the Tastee Freeze on Saturday, between customers. Daddy was too dumb to notice, or noticed and didn't care because he liked to get Marie all the conveniences of modern life so she could lay back there on her bed like The Queen of Sheba-with-a-book and he could tell the other men his wife didn't have to do anything now all day but read everything on the bestseller list and eat chocolate candy. Marie had got glasses, which she didn't even need. Joined Book-of-the-Month. "I might have missed my education," she was always telling somebody, "But I'm educating myself now." She'd bring home half the library once a month. *Below the Salt, Exodus, Poor No More, The Status Seekers. Inside Russia Today. Mine Enemy Grows Older. Stay Alive All of Your Life.* Some of them were interesting—Dr. Kinsey. *Coming of Age in Samoa*, by Margaret Mead. *Lolita.* But most weren't, and Marie acted like she was orbiting the moon most of the time.

It's a wonder I grew up at all, Lily thought. I'm almost out of high school and I've got a mother who is barely thirty years old.

I feel like I'm going to catch up with her, pass her, anytime now.

Lily dipped into her cleavage and brought out a little comb. She might as well untangle some of this mess and see how it looked. Her hair wasn't getting very light at all. She should have put more Clorox in the peroxide. You needed really light blond hair to get anywhere in life. She wondered why every girl and woman didn't bleach their hair. It wasn't hard, if you could keep your roots touched up. It didn't take but above five cents worth of ingredients and some sunshine. Everywhere you went, people looked, whistled, tried to find out who you were. Even an ugly girl with light blond hair was going to get some of that attention. It was like pushing a button. And yet girls would walk around with the mousiest hair—Tollie Ramsey was one of them—and why? She couldn't figure it out. She'd look at girls at school, sitting in their mouse-colored clothes, wearing their old black glasses, and she could see a miracle ready to bloom, if they'd just put a little work into themselves. Take off the glasses—what was there to see in Hope Mills?—bleach their hair, use some make-up, get some bright-colored clothes. She'd seen it all in a flash one day: mice-in-glasses, everyone of them sitting in the first two rows of seats, gazing into the face of a-mouse-who-grew-up-to-be-a-rat at the blackboard—a rat who *made* everybody in class cut up a stinking old frog and a stinking old cow-eye. She herself had been sitting near the back of the room. Jimmy Long, the football captain, had been rubbing his hard knee against her butt through the hole at the back of the desk—she knew she shouldn't let him. He had a girlfriend, Cindy Wiggins, who was a cheerleader, who lived in a big white house that would never be gone with the wind. But it felt good, and she wouldn't mind if a boy like Jimmy Long got to like her. He was cuter than any other boy in school. They were coming down from Duke, Carolina, Wake Forest to watch him play football. He was a Mill Rat too, but you'd never know it now. That was one thing that could change your life, if you were a boy: nobody, nobody in this world, would deny natural football talent. You could possibly be a good football player and get away with murder. Jimmy Long *was* going somewhere. She didn't think it was anywhere she wanted to go, but you never knew.

She turned the newly bleached streak this way and that way, ratted the hair under it a little and smoothed it back. She could imagine Jimmy telling Cindy that they were going to have to break it off because he couldn't resist Lily Jones another day. She could see Cindy crying, her tears slipping down her stupid pouty face and ruining her $40 cashmere sweater—"Lily JONES! I never knew you were susceptible to the fatal charms of Lily Jones. . . . She'll break your heart into little bitty pieces, Jim-mee. . . ." Lily pulled a wave down over one eye. Cindy herself could look a lot better if she had the sense to go blond. Cindy didn't have much sense at all. Everybody said that she'd had an abortion. Not in the back room of a rusty old trailer out in the boonies or in a shack on B Street, but in the office of some doctor who was her daddy's friend and taught up at the Medical School. How had people found out a thing like that? If you were Cindy Wiggins, did it matter? Those girls probably could go back and forth, yes and no and no and yes and no and nobody would ever tear their dress half off them and leave them to walk home. Unless it was somebody who was as rich as they were.

" . . . Oh Jim-mee," she could imagine Cindy whining, "I was going to go to school up at Peace, just to be close by and watch you play football for four years. . . ." Jesus Christ on Cavalry's Cross. Some people's teeny little plans for themselves. She was glad Jimmy Long had never got to like her. She hated him. He'd told everybody she'd let him rub her butt with his knee. Now she had to sit in the back row every day, just when she was finding some stuff she was interested in, Geometry and Geography, just so some shithead couldn't get at her butt. Those people had small minds, that's all there was to it. If you weren't supposed to do something, why would it feel so good to you? Look at those little girls in *The Coming of Age in Samoa*. Nobody made them feel like they were whores for doing what comes naturally. Of course expectations were different for white girls. She guessed that was the only good thing about nigger—ne-gro—life: nobody cared if the girls did what came naturally.

Lily tucked the end of the wave behind her ear. She looked just about perfect. But she felt sort of sick. Remembering what white girls couldn't do without suffering for it reminded her of the only boy she'd ever been stupid enough to fall in love with, Wayne Dixon.

Wayne had been so cute, and so sweet, everything about him the color of sand except for his baby blue eyes. He could have been in the movies. He'd come around to take her riding in his mamma's Chevrolet, to a dance or a show, for a cheeseburger basket at the drive-in, and he'd always tell Marie where they were going, what time he'd get her back, and stand there like he was waiting for Marie to say it was okay.

72

Marie would raise her eyes up from her book and look at him over her glasses like she'd heard him. Then she'd give him a little smile. Wayne said he thought Marie looked just like Jeanne Crain. "I just come to see you so I can see her," he'd tease. Yeah. Ho. But he was nice to say it, to show respect for her parents, rather than making her suffer for them like everybody else did. Finally they'd gone over to his house while his mamma was at work, and then back into his room, which was still a little boy's room, with model airplanes and destroyers all over the place. Wayne's daddy had been killed in the War, and his mamma kept the books for some Wiggins or other, which meant that the house was empty after school five days a week. He'd had the hardest, coolest little mouth, and when he'd got that catch in his breath, it almost drove her crazy. And still she hadn't been able to do it, though they almost had. She'd been "saving herself"—! Like everything she'd ever heard or read on the subject (except Margaret Mead and Dr. Kinsey, who were kind of vague) said you should do. Finally Wayne had given up on her and gone down to B Street and lost his cherry to a $2.00 whore. She'd never forgive herself for that. She'd never forgive him for telling her about it, either! He said she'd drove him to it, and that if she didn't let him, he'd go back. But after what he'd just told her, she couldn't let him—it would have made her throw up: Wayne's skin the color of pale sand ensnared in those black, black arms and legs, his pink little thing snaking into something that she imagined as red—red-red, the color of a wound. She'd never forgive Wayne for giving her a picture like that. And she'd never forgive herself for saving herself, driving him to it, finally driving him away.

Saving herself for what? That s.o.b. that had held her down in the backseat at the drive-in movie and jabbed her like she was a pork chop or piece of chicken? Then tried to make her do it with his friend, with her bleeding all over her clothes, and crying her eyes out? And then telling half the town, like *she'd* done something wrong?

After that, half the world thought she was a whore, she might as well have some fun.

Now Wayne had his own car, a 1949 Mercury that he'd lowered the tail down to the ground on, fender skirts, mudflaps, two antennas on the back, twin carbs and four cams. He had a new girlfriend too, a little mouse with big tits, Marcia—which she made you pronounce Mar-SEE-ah. She was a year older than Wayne and had a scholarship to some college or other for next fall. That would be the end of that . . .

73

unless it wasn't. Wayne would get a scholarship too, because of his daddy being killed in the War. Sometimes she daydreamed about next year, when Marcia would be off to a college, about Wayne forgetting Marcia and coming around again. She'd forgive him for going down to B Street and he'd forgive her for Big Mack and the others and they'd ride off into the sunset in his Mercury and never look back.

That was shit. That was never going to happen. She'd probably outgrown him anyway. She thought his car was immature. He probably still had model planes all over his room. Was he screwing Marcia in there? She knew he was. That girl looked like a mouse but you didn't grow big tits like that unless something was going on, or at least that was what they said at school. That you could look at somebody's tits and tell if they'd let you feel them up, look at their ass and tell whether they'd ever done it or not. That *had* to be junk! Still, she knew girls who wouldn't even wear a tight skirt because of that. Where did they live, Transylvania? Prim-i-tive.

Lily checked under her eyebrows for any stray hairs. Nope. Not one. Not on Lili Lorene. That was the name she'd decided to go with, once she was in Hollywood or New York City. Double initials seemed to be an advantage in the stage and screen business, whichever one she got into. She wasn't going to stop until she'd lost her name completely, until she was just LL and everybody knew who was being talked about, like MM and BB. She smooched her lips toward the mirror. Actually, she'd never be satisfied until she looked exactly like Brigitte Bardot. She'd let every boy she was going out with at the time take her to *And God Created Woman,* just to study. She knew she looked something like BB already, because she could see people looking at her when they were walking out of the theatre, what else but catching the resemblance when she pouted her mouth a little and looked bored?

Which she usually was: bored as a board, just waiting to get on a train or bus. She was going to go straight to Broadway, or else Sunset Boulevard. She might not even mess with Junior Miss or any of that. They were prejudiced down here anyway. The girls that won those things were cut with different scissors, or something. How would she ever get the wardrobe, even, that she needed for those contests? Marie? Jesus of Nazareth. Cindy Wiggins had gone all the way to Raleigh, just to get her old Miss Hope Mills High gown, even The Dome wouldn't do. That's what you had to do to win. The gown had been a soft draped satin dress, as plain as could be, the color of cream that somebody had put about a tenth of a drop of strawberry juice in. Strapless and almost too low, which only a girl like Cindy could get away with. It was an eye-opener: elegant. Suddenly all the net and ruffles and the cloth roses and the little sparkly things were put in perspective—an education. Her own rows of gathered net, badly made from a McCalls pattern, the flouncy skirt, still flecked where Marie had pricked her fingers a hundred times—it seemed cheap, overdone. Even if all the other runner-ups were ruffled and flounced too. Even Marie, sitting in the audience with her hands clamped together like she was praying, had seen it.

"I think we'll make you something simpler next time," she'd said later that night, after sitting at the kitchen table without saying a *word* for about an *hour*—never mind that her daughter had managed to get first runner-up in a homemade dress, in spite of being a little whoring Mill Rat! Sometimes it all made you so tired you just wanted to lay down and die.

Lily re-rolled her hair without thinking—she'd thought enough to-day to last her for a year. It was Tollie's fault, all that stuff about ne-groes . . . "organs" and "passions." That was exactly what ne-groes ought not to have, men anyway, if they wanted to stay alive in Hope Mills. She remembered that old play too, old Thornton reciting, look-ing like Ichabod Crane in that Disney cartoon show. Old Ichabod Thornton hadn't said a word about negroes. That was just Tollie Ram-sey, who was going to think herself into a early grave about stuff that didn't have anything to do with her.

Lily stuck the comb back into her bathing suit and checked herself in the full-length mirror, centered one of the cut-outs over her navel. She cocked one knee over the other, like women did for pin-ups. Looking sharp!

"You'll never be able to wear that suit on a Southern beach," Marie had said.

Just you watch. I'm going to be wearing a French bikini before it's all said and done. Why was Marie so upset? Her generation had worn two-pieced suits. Lily had a picture of her mother in one, white, with a halter tied around the neck, a modesty panel rippling a little on the bottom piece, like cheap cloth would do. Marie had looked pale, young, squinty. A faceless male's arm was around her shoulder, every-thing else cut out by the camera. Was it Daddy? Probably. Marie had barely opened her eyes before she got married. If it was Daddy, Lily thought, I'd like to reach into that picture and flip his arm back where it belonged, tell Marie to straighten up her posture, get a tan, bleach her hair, smile and get herself a rich man. But little Marie was frozen there, slumped and frowning against the sun, defeated way back then.

Lily turned to go and spied her Sweetheart ring still resting above the sink. She put it on her finger. It felt cold, tighter than ever.

Out in the bright sunshine, she squinted till she made out her order waiting on the food stand's counter, the wax paper on the hot dogs covered with flies.

"At least you could have waved the flies off it," she said to the man at the grill. "I wasn't gone that long."

"No flies on you, are there, Sug?" the man said, grinning. He had a five-o'clock shadow. She'd be glad to move to a part of the world where the men didn't call you Sug. Beside the food stand there was an old game booth, like you'd see at the county fair or a traveling carnival. A rusty old "Wheel of Fortune" waiting for somebody to put money down on a spin. To the side was a rack of dirty old panda-bears. She'd never yet seen anybody minding the wheel, nor anybody lined up to play. Why would you? Who'd want one of those old pandas? Somebody had stuck a Tootsie Roll between the legs of one of them. God. What a place.

She picked up the food. Behind this creep she could see a part of the lake that was more or less empty, just a couple of guys fooling around with a girl, ducking her down in the water and holding her head under until she could claw her way back up. The girl rose up in storm of spray, whipping her long hair from side to side. Then before she could catch her breath, they'd duck her again. She's going to end up brain-dead, Lily thought, as the girl came up again, thrashing her arms like a windmill. She was squealing and trying to laugh along with the boys, gasping for air and pulling up the straps on her bathing suit, which kept slipping back down on her arms. The lake looked olive drab. Lily knew it was the temperature of pee and thick as puke. The mustard-and-onions on the hot dogs was beginning to smell like something old and awful as time itself, like something coming from way deep down in the ground. She set the food back down. "I'll be back in a minute," she said. "I forgot something in the ladies room."

"I'll keep things hot for you," the cook said, winking and showing a row of tiny white teeth. "*Like* that bathing suit, Sug. Any more at home like you?"

"Just keep the flies off it," Lily said.

"You do the same," the man called after her.

Lily made it to the john and bent over, folding her arms across her middle. She vomited, heaved, then vomited again. Her stomach seemed to have collapsed in on itself. Then it threw up more. I feel like I'm going to actually puke my guts out, she thought, frightened. She flushed the toilet and let the swirling water go out of focus. It was just murked-up color, she reminded herself, a shimmying, shrinking funnel. Then it was porcelain white, a steady circle, expanding until it was a perfectly regular shape. She was in the ladies room in a big Beverly Hills hotel. She'd just thrown up from drinking too much champagne and eating too much caviar and crepes suzettes and baked alaska. She was lucky she hadn't ruined her expensive dress, designed for her alone by Edith Head, dressmaker to the stars. Outside they were waiting in the dining room full of potted palmtrees for her to finish "powdering her nose," so they could take more photographs. Her hair was as dazzling as a winter sun. They'd need sunglasses, just to take her picture.

She rinsed her mouth at the sink, wiped her eyes and took a deep breath and held it, concentrating on the nausea and forcing it back down, and then out of the range of her senses—where it belonged, mind over matter! She was glad she'd brought that jar of grain alcohol along. She was going to want a drink.

She left the damp restroom and went out into the sunshine. She inhaled again, laying claim to the hot air that she knew in her bones everybody had an equal right to. They couldn't take that away from you, unless they killed you.

She took several more deep breaths. She imagined her lungs inflating, like powerful balloons. Like mighty blimps that, if you just had it in you—and she absolutely did!—could take you to the stars.

Déjà vu.

Tollie was half-dreaming of the cute boy she'd seen on the beach, half-thinking a phrase that Lily had half-relayed to her from French class, when she heard a key turn softly in the lock of her bedroom door. Through the crosshatching of her eyelashes, she watched Janice in her thin cotton nightgown come into the room and move across it on tiptoe in the white morning light. Janice unplugged the radio in the middle of "What a Difference a Day Makes," a song you couldn't get away from, whether you were listening to the local stations, Negro or white, or to the Clear Channels. She watched Janice retreat with the radio in her hand: *Déjà* view.

When the door closed, Tollie opened her eyes all the way and looked at the ceiling where an old water stain formed a tea-colored cloud. Why was it that Janice never thought that she, Tollie, would realize that the radio was gone, that the room had been locked the night before? On the other hand, if she confronted her mother with knowledge of the key hidden on the ledge of molding outside the door, then Janice would probably feel free to barge on in, any time of day or night.

I guess I'll just let her think I'm dumb as a doornail, Tollie thought, getting the knot of sheet off her feet. She fanned her gown up over her legs. Another hot day. The sun behind the blind felt like a heat lamp already. She wiped her forehead with her hand and gazed back at the ceiling. The cloud looked like a dog, sort of.

79

That was something: making a cloud out of a water stain, then making a dog out of what wasn't a cloud. She did that all the time, though: looked for new shapes in that old stain. It was something to distract her, anyway. What was it she was trying to distract herself from today? She knew it was something.

She was surprised that she'd dreamed about that boy. It didn't seem like she dreamed much anymore. She didn't remember what she'd dreamed about him. She just had the impression of him in her dream, less an image of him than something deeper, that you couldn't see but could only feel. Or inhale: an *essence*, like the invisible basis of your cologne or bath powder, except it wasn't a smell.

It was nice, the dream. She didn't daydream much anymore either. It had started to seem like a waste of time. Of course if you weren't supposed to use your ability to daydream, why would you have it? It was what the thoughtful species got in The Scheme of Things to save their lives, she reckoned. And here she was, giving it up. That was a sad state of affairs! Maybe she was taking up Art instead, and didn't know it. Making a cloud, then a dog, out of a water stain. A *kind* of Art, something rising up out of the last signs of destruction, a bird out of the ashes, a dog out of the mildew.

She, Tollie Ramsey, the legitimate daughter of an imaginary dead man, the Unknown Soldier, was lying in her own ashes. Getting ready to be born again as the bastard of some old yankee tomcat who was probably still alive, somewhere. Which made it worse. Dead men could tell no tales. You could make up whatever you needed and they couldn't ever contradict you.

Poot, Tollie thought, flipping over on her stomach and wiggling her heat rash against the sheet for a blissful second. I guess I'll rise up out of my ashes like the legendary Phoenix, any minute now. I just need to get a grip on myself. It would be a lot easier if every day you didn't have to wake up to weather so hot it made you sick at your stomach.

She could hear her mother's bathwater running and a few notes from the radio music. Why was it that a woman who made a religion out of unplugging things would plug in a radio right next to her bathtub? There was no way a person could go back to sleep with something like that going on. In seventh grade poor little beanpole Molly Raney had set a plugged-in radio on the edge of her bathtub and been electrocuted when it toppled over into the water. Tollie would always remember Molly the way she imagined her in her bathwater, turning to pure light. Molly's two ponytails blazing straight up, a look of surprise on her freckled face, before it turned to light too. A radio could take you farther away than you'd ever intended to go. Didn't Janice remember anything useful? Could her mother survive this world . . . this time around?

I don't think she does remember anything useful, Tollie decided. I think she just remembers the useless old sad stuff that wears you down over time, prolonging the agony and spreading out so that it attaches to everybody around you.

The sound of the bathwater's running stopped. Janice had found her station. The Oldies from her day. Tollie closed her eyes. She listened for a while, to "The Last Time I Saw Paris," "It's a Big, Wide Wonderful World," and "God Bless the Child That's Got It's Own." She dozed off for a few minutes and then tuned in again: "You'd Be So Nice To Come Home To," "Don't Get Around Much Anymore," "Don't Fence Me In." Then, "Long Ago and Far Away." Good. That would make Janice happy. But wasn't she getting waterlogged in there? Tollie could never understand how her mother could bathe almost all morning long if you didn't get up and start stomping around. Which eventually you had to do, to confirm that she hadn't drowned herself.

Suddenly Tollie heard the front door slam. "Janice?"

Whew. It was just Arlene. She wished Janice would lock the door after Les left for work. Someday somebody was going to walk in and put them both out of their misery.

"Janice?" Arlene called out again, moving down the hall. The volume went down on the radio.

"Arlene?" Janice called back weakly. Tollie heard the bathroom door open. She imagined Arlene's head with its red Italian-boy haircut poking into the bathroom, Janice's thin naked body exposed in the bathwater's creepy light, like something dead. Tollie got up and tiptoed to the wall and cupped her ear there.

"Here you are," Arlene was saying. "Sorry to pop in so early, but I thought I'd go out to Mamma's and pick up those bedding plants she says she's got for me. You mind if I cut this racket off—?" The radio music stopped. "There," Arlene said. Tollie imagined her sitting down on the commode. Where else?

"Boy, you look skinny," Arlene said. "I mean skinny-skinny. Are you eating yet?"

"Like a dog," Janice said. Tollie could tell her mother was annoyed. She didn't blame her. Arlene was sweet, but she wasn't always tactful. She was one of those people that prided themselves on being honest, which Tollie thought was just an excuse for being as rude as they wanted to be without apologizing for it.

"I can't believe you're going to try to grow more flowers," Janice said lethargically. "Tollie read in the paper they're going to restrict the use of water."

"Then you'll have to get out of the bathtub, won't you?" Arlene said. Tollie could tell Arlene was annoyed too. "I don't care if they do restrict it. I've already dug the beds. With a little luck they'll make it. Flowers aren't as delicate as people think. Look what I brought you."

There was a silence and Tollie tried to imagine what Arlene had brought her mother. Food?

"*McCalls, Vogue, Town and Country,*" Arlene said. "The clothes are so pretty! Houses on the rocky coast of Maine—Look."

Tollie could hear the rustling of magazine pages.

"That'll cheer me up," Janice said. "Looking at what people have got that I don't have."

"Well, look at it this way. If you don't have it, you don't have to take care of it. It's a lot easier to look at the pictures and imagine having it, then put it all out of your mind."

"You sure have a perspective on life," Janice said.

"I do!" Arlene said firmly. "You need one too. A better perspective. Adversity builds character. Hard times make you stronger, and build you up."

"That's just something somebody said." Janice's voice sounded more than tired, Tollie thought. "It's not true."

"I think it's true!" Arlene's voice rose.

"Sssh-sh. You'll wake Tollie. And adversity wears you down." Tollie imagined her mother slipping deeper into the water with fatigue. "It wears you out and ruins you. If it's adverse enough."

Arlene didn't say anything for a minute. Then, "I guess I've got a more cheerful disposition."

"Lucky you."

"Goddamn you!" Arlene exploded. "What have I got in life? I've got a husband who's going to get laid off just like your husband, but who's too proud to let his wife get a job. I've got a high school education with four years of Latin, top of the class, and I never got to use a bit of it. I haven't got a pot to pee in. We can't even afford to have kids. If we did, I couldn't even have a dress now and then or a magazine or any kind of a car, not even an old one like I've got now, that breaks down every time you get walking distance from home. But I don't let it get me down!"

"I guess you've got real fortitude."

"Don't you condescend, Janice. You'd better snap out of this stuff or you're going to lose what little you've got left, I'm not kidding." Arlene sounded furious.

"I know it," Janice said after a moment. "I can't help myself. I'm worn out."

It was quiet. Tollie wiped her wet eyes with her nightgown. Damn it. Damn it.

"I love you, Janice," Arlene said. "I know I'm not Rowen Faircloth—not that he seems to be making you a bit happy—but you and I have been friends a long time and I've got to be honest with you. You understand? I love Tollie too, and she's being neglected, and I hate to see it. She's going to get into something, you can bet on that. I loved that little boy, but he's gone. I can even tolerate Les. I'd like to see things change for y'all, but you won't do what you could for yourself, and you won't show me a thing I can do for you."

Arlene is right, Tollie thought, sinking down on the floor and wiping her nose on her gown. She rested the back of her head against the wall and looked up at the ceiling. The old dog up in the sky looked like something else, something puddled in itself. Arlene's words sounded like a prophecy. What am I going to "get into?" Tollie wondered. She didn't even want to know. She felt like Janice, like she couldn't handle one more bad thing. Not this summer. And she wasn't even going to try to handle "Rowen Faircloth."

"It just burns me up!" Arlene burst out. Tollie quickly swiveled back to the wall and put her ear there.

"I believe it," Janice said slowly. "And I appreciate it. How you feel. But why is it that nobody, nobody in all of General Eisenhower's America, from one shining sea to the other, will believe that sometimes, in some situations, a person just can't do anything to help themselves. I can't do anything, Arlene. Stop giving me sayings. They aren't helpful."

Her mother's voice had grown lower. Tollie strained against the wall.

"I'm afraid you're going to die," Arlene said. Tollie felt a chill. It felt funny: to be suddenly cold when you were dripping with sweat from the heat.

"Me too," Janice said quietly. Tollie's heart felt prickly in her chest, like it had gone to sleep, the sleep of the Dead. Damn it. God damn it.

"I wasn't kidding about Tollie," Arlene said. "I'm afraid about her. I remember when she was a little girl. You'd dress her up so pretty. Those little pinafores. Rompers. You'd sew all those things, making do with the little bit you could get your hands on. Remember that little plaid book bag you made her when she started to school? It looked like something you could have bought in a store. You haven't even made yourself a dress in years. I don't even think it was the baby dying that did this to you."

"I think you should go on over to your Mamma's," Janice said. "I'll try to think of something I can do."

"Okay. I can't sit in here and get any more depressed. I've got to go get those flowers. Maybe it'll rain."

"Maybe," Janice said.

"After I leave Mamma's, I'm going to Madame Lucretia's. I'll ask her about you. Maybe she can read your cards without you being there."

"Get me some more belladonna," Janice said.

"I wish I'd never done that in the first place," Arlene said.

"Would you turn my radio back on before you go?"

Tollie walked slowly along the dusty shoulder of Vine Street in the afternoon heat. She passed by the last of the old millworkers' houses, from back in the days when there was more than one Hope Mill. From where she lived, near the last Hope Mill, it was almost a three-mile walk to downtown, but she was young: she could take it. She might take the bus home, though. If she could bring herself to spend a nickel.

Up ahead, on the next block, the businesses started, and the sidewalks. Of course by then her shoes would be totally covered with dust. Which was too bad, since she was on her way to the new thrift shop, Pandora's Box, to apply for a job. She was fifteen today, the legal age to work enough hours to make it worthwhile, with your parent's consent. She figured she could get Janice to consent to about anything these days.

I'm not going to think about her all day today, Tollie resolved, crossing Mill Street and stepping up onto a sidewalk, at last. Up at the end of the next block she could see the big sign of the car dealership on a building that looked like a jukebox, built back before the Depression—tacked onto an old feedstore that was still in business. The Wiggins New and Used Cars and Feed. Fifteen was the legal age to get a learner's permit, too, with your parent's consent. Not that I'll ever get a chance to drive a car in or around Hope Mill, she thought bitterly. The Wiggins will never make a cent off of me.

What kind of a thing was that for a young girl to think? You were supposed to be able to imagine yourself driving the best-looking car in the universe when you were her age. Something had gone really wrong with her life.

The heat rose off the asphalt in a dreamy iridescence. She passed the empty lot where they used to sell mobile homes, one of the many businesses that had relocated out on the by-pass. She passed a single shoe on the side of the road, dust-covered but still good. That was one of the mysterious things in life, how often you'd see a single, perfectly good shoe on a road. Like somebody had been jerked out of it. What happened to all those people? Nobody threw away a good shoe. Even somebody disturbed enough to do such a thing would most likely throw away both shoes. A shoe on the road was about the creepiest sight in the world, she guessed, passing this one by, a ballerina flat.

She came to the Tastee-Freeze where Lily worked part-time. A bunch of little kids outside it were licking their frozen custard swirls, vanilla lines snaking down their tanned arms. The sight of it made Tollie remember her dead little brother for a second, who would never again feel heat that would melt ice cream, but was himself cold as ice, in his cold, cold grave. I'm not going to think about that today or any day! she thought, shaking her own hot body a little to recollect what was of this world and worth thinking about, shaking off what was gone and might as well be forgot.

In the little parking lot of the Tastee-Freeze, a couple sat up on top of each other, kissing, in a 1950, '51, Mercury, lowered down to the ground, fender skirts and mudflaps, its chrome blazing. "The Sea of Love," number one on the charts, was blaring from the radio. How did they stand sticking themselves together like that in this heat?

Tollie squinted through the window of the Tastee-Freeze, but didn't see Lily, just that poor girl from school with the bad skin and the old creep who owned the place.

She'd better keep walking, she thought, even as she moved into the shade of the Tastee-Freeze's overhang. Just for a minute. She still had four blocks to go, past the car lot, past the old Mill-founder's home, now a funeral home with a big clock outside. That was about the most insensitive thing she'd come across yet. *"Tempus fugit,"* Arlene had said, shrugging, when Tollie had said as much one day last year when they were driving by, in cooler weather, licking their own frozen custard. "Don't give much thought to that kind of thing or you'll end up like . . . somebody you don't want to end up like."

Of course she meant Janice. Tollie was kind of ticked at Arlene, in spite of the birthday present Arlene had left on the tv this morning. A view of the two women in the bathroom rose in Tollie's mind. Arlene on the john, giving advice. Janice stretched out in the tub like it was some old psychiatrist's couch. They ought to be in a cartoon. Cartoons favored psychiatrists and psychologists as subjects, Tollie had observed. And psychologees.

Well. She wished she hadn't eavesdropped, for several reasons. Arlene had said "Rowen Faircloth," that was one reason. Lily had been saying Janice was fooling around with Mr. Faircloth all summer, and Tollie had thought she was crazy. How could it be? And yet Arlene had said as much too, right to Janice's face.

I won't believe that on the day I die! Tollie vowed, shaking off the whole evil mess of thoughts that rose up in her mind with the man's name, including his lanky body in his jeans and workshirt, his tan and thin-lipped smile with the teeth that lapped over just a little, his sunglasses. He was good-looking, anybody could see that, even if he was middle-aged. She didn't know much about him. People in town didn't pay much attention to people outside of town, but in a place like Hope Mills everybody knew the basics about everybody who had something in life. Mr. Faircloth's family owned a gigantic farm operation near Rockfish Creek, with a big fresh vegetable stand down on the road that ran past it. Janice and Tollie used to go to buy produce in the good old days when Janice would drive the car. The couple of times Tollie had picked crops for him, he'd kidded around with her in a nice way, saying she was on her way to becoming Queen of the Hop, anybody could tell. He'd gone to college and studied something interesting, maybe philosophy—or psychology? *That* would make sense!—but then had come on back home and taken over the farm when his Daddy had had a stroke. That was as good as anything else he could have done, Tollie reckoned. What could you do in 1959 with a degree in something as out of date as philosophy? She felt sure that it had been philosophy. That was just one more thing rich people could do, study for fun. Something she and Janice had had to give up on, no matter how good they were getting to be with words. It surprised her how much she thought about college sometimes, even if she didn't have a chance in Hades of going. She paid attention to who had gone to college in Hope Mills, and who was planning to go, and where. Mr. Faircloth had gone to Duke.

There was another reason Tollie wished Arlene had stayed home this morning. She'd always thought that Arlene sought her out to go places, like the Tastee-Freeze, because there was something interesting about her, Tollie, even as young as she was—something she herself hadn't discovered yet. But the conversation she'd heard through the wall made her sound like Little Orphan Annie, a charity case! Or a juvenile delinquent: Tollie's going to get into something. . . .

The birthday present was nice, though. A little gold ankle bracelet with two hearts on it. Probably not real gold, but that was just as well. The last thing she needed was to feel indebted to another older woman whose life hadn't turned out right.

Which made her think of her Aunt Gracie. Her aunt had sent a card from Whiteville. Tollie didn't know why she felt responsible for her aunt, living alone in the big old house down there. She hadn't even seen Aunt Gracie in about eight or nine years. There had been a dollar in the card. That depressed her too. A dollar wasn't quite a present. You had a feeling that if all anybody could give you was a dollar, they probably needed it more themselves. Which Aunt Gracie probably did.

I'm going to spend it this afternoon, Tollie thought. It's burning a hole in my pocket. I just want to spend it and forget it, on something that I can forget. She knew she was going to have a Black-and-White Soda at the Rexall. One of their most expensive single items: Thirty-five cents. Why? Who knew?

She'd like to have a Tangee lipstick, too, but then she'd have to think of the dollar, or a quarter of it, every time she colored her lips. It was a problem. She should have spent a nickel to ride in on the bus, just to be rid of it. You couldn't eat but so much in the middle of the afternoon in this weather.

"A small coke," she said stepping up to the window before she had much time to think about it. She was thirsty, sort of. It would take care of a nickel. The girl with the bad skin brought her the coke and laid out her change, three quarters and two dimes. The girl's nails were bitten down to the quick, her hands small and short-fingered, stunted-looking. "Thanks," Tollie said, searching for the girl's face through the glass, but it was covered by a sheet of paper listing the prices of hot dogs and hamburgers, barbeque sandwiches, french fries, frozen custard.

Tollie put the change in the pocket of her dungarees and turned away, peeling the end of the paper off a straw with her teeth and then blowing the paper away from her, hitting the oil-drum trashcan: Bingo.

She stood in the shade for a few seconds, sipping her drink. The couple drove off, taking "The Sea of Love" with them. Tollie was glad. It was a spooky song: like some old ghoul had risen up from the Black Lagoon to try to hypnotize you into walking into the water so he could drag you down into its depths. That was another funny thing for a girl her age to be thinking. Most girls her age had been dreaming happily about drowning in The Sea of Love for a couple of years.

I wonder why I've never been in love, Tollie thought, stirring the straw into her melting ice. I'm old enough. I've *been* old enough. I sure wasn't in love with Ramírez! I guess I've never had the peace of mind.

Across the street was a little bit of the old lake, almost lost in the haze. Across the old lake, on the other side of a narrow strip of land planted with pines, there was a new lake, newer than even the one old Rolando had built, which was way out of town. Everybody in town knew that the new lake behind the old lake was where the Managers' houses were, and the houses of other people with money. Most of them with boats tied up at little docks. Even when it wasn't lost in the haze of summer heat, the new lake seemed far away.

A sudden breeze lifted Tollie's bangs for a second, surprising her. It felt good, even though the breeze was hot. She squinted at the water of the old lake, what she could see of it, trying to sustain the feeling of relief. Water still gushed down from the original flume. She strained to hear it. She thought she could. She could see some timbers sticking up nearby, the remains of one of the old mills that had gone up in flames. Down the lake she knew there were stones still stacked up, looking like that place in England you always saw pictures of, shrunk down to Hope Mills size. They were the foundation stones of the mill that General Frank Blair of Old Sherman's Army had blown up when he'd marched his troops through Hope Mills in the War Between the States. There was a lot of history in Hope Mills, she guessed. A lot of buildings. Churches: First Baptist, Second Baptist, Southern Baptist. Presbyterian, Methodist, Episcopalian, more Baptists, Church of God, and a couple of holy-rollers Tabernacles, one of which Lily's Daddy belonged to. The old White schoolhouse, now the Colored School, still in use under a sagging roof.

She took the last swig of her coke. What would she say to the person at Pandora's Box? List her experience babysitting. The few hours she'd worked at Kresge's last Christmas. Should she tell that she'd worked in the fields? It showed responsibility. Then again, white girls—nice white girls—didn't do field work. She'd better keep it under her hat. She wished she'd worn a skirt! She didn't act like she had good sense these days. Then again, she wasn't putting in her application at The Dome, just a thrift shop. She didn't think they'd ever had a white person's thrift shop in Hope Mills before, not in her recollection. It must be true that times were going to get hard, for more people than Les.

Tollie moved over to the oil drum, slurping at the empty cup, and prepared to go back out in the sun. Just then, a little red sports car zoomed by with its top down. She had turned toward the noise, then she stood still, her empty cup suspended. It was him. The boy from Rolando's Beach. He hadn't seen her. That was good, she thought slowly, confused by the prickly feeling inside her chest. She'd hate him to see her with her dusty shoes, sweaty hair. He wasn't wearing a shirt, she noticed as he turned the corner on the other side of the car lot and disappeared. Just sunglasses, like a movie star.

Dumb, Tollie thought, in self-disgust. The last thing I need is to start thinking like Lily Jones. I'd be wearing sunglasses, too, if I had any. I'd better get to Pandora's Box and see if she's got anything for me. I haven't got any business slowing around, drinking coca-colas. I'm probably going to turn out just to be a dawdler in life.

She started walking, picking up her pace. She couldn't afford to slow around!

She looked way ahead as she walked—beyond the car lot and the funeral home and the big old houses with columns that were tourist homes now, and boarding houses, one even with a concrete addition to the front, a mechanic's garage—up to where the main part of town began: her destination. Up there, cars were parked on the diagonal on both parts of the street for several blocks until the town petered out into the beginning of the Negro houses. First, she'd pass the appliance store with its big Kelvinator sign and a couple of insurance offices and lawyers offices, the Western Auto. Then the heart of Hope Mills, where almost every shop had an awning, luring you into its inviting shade: Kresge's, Barefoot's News and Camera Shop, six cheap dress shops with names like The Diane Shop and Marilyn's and Milady. The Jewel Box, a coffee shop, The Teen Shoppe, Belk's. The Twigg Shoppe, The Gentleman's Closet, The Palm Court Restaurant, and finally the one big department store that nobody she knew could afford to shop in: The Dome.

She walked faster. Already she could imagine getting her interview over with and heading back with something to show for herself: a job. She imagined her return through town, swinging into the Rexall, past the penguin with its frosty "Kool Inside" painted on the glass, moving confidently through the cold air and the smell that only drugstores had—Tollie Ramsey, Salesgirl. She closed her eyes for a second and inhaled as she walked, imagining the drugstore's delicious, promising smell. Sort of peppery. Impossible to describe. She'd sit at the counter and have her Black and White Soda. Then she'd spend the rest of her money on a lipstick, and sunglasses. When she got paid, she'd send her Aunt Gracie five whole dollars! Maybe she could still dream after all.

"Hey, Hot Pussy!"

A car with three men in it had swerved near the sidewalk. An arm reached out the window and a hand grazed Tollie's elbow. "Whee-oo!" one of the men yelled as the car lurched away.

I'd better watch where I'm going, Tollie thought, opening her eyes. Strange men in cars were a hazard these days. Making you feel like two cents.

She stepped with relief over the sidewalk's crack. Lucky, Tollie thought. I opened my eyes just in time. I wouldn't want her to have less of a spine than she's already got.

Immediately, she prickled with guilt. Hadn't Janice left her a birthday breakfast, the usual strawberry preserve and margarine sandwich cut into quarters and wrapped in waxed paper supplemented by a little pile of peanuts and raisins and honey perched on a piece of canteloupe, a note that said there'd be a present this evening?

That was another reason to watch where she was going. Janice had come downtown on the bus. The note said that too. She'd better watch out or she'd run smack into her and spoil the day. Spoil the *surprise,* she corrected herself.

No, spoil the day. She hardened herself. After all, Janice had got so gloomy in the bathtub that a person couldn't even remember it was her own birthday until noontime! That had never happened before. Why couldn't you daydream about fifteen minutes into your future without feeling like you'd left your mother in the Jaws of Hell to fend for herself while you escaped?

She was approaching the corner of Hope and Vine, the car lot/feedstore, jukebox and checkerboard designs. It used to be just Wiggins Feed Store, Les said, but not in her lifetime. Vine Street went on and on, winding out of sight into Negro Town (*other* people might say Niggertown, but she'd been brought up more civilized, by the old Janice, thank her lucky star, if she had one). Vine wound out of sight back in the direction she'd come from, too, looking like it could just keep going on and on in both directions. But Hope ended right here, where she was walking. Before it reached Vine, there was a cluster of bars and flophouses that the soldiers swarmed to on payday. But once it reached Vine and crossed it, Hope Street was just a bed for a road that never got laid. Clay and ruts, shooting up toward the old lake and disappearing in scrub pines. Back in the pines all you found were about a dozen old rusty trailers covered with fallen pinestraw, which everybody knew was covered with red mites. The trailers were an eyesore some people were trying to get rid of, even if you couldn't see them hidden in the pines, but Rolando McLaurin rented them out and protected his interests.

Tollie crossed Hope and stepped up on the sidewalk where a stocky man in the car lot was leaning against a truck with his back to her, talking to somebody hidden behind the truck's cab. The man was Little Wiggins, old man Wiggins' middle-aged son.

"Ramsey, I don't think I can give you much, cash-money, for that thing," the man said. Tollie stopped and pricked up her ears.

"I don't see why." It was Les's voice. Tollie bent down and crept up on the other side of the truck's cab. What was he up to?

"It's not much more than four tires and a steering wheel," Little Wiggins said.

"Runs good," Les said. "It's never give me a minute's worry. Got a radio. New brakes. New belts."

"Yeah, and I bet you did it all yourself. Look, I could give you something on trade-in, if you wanted a new Ford. But I don't see you buying a new car right now, Boy. The way things are going."

"I ain't wanting new. I'm wanting different."

That was Les all right, Tollie thought.

"Even different's going to cost you," Little Wiggins said. "They ain't going to save the Mill."

"I heard they might update it to Easy-Care."

"Not this one. They got other mills to update, in other towns. I hate to see it. It's going to cost us plenty. Six months from now we'll be back in the goddam feed bid'ness alone. At least in Hope Mills. We didn't have that Lincoln dealership over in Aberdeen, we'd be hurting. Get the golf people from up North over there. They'll take a train down here, then decide they have to have a car after all. I could blow the old man's brains out. He was an original stockholder of the old Hope Mills, three or four of them. When the Industries started buying up, he could have had new stock. He took cash-money! Now they're going to make a billion, billion dollars with that new cloth, all around the state, except here. Jesus."

"I want to try out that Fairlane."

"Shit, Ramsey. You act like a nigger on Saturday night. You can't afford that car."

"I want to try it out," Les said, coughing a little.

"I ain't got time for dry runs. You cough in my face one more time, I'm going to beat the shit out of you. You old boys don't take any care of yourself over there. Every one of you has got rotten lungs by now. Why don't you just tie a rag over your nose and mouth on the job? Act like you ain't got sense to come in out of the rain."

"I'll just drive it around the block," Les said.

"The hell you will. I can't fool with you anymore. You were talking cash-money. I thought you were ready to get what you could for that thing and start walking to work. Hell, you can see the goddam Mill from y'all's houses. You practically living on company property. I'd walk, it was me. It won't be but a few days a week, for a couple more months, take my word for it. You off today, ain't you?"

Little Wiggins turned and looked out to the street. Tollie ducked down. But not before she'd seen his face: Something bright-white capped on his teeth. Blue-black dyed hair combed over his naked skull. Mean little red eyes.

"How much could you give me? Cash-money," Les asked.

"Come on, Ramsey. I can't mess with you all day. First you say cash-money, then you say a different used car, now you say cash-money again. I think you'd be making a big mistake to buy any kind of car right now. Keep your money and pecker in your pants and everything'll work out bye and bye."

"I'm interested in cash-money."

"I don't know. I'll have to go ask Daddy, but not a whole hell of a lot. We don't have much call for junk like that."

"Well. Go ask him then."

"Keep it in your pants," Little Wiggins said. Tollie could tell he was ticked. She inched up and looked through the two glass truck windows to where Little Wiggins was waddling off.

"Tollie!" Les said.

Tollie shifted her eyes and stared at Les through the windows, then walked around the truck to where he was standing in his khaki work clothes and a black cowboy hat.

"What are you doing down here, girl?" Les asked.

"It's a free country," Tollie said, irritated. "What are you doing, selling off the only piece of property we own? Does Mamma know what you're up to?"

"I'm just practicing," Les said defensively. "Horse-trading. I got to get into another line of work any day now. You see that son of bitch's pants?" They watched Little Wiggins' big butt disappear into the jukebox-front of the building. His khaki pants had a buckle on the back, below the waistband. Some of the boys at school wore that kind of pants, boys in the college preparatory courses.

"They call the style Ivy League," Tollie said.

"I wouldn't wear a pair of pants like that," Les said. "What's the point? Looks like the only purpose that buckle could have would be to tighten up the ass of your pants. If you're rich enough to go to an ivy league college, it looks like you'd be able to buy a pair of pants that fit you in the first place. Not that Little Wiggins ever did go to that kind of college."

"I think I heard he took a year's worth of Business over at State," Tollie said.

"Yeah. Figured a year was enough to teach him how to jap and jew and gyp the rest of us for the rest of his life." Les took off his hat and wiped his forehead. "If I'd had his advantages I wouldn't have been working when I was ten years old, messing up my lungs so I couldn't get into the War."

"Here we go again," Tollie said.

"You do things right in Wartime," Les said, putting his hat back on, "you can come out better than the ivy league. Doors open for you. Money and jobs fall into your hands from out of the blue."

"Who says?" Tollie said. "I wish you wouldn't feel sorry for yourself all the time. It's unbecoming."

"If you do like Audie Murphy done, they make you a movie star. Riding the purple sage and heading them off at the pass. Making a fortune."

94

"Have you been talking to Lily? Can we move into the shade?"

"I'd rather be Audie Murphy than anybody I know of," Les said as they walked toward the shade of the building. "Somebody would probably just give him a new Ford if he was in the market for one, or a Cadillac, or an Arabian mare. Everybody thought I was dogging it but what was I supposed to do: wear a sign that said I'd rather be over there shooting japs than driving a son of a bitching cotton truck but I got lung disease? Aw, yeah, sure you have, and I guess you can't walk ten yards with them flat feet, either, and I guess that's the jaundice running down your backside, that's how they'd have felt about it. Of course, if I'd had Wiggins' money, I could of dogged it and nobody would of thought a thing about it. That's the way it goes. Nobody gives the Les Ramseys of the world the benefit of the doubt."

"Stop it," Tollie said.

"Not that much to fight for anymore," Les said grimly. "Unless you can come out of it and go into the western movies, a hero playing a hero. Double-hero."

"You're talking junk," Tollie said. "What are you up to?"

"What are you up to?" Les asked suspiciously. "Dragging around downtown in the sun in the heat of the day? I asked first."

"None of your business," Tollie said. She wished she had another coke. She felt like she and Les were on "Death Valley Days."

"Sneaking around to meet some soldier, I reckon. You're going to end up sorry you were ever born."

"I don't have much to go," Tollie said. "Leave me alone. It's my birthday."

"Happy Birthday," Les said, looking over at the lake. "I ain't forgot. I got you something for this evening."

"You don't have to," Tollie said, softening. Les always had got her something nice for her birthday, even if it was just a little something. "I know you're on part-time now."

"You see that son of a bitch's shirt?" Les said. "Made out of cotton from India! Just when the USA is getting out of cotton. Somebody from work said them shirts don't even hold their dye when you wash them and that's what rich old boys are buying them for."

"Bleeding Madras," Tollie said. "You have to iron it too."

"Fourteen, fifteen dollars a shirt," Les said incredulously. "Jesus. Groceries for a week. More than a week. He thinks I'm going to give him my goddam Ford. They say 'trade-in,' then jack up the price on the other car so that they get yours for nothing, then turn around, and sell it the same way. I think he ought to be in jail, him and his old daddy both."

"Calm down before you have a stroke," Tollie said.

Les took off his cowboy hat and pulled out his handkerchief. Thinks he's Rowdy Yates, Tollie thought as she watched him squint across the parking lot and wipe his forehead. No. Thinks he's Gil Favor, Trail Boss.

"I'd give a year's pay to have that," Les said, nodding at a new white pick-up.

"Well, if you would, I guess you could have it," Tollie said.

"Don't be a smart-ass," Les said. "Like your mamma. A family man's got to have an automobile. A truck's a luxury. Look at that thing."

Tollie looked, then looked away.

"A family man's got to stay put, however much shit he's got to take," Les said, putting his hat back on and adjusting it with both hands.

Josh Randall, Tollie thought. He *wishes*. Bounty Hunter.

"Daddy did," Les said. "Stayed put and worked in tar, pitch, and resin till them lonesome pines killed him dead, keeping food on the table for a bunch of snot-nose kids that never amounted to anything."

"Now you're begrudging the food in my mouth," Tollie said. "Such as it is."

"Whose fault is that," Les said. "She must think she can mop up the floor with me. One of these nights I'm going to go on back there and roll her over on her back and take what I've got coming."

"Stop it!" Tollie said, slapping her hands onto her ears. "I'm just a kid. This is inappropriate."

"Sorry," Les said. "You're right."

"I got to get going," Tollie said, jamming her hands into her dungaree pockets, fiddling with her coins.

"You still ain't told me where."

"And I'm not going to."

"You'd think I'd deserve that much." Les fixed her with a look. "Just for putting food in your mouth. You'd think I could ask anything I want. Trust you not to slip around. Keep your knees together till you're out from under my roof."

"Come on!" Tollie moved away from Les.

"I keep my ear to the ground," Les said.

"Ho, yeah. I've got to go."

"Naw. Stay with me a minute. Watch how I do with Little Wiggins."

96

"I've got to go. I can't stand around all day messing with you. Especially the way you talk about her."

"I'm sorry," Les said. "I'm just a fool in love. In love with a cold, half-crazy woman. Hey, Mr. Hawkins." Les nodded at a heavy-set man with wiry hair the color of Crackerjacks.

The man nodded back and kept on his path to the front of the lot. "What's your price on that Fairlane?" Les said.

"Six hundred. Firm."

"How about five hundred?" Les said.

"Don't waste my time," the man said, pausing. "None of you old boys is gong to be buying."

"You got to clear five hundred with old man Wiggins first, is that it?" Les said, grinning, winking at Tollie.

Oh, Boy, Tollie thought.

"Hell, no," Hawkins said. "What do you think? I been working here thirty years. I'm the goddam manager."

"How about five hundred?" Les said.

"Les," Tollie said.

"None of you old boys is going to be buying," Hawkins repeated. "But if you was, I'd let it go for $550, firm, and I don't have to check it out with anybody. Now stop talking shit and get on out of here and let a man work."

"Thank you, Sir," Les said to Hawkins' back. "Appreciate your time."

"What are you up to?" Tollie asked. Little Wiggins had come out of the door the man had gone into and was coming toward them.

"Watch this," Les said.

"Daddy said seventy-five dollars," Little Wiggins said. "But I think he's crazy. I wouldn't give you more than fifty if it was up to me."

He didn't even acknowledge me, Tollie thought. The shit.

"Then I'm glad it ain't," Les said. "I'll take it. Here's the title, already signed."

"Les," Tollie said, but Little Wiggins already had his billfold out of his back pocket. He counted out some bills for Les and put a quarter-inch stack of money back in his billfold. What did he mean he was going to be hurting too? Tollie thought. With that kind of money in his pocket.

"Just in case your ship comes in, you can bring this money back and I'll give you eight-five trade-in on the Fairlane," Little Wiggins said to Les.

"You still owe me five," Les said, counting the money. Wiggins brought his billfold back out and gave it to him, no sign of remorse.

"How much is that Fairlane," Les asked.

"It's seven hundred, firm. But you could have it for six twenty-five. Thirty days to pay."

"Thirty days?" Les said. Tollie could see panic in his eyes. "It used to be twelve months."

"That's use-to-be," Wiggins said.

"I can't pay for nothing in thirty days," Les said.

"That's what I been trying to tell you, Ramsey. Give my regards to that hot-looking wife of yours. Come on back when you need some feed."

Late that afternoon Tollie was riding with Les in his old Ford, going where, God only knew.

"I can't believe how you've ruined my birthday," Tollie said. They'd spent the whole afternoon haggling with Little Wiggins, and it had still cost Les a hundred dollars to buy his car back. "I wish you'd come in here every day of the week," Little Wiggins had said when he'd handed over the keys, grinning like a jack o'lantern. "I could make a living wage off of you alone."

Les had pushed Tollie into the car and taken off. "Like I don't have a right to any plans of my own," she'd protested. But he'd been so mad it had taken her this long, almost out to the Rockfish Creek, to get through to him and really let him have it.

"I think you've gone crazy!" she yelled, punching him in the arm. "I want to go back to town."

"If I have—gone crazy—I guess I'd be like everybody else in the house. Don't you ever hit me, girl. I'll wear you out."

"I'm sorry," Tollie said. But she wasn't. She'd like to hit him again. And again. "Where are you taking me?" she demanded. "I'm fixing to jump out of this car and go call the law on you, I swear it."

"Hush up," Les said, pulling into The Last Outpost, a store and service station.

"I'm going to run for it," Tollie said, jerking her door open. Les caught her arm.

"No, you ain't," he said. "You're going to come on out to the woods with me and see what's what. Why should I go through everything I have to go through without anybody to keep me company?"

"I can't believe you," Tollie said, amazed. Was he going to make a pass? She'd heard a person's stepfather would, but Les had never tried anything with her. He'd never even spanked her. Never even kissed her on the cheek.

"I can't believe much of anything that's going on in my own life," Les said. "Stay put. We're going to sneak up on your mamma and her boyfriend, and if you're with me, maybe you can talk me out of blowing both their goddam brains out."

Tollie watched Les go into the station. So even Les thought something was going on with Janice and Mr. Faircloth. Blow their brains out—He ought to be shot, himself, for saying a thing like that. Kidnapper.

She felt like she was living on the Forbidden Planet.

After a few minutes, she watched Les come out of the store with a brown paper bag, which he stuck in the backseat. They took off, almost hitting a big white sign with a red hand on it, advertising Madame Lucretia's palm-reading services. The hand was divided by several thick black lines.

"Give me a beer," Les said, when they were pulled up under some pines off the road that ran alongside the Faircloth's farm, with a clear view of the house and yard and outbuildings. Tollie could see a couple of people moving around there, a couple of cars, some farm equipment, Mr. Faircloth's nice white pick-up truck pulled up next to a shed.

Les reached up under his seat.

"Don't get your gun out," Tollie said in a panic.

"Church-key's in the glove compartment," Les said, bringing out a pair of binoculars that he used to use for hunting. He scanned the Faircloths' farmyard and put the binoculars on the seat between him and Tollie. "It's a little early for the bus," he said, taking the beer Tollie had opened for him. "That's how she'll be coming. Why don't she have the son of a bitch pick her up somewhere? Not to save *my* face! Get me my magazine. It's in the bag."

"What do you think I am, your slave?" Tollie said, but she got up on her knees and reached over into the bag on the backseat, coming up with a copy of *Fury*, a man wrestling with an alligator on the cover of it, up to his waist in dark water on which the titles of articles were spelled out in red: "Hell in the Everglades" in big letters, with "What

Women Want" and "The Real Khrushchev—As Seen Through A Vodka Glass" in smaller letters.

"It's probably the last one I'll read," Les said. "I can't waste too many more quarters on magazines. Not when a quarter'll buy you two packs of cigarettes, or a pound of hamburger, or a gallon of gas, with change left over. That's all right. These damn things have got so they depress me, anyway. Everything's about the past. Old Wars. Old West."

"You're a fool for the Old West," Tollie said. "You say it every day of your life. Even today. Besides, this one's got a story about Khrushchev. The present."

Les looked back at the cover. "They sure are letting that old boy have it," he said. "Why? Everybody in Russia has a job, I read in the news. Course the news said that was bad because you didn't get to pick your job, government picked it for you. Well, shit—blow the suckers up with the A-bomb *and* the H-bomb! Les Ramsey, American, got to pick his job." Les rolled up the magazine and whacked it against the dashboard, making Tollie jump. "He picked to go to work in a mill when he was ten years old, open his lungs and let them fibers float on in—part of the job *he* picked, mind you—"

"Stop it," Tollie said.

"*Picked* to drive a cotton truck instead of going to the War when his lungs got full, picked to work at another mill when his lungs cleared out a little, and now that they're getting full again, he's done picked to get out of a job altogether. That's the *American* way, can't beat it!"

"Shut up. Let's go home. This is stupid."

"You can pick a job or pick being a bum, here in the land of the free. Naw, I wouldn't give up the right to pick and choose like Americans can do for anything on this Earth. I'd rather be dead than have some old Red Russian picking my next job out of a hat. I'd rather starve to death, which I probably will. You too."

"If you hadn't *abducted* me—which you did," Tollie said, "I'd be down at Pandora's Box, signing up for a paying job myself."

Les took a swig of his beer and flipped through the magazine. "Ain't nothing worth reading in this thing. Looka here. Learn Radio-Television Repair by Practicing at Home in Spare Time. New Shop-Method Way to Learn Auto-Mechanics at Home in Your Spare Time. Mail Order Business, Your Big Opportunity! Shoe Repair Course. How to Write and Sell Songs. How to Get a Good Job." He coughed.

101

"One of these days I'm going to kick the bucket and nobody, nobody at all is going to notice or give a shit."

"Awwww," Tollie said. She did feel a little sorry for him, though. It was probably true.

"Hell, half the time, I don't give a shit myself," Les said. "What for? Nothing's gone the way I'd hoped it would."

"Don't feel like the Lone Ranger!" Tollie fumed. "You don't have a gun with you, do you?"

"Maybe I do."

"You don't!" Tollie said, realizing he didn't. "I should have made a run for it back at The Last Outpost. Jesus. It sounds like we've ended up in some old Western movie together. I could shoot *you*."

"I'm going to look around," Les said, dropping the magazine on the seat and picking up the binoculars. He got out of the car and walked a few steps away, finishing his beer. Tollie watched him drop the bottle in the pinestraw and lift his binoculars. It was just as well she was out here. At least she'd find out something definite about her mother and Mr. Faircloth. Maybe.

She picked up the magazine and studied a lingerie ad, "Make Her Over to Please YOU!" #811 Sweetheart Pants, heart-shaped nylon underpants. #96 Up-and-Out brassiere. #1310 Curves Adrift, a garment it would be hard to find a name for. She couldn't see Janice in any of these things. Did Les? Janice was losing so much weight it would be a sad sight. Tollie couldn't see her mother in #779 Whiplash, or #144 Better Half, or #781 Good Girl, a baby-doll pajama. And even so. . . .

Janice and Les were both losing weight. Maybe they were just wasting away on her and one day she'd be a complete orphan. Maybe that wouldn't be so bad!

"That bus is slow as mole-asses," Les said, reaching into the backseat for another beer, then getting back in behind the steering wheel. "That's what those old boys say at work. 'Ramsey, you slow as mole-asses. We keep cutting back, you going to be the first to go.' I'd like to blow the damn place up, I tell you."

He turned on the radio and he and Tollie listened to the news. More on Khrushchev's visit, the payola thing, a human skull that was almost two million years old found in Africa.

"That's depressing," Les said.

"What?" Tollie said.

"That skull."

"I don't think so. I think it's interesting."

"I don't know," Les said, fiddling with the binoculars. "Man might be as old as two million years. For some reason, that depresses me mightily."

"Let me know when something happens," Tollie said, laying her head back on the seat and closing her eyes.

"Right now, there's just a couple of old crows resting on the fence," Les said. "I hope I can tough it out till she gets here. My ass is getting so bony it hurts to sit on it. I'm swimming in my clothes like a trout. I bet I've lost thirty-five pounds this summer."

"More than likely crows are all we're going to see," Tollie said, keeping her eyes closed, trying to listen to the interesting commercial for Madame Lucretia, "She hope me, she'll hope you. . . ." On the white station, now. Think of it.

"I hear a lot," Les said. "That's for sure. Men at work saying, hear that kid of yours is running around with jungle bunny-spics from out at the Base."

Tollie opened an eye and looked at him, then closed it. "I guess that must make you glad I'm not really your kid, then."

"Hear that crazy wife of yours is sneaking up to Rowen Faircloth's on the bus in the afternoon."

"I'll believe it when we see it."

"Hear this, hear that, hear the other thing. It's hard for a man to take."

Tollie opened her eyes and sat back up. You couldn't get a minute's peace in this world. Outside the window the crows flew away, one after the other one.

"Bad enough to have everybody know she took the blade to herself," Les said.

"*Shut* up!" Tollie said. "I swear—"

"People don't understand a thing like that," Les said, drawing on his beer. "They don't see it like the worrisome thing it is and feel sorry for you. They see it kind of like whoring around, a mark against you. Of course I wasn't worried what people would think when it happened, I just thought: Good Lord, don't take her away from me, Give me another chance to do right by this woman and her little girl, But if you got to take her, take me too, I ain't got one other damn thing worth living for."

Les fumbled in his shirt pocket and brought out a cigarette and lit it. Tollie felt her heart go to pulp—for Les! Goddamn it. What next?

"You worry too much about what people think in general," she said. "Let them think. They *can't* think much, most of them."

"If you don't have your reputation, you don't have much," Les said.

"Jesus," Tollie said.

"It's easier on you to lose your job than your reputation. Women can ruin a man's reputation for him, quicker, whoring around or giving people the idea they're whoring around, than about anything else."

Big Mack came on the radio and announced it was time for Platters Without Chatter—A Solid Hour of Rock 'n' Roll.

"I hate that s.o.b.," Les said. "It's the best time of the whole afternoon, when that son of a bitch shuts his fat ugly mouth and lets the music play. How a man can wear a beard in this heat is a mystery. I saw his old ugly picture in the paper, looking like the Devil."

"I'm surprised you listen to WMIL," Tollie said.

"Habit. Young boys from work listen to it on break. I like country music myself." He turned the dial. "Let me see if I can find us some." After a minute of static, he went back to WMIL and turned down the volume even lower. He threw the cigarette out the window.

"Tastes like Hell," he said to Tollie. "Nothing tastes worth a shit anymore."

He leaned over the seat and got a bag of pork rinds and another beer out of the paper sack and opened them.

"You want something?" he asked Tollie, moving the pork rinds toward her.

"Nothing you got," Tollie said.

"They taste kind of rancid," Les said, finishing a pork rind. "I guess I'll eat them anyway. Can't afford to waste much now."

He finished the rinds and tossed the wrapper out the window.

"Litterbug," Tollie said.

Les sipped on his beer and watched the farmyard. "Beer tastes like horse piss," he said. "Hot already. I had to pawn my damn cooler."

"You mean the one you got with the green stamps you hid from Mamma?" Tollie said.

"I didn't want much," Les said. "A cooler full of shaved ice, the necks of Schlitz bottles sticking up like star-points, at the end of a day's honest work. Drive out to the woods, pop a few cool ones, maybe go over to the lake and take a swim and wash the Mill off. Listen to a little country music. Go home and have your wife come kiss you at the door, your kid get you a sandwich to tide you over till you got to that home-cooked meal that was smelling up the house like perfume. The Life of Riley. Why was it so hard to get so little?"

"You're the depressing one," Tollie said, sick to realize how close her own dreams were to Les's: home-cooked food, an easy home life.

"It seems like there'd be enough to go around," Les said. "Perry Como got 25 million dollars to sell Kraft cheese! I heard it on the radio. They're sending satellites up into Outer Space. They got something they call a Heat-Tracking Missile, cost millions of dollars."

"It'll probably track its way to Hope Mills, given how hot it is this summer," Tollie said, fanning herself with the *Fury*.

"How much could it cost to convert a mill to Easy-Care? A drop in the slop."

Suddenly Les threw his beer bottle out the window and threw open the car door. The bottle hit a pine tree and sent beer foaming on its bark.

"What's the matter with you?" Tollie said, scared again.

"I'm going downhill like a snowball going to Hell, that's what!" Les said. He hit the dash of the car. Then he hit it again, harder.

"You're going to bust your hand," Tollie said.

"I don't give a shit!" Les said. He hit the dash again. "That baby just died in the middle of the night. It stopped breathing without making one goddam sound that you could hear. She went in there the next morning with his bottle and found him laying on his back, cold and gone."

"Les—"

"I was just shaving, like it was a regular day. I saw her standing at the door, looking like somebody had clouted her upside the head. That's what I thought it was, that somebody had got in the house. Then she started to moan, not a tear in her eye, just that long, long, long moan—"

"Stop it," Tollie said, putting her hands over her ears, which didn't help at all.

"Like she was reaching way down inside herself for everything that was there so she could empty it out. I knew it was him then. I ran in there, thought at first I was wrong. He looked like the picture of a baby in an advertisement, toes curled up in the sock-feet of his pajamas, hands back to either side of his head. But he was dead."

"Cut it out, Les!" Tollie felt her eyes stinging. "We know all this." But Les seemed out of her range, transfixed. Maybe he's gone crazy too, she thought. Maybe all of us are going to be crazy.

"He was as dead as anybody ever was in this world," Les said. "I was crying and running back to where she was and got there just in time to catch her when she sank down. I pulled her back up to me and held her tight to me like that, like something off a movie poster. Crying till I could stop. Then I could tell she wasn't there any more, not my Janice. She'd done emptied herself out."

Les looked at Tollie, teary-eyed. He took her hand and squeezed it. She pulled it away and put it to her face.

"You were standing in the hall in your nightgown, looking scared," Les said. "Arlene was at the front door, banging. She'd called the sheriff."

"Y'all started drinking," Tollie said, wiping her eyes. She knew it all by heart too.

"Yes," Les said. "While we were waiting for the meat wagon, Arlene and me had a boilermaker, even if it was seven o'clock in the morning. Arlene kept going into the living room every couple of minutes where Janice was sitting on the couch like a zombie. I watched them from the kitchen table, through the door. 'Janice, Honey,' Arlene would say and put her hand on her, then pull it away. A few minutes later she'd go in there again, 'Janice, Honey'. . . . "

"Then you came down to his room," Tollie said, shivering, saying her part.

"You'd pulled up a chair next to the crib," Les said. "You were sitting there with the bottle of milk in your hand. I could see his elbows poking at the pajamas like two marbles, the creases in the palms of his little hands. I never been more miserable a day in my life. His little bunched-up diaper under the pajamas, where his legs came together. Seeds dead in their pod, end of the line."

"You would think a thing like that," Tollie said, snuffling.

"Maybe it's just as well," Les said. "Why would you want to roll out a whole line of anything from an old out-of-work, out-of-luck hopeless snowball-to-hell, rotten-lunged piece of shit like Lester Ramsey that can't even take care of his family?"

Les cut off the radio and wiped his eyes. Tollie could see that the crows had returned to the fence and had brought their friends.

"I'd never shoot her," Les said. "You don't need to worry about that. You don't need to worry anymore than we've already worried you."

Tollie watched the crows swoop down on something, maybe something dead in the field.

"Even if she was to put horns on me with every pair of pants in Hope Mills and out at the Base," Les said. "Stomped my name down in the dirt so far I'd never be able to lift it up again, I wouldn't hurt her. I'd

106

cut my throat before I'd hurt her any more than she's already been hurt. That woman has been hurt enough to last her all her days, and then some."

"I agree," Tollie said. "I need a tissue." She fumbled in the glove compartment until she located an old napkin. She wiped her nose and eyes. "I'm not going to hide around out here and watch for her, either. Let's go. Maybe I can still get down to Pandora's Box before it closes. This isn't doing anybody any good."

"I got to know," Les said. He turned back on the radio.

"I don't," Tollie said firmly, opening her door and getting out of the car.

"It's a long walk," Les said, leaning over to look up at her with his teary eyes.

"I can use the exercise," Tollie said. "I'll take a beer for the road, though." She reached into the back and hooked a bottle of beer.

"Naw, I wouldn't hurt her," Les said. He leaned his head back against his seat, Tollie's long walk home apparently forgot. "I guess I'm glad to know that about myself."

Tollie was glad to know it about him too. She closed the door and opened her beer, put the church-key on the dash through the open window. "Bye," she said. She walked around to the back of the car and poured the beer on the pinestraw, which was smoldering where the cigarette Les had tossed out had landed. Let him sit peacefully in some good knowledge about himself, she thought. As long as he could. A minute's peace was a hard thing to come by. Already she could see the bus coming into sight down on the road.

About a quarter mile from where Les had parked his car, Tollie—out of sight of Les's car, Les out of her mind!—hid in the trees and watched the bus come to a stop. Somebody was getting off. Squinting, Tollie could recognize the sundress, even this far away. Janice stopped to say something to whoever was tending the vegetable stand—a little boy, it looked like—then started up the lane, carrying something as big as a suitcase. Had her mother run away from home? To move in with Mr. Faircloth? The idea made Tollie cold inside.

It's probably just my birthday present, Tollie realized with relief. In one of those big shopping bags with handles.

When Janice was about half-way up the lane, a little red car turned off the road and followed her, kicking up dust. Tollie's heart jerked. Him. She recognized the car. What was going on?

When the sports car came up to Janice, it stopped and she got in and rode on up into the farmyard. Janice got out and then lifted her bag out. The cute boy got out. He had on a shirt now, a blue one, and jeans. He walked to the house and went inside.

A woman emerged from some shrubbery and went up to Janice. Tollie wished she had Les's binoculars. The woman had dark hair, with something red in it, a bow maybe. She was skinny, wearing a white blouse and some kind of skirt, moving up close to Janice, then jumping in front of her when Janice tried to get by. The woman grabbed at Janice, hooked onto her arm. She was saying something, and Janice was saying something back, but Tollie couldn't make it out. Then somebody came out of a shed, wiping his hands on a rag. Mr. Faircloth, it looked like. Janice said something to him and he reached in his pocket and handed her something. Janice set her shopping bag down and took out a box. Tollie squinted. It looked like her mother cut a ribbon from the box and gave it to the woman. Then Janice handed something back to Mr. Faircloth, probably a pocket knife, and the two of them walked to the shed and disappeared inside. Tollie could hear the woman calling something after them, but she couldn't make it out. Then the woman went around behind the shed.

Tollie stayed put. She ought to go on home. She was as bad as Les. It was good there were so many people around. At least Les couldn't sneak up on the shed.

After about fifteen minutes, with nothing happening, Tollie was interested to see some movement. She watched the cute boy come out of the house and get in his little car. He revved the engine, then drove back down the dusty lane and headed the opposite way he'd come, away from town.

"Who're you?"

Tollie whirled around to the voice that had come from right over her shoulder, almost giving her a heart attack.

It was the woman who'd been talking to Janice in the farmyard. You could see the woman wasn't right. She looked about the age of Janice, but she also looked like a little girl. She had a stick-like girl's body and a large bobbing head. She wore her thick black hair straight, pulled to one side and caught with a large bow, not a red one anymore, but a lilac-colored one, tied crooked. "Who're you?" she said again.

"Nobody," Tollie said. A blood-colored lipstick was smeared around the woman's mouth and the ends of her hair were cut Dutch-boy style, so straight the hair seemed to cut a line across the white collar of her blouse. The blouse had several slashes of grass-stain on its front and it seemed in danger of slipping out of the woman's red plaid skirt. She was wearing loafers and anklets, their tops rolled down just once, as neat as the ends of her hair.

"I'm somebody," the woman said. "I'm Wiggie. Don't you have a name?"

"Tanya," Tollie said, giving her real name. Then she wished she hadn't. It was as unusual as "Tollie" in Hope Mills. She should have made up a name.

"Do you like my new ribbon?" the woman asked, tugging on the bow in her hair until it drooped and looked like it would fall. Each fingernail on the woman's hand was outlined in grime. "Janice gave it to me. I told her it was my birthday, but it isn't."

"Who's Janice," Tollie asked carefully, looking down the path and then back in the woods, looking for a way to get away without this woman getting her in trouble for trespassing, spying.

"My friend. She goes in the shed with my brother."

Tollie felt sick. "I've got to get home now," she said. "It was good to meet you, Wiggie."

"I told her I'd tell, if she didn't give me a present, and she said I couldn't tell because they don't let me go into Hope Mills. But I said, yes, they do. I do so go. I go every month to the beauty shop for my cut. I go to Belk's and Kresge's to buy my clothes and make-up. She wasn't nice at all."

Tollie could see a storm gathering inside the woman's eyes.

"I'd better get going now," Tollie said. "Happy birthday, whenever it is."

The woman brightened. "I can pretend it's today. I got a present from Janice, and I made Rowen do Bugs Bunny. I kept telling Janice I was going to tell, even after I had the ribbon, until Rowen said, 'Th-th-that's all, folks, goddamn it!' and then it was perfect."

The woman smiled wide, her lipstick stretching out like a blurry wound. She lifted her arms up and waved them around, pulling her blouse all the way out of her skirt. Her skinny legs were knock-kneed, Tollie noticed, awkwardly broken by the skirt and anklets. She looked like a marionette hung crooked on its strings.

"Well, goodbye," Tollie said, backing away, eager to get away from Wiggie. She looked like . . . a vast dis-order—the middle of her: the line of haircut chopping off her head, the lines of the anklets chopping off her feet. It gave Tollie the creeps.

Tollie turned and hurried down the path toward the road. She'd better really hurry. The trees were thinner here. Somebody might see her. What if that woman followed her?

"I'll never tell, now," Wiggie yelled after her. "I won't tell at the beauty shop and I won't tell at Belk's and I won't tell at Kresge's."

Tollie could see the road up ahead. It was her goal, but it was also going to expose her. That seemed like her life, all the way around. Her heat rash was eating her alive inside her dungarees. Now there was no doubt about her mother and Mr. Faircloth!

Well. She guessed even Janice had to get out of that house sometimes. She and Mr. Faircloth. Tollie and Ramírez. It would probably end the same way too. . . .

Tollie studied her shoes moving beneath her. They looked like they were made of dust. She looked over her shoulder. Wiggie was nowhere to be seen. Nobody at all at her back. She looked ahead. Maybe Les would come by and pick her up.

At the road, Tollie turned away from town. She was going to have to go back the other way or somebody would see her passing by the house. At least the kid at the vegetable stand would see her. She'd seen him pretty well before she made her turn: sitting under the shed in a straw hat, among the boxes of stunted sweet corn and crook-neck squash and tomatoes, the puny harvest of drought, looking like Huckleberry Finn reading a comic book. Any minute Janice might come back down the road, or she and Mr. Faircloth might drive down it in his pick-up. She could hear her mother now, "Tollie! What in the world—"

Where in the world was Les, that fool? The highway stretched out in front of her forever, the horizon invisible in the haze, the heat like High Noon, even this late in the day. Oh, God.

The little red car came out of the haze at the same moment she recognized its sound. Tollie stopped in her tracks, looking around her. Nowhere to hide. Not even a ditch to lie down in.

"Hi," the boy said, loud, over the motor, once he'd stopped next to her, not even bothering to pull off the road. "You're a long way from Rolando's Beach."

"Hi," Tollie said, looking behind her. The kid at the vegetable stand had looked up, then he went back to his comic book. The house and Rowen Faircloth's notorious shed were out of sight behind the pines.

"Can I give you a ride somewhere," the boy said. "My name's Raeford Faircloth."

"I wouldn't want to take you out of your way," Tollie said—meaning, I wouldn't want you to get a good look at me on the worst day of my life! "My name's Tanya Ramsey," she said.

"Let me turn around," Raeford said.

"No. I'm actually going the way you're headed," Tollie said, wrenching open the door of the car, already sorry about the dust she was getting ready to bring in it. "I just get turned the wrong way sometimes."

Raeford grinned at her beneath his sunglasses as she settled into the seat. He put the car in gear. "I can tell you're smart enough to know the difference," he said.

In the kitchen, late in the day, Janice's hands shook when she moved the hastily made paper tube with icing in it across the top of the cheesecake, making a large pink rose. She had another tube filled with green icing for the leaves and for "Tollie." There wasn't going to be room to write "Happy Birthday," and that was just as well. Now that Tollie knew more about her birth, "birthday" wasn't innocent anymore. Tollie was always listening for what words said that a person could overlook. She wouldn't see the *wish* in "Happy Birthday," Janice thought, giving the rose one last wobbly leaf. She'd imagine somebody coming into my hospital room and saying—sarcastically, given the circumstances—happy birth day? That was Tollie. There ought to be something she could do in life with that brand of imagination.

Janice took a deep breath. Now was the test: could she get the Tollie on right? A rose would look like a rose, as long as it was pink and on a cake. But the name—

She held her breath and made the T. She'd print. She'd never manage cursive. She hesitated. Should she write Tollie or Tanya? She bent to sniff the cake, hoping the earlier heat and then the freezing hadn't hurt it. It smelled okay to her. Not like a flour cake, but okay.

Janice steadied her tube. Why not Tanya? Tollie was growing into it. Maybe it could change her luck, or even the gloomier parts of her personality.

When the cake was decorated, Janice put it in the refrigerator. She could hear Tollie stirring around back in her room—not banging things around, thank god. When Janice got home, she'd gone directly to Tollie's door, which was locked, giving her a chill. She'd knocked on it until Tollie had snapped at her to go away. Janice was still a little afraid that, after all she'd managed to do, the birthday would be ruined. Knowing Tollie, she would think of it as the anniversary of the next-to-saddest day of her mother's life, nothing to celebrate.

Janice opened the refrigerator again to see what they could possibly have for supper. In all the effort of the day—picking up the dress on lay-away, going out to the country on the bus, getting back home, the cake—she'd forgot about supper. She was too tired to make anything complicated. She found a package of ham, an onion, a few green olives with pimento, mustard, a can of pork and beans in the cupboard. She turned on the oven, put the beans in a casserole with the sliced onion and some brown sugar. She spread each piece of ham with mustard and rolled it up, skewered it with a toothpick and buried the rolls in the beans. She put the casserole in the oven and cleaned off the counter. After the ham and beans baked, she'd stick an olive on each toothpick before she took the casserole to the table. It would look festive, and it was all she could manage.

"Mamma?" Tollie said from the door.

Janice looked up.

"I'm sorry I was so mean. I was just waking up."

"Your eyes look red. I'm sorry I woke you up. I just wanted to know you were all right."

"I wish you wouldn't worry so much."

Janice smiled at Tollie. "Happy birthday, sweetheart."

"Thanks," Tollie said. "I got a card from Aunt Gracie."

"That's good. She never forgets you, does she?"

"Nope. She never does. It smells like you're cooking."

"A special casserole! But the really special thing is in the frigidaire— don't open the door till it's time."

"I need the cornstarch. I put it in there because I thought it might help my heat rash more if it were cold."

"Why don't you use your new bath powder?"

"I don't know. I feel like I ought to save it."

"Don't!" Janice said. "We've been thinking that way too long as it is."

"I guess," Tollie said.

"I've got a present for you," Janice said.

"What is it? Cornstarch?"

"You look like you mean it! Of course it's not cornstarch. Here—" Janice went over to the table and brought the shopping bag back to Tollie. "We have to go in on the couch so you have room to spread it out. I'm sorry about the bow. I guess I lost it on the bus, some way or other."

On the couch, Tollie lifted the sundress out of the box and laid it in her lap still in its tissue paper, folded back to expose the bodice of the dress.

"Oh, Mamma." She sounded stunned with pleasure. That's what I was after, Janice realized. I just wanted to give her back, if just for a minute, a . . . capacity.

Tollie sat with the dress on her lap, touching the fabric with her finger. "Is it some kind of new Easy-Care?" she asked, skeptically.

"Of course not! It's about the best grade of cotton I've ever seen in my life, and that's from the daughter of the best cotton-grader in the southeast United States."

"Well I didn't know," Tollie said, lifting the dress out of its paper. "I've never felt cotton like this. It's so soft I bet you don't even have to iron it, just wash it and let the breeze blow out the wrinkles." She smiled at Janice. Then she raised up and leaned over to kiss her lightly on the lips. "Thanks, Mamma. This is the nicest thing I've ever owned."

"Well, I hope it's just the beginning of nice things for you, Baby. I really do."

Janice heard Les's car pull into the driveway. "There's Les. Put the dress in the box for now and put it in your room. Just let him think I gave you what's in the frigidaire. It'll be easier."

At the table, after the casserole, which had survived the oven without the toothpicks catching on fire, Janice was relieved to see— furious with herself that she'd been so stupid: they were charred black—Janice brought the cheesecake to the table.

"How did you have time to make a cake today?" Les asked suspiciously. "I thought you might have gone to town."

"I did," Janice said. "I bought it. It didn't cost but a dollar."

"A whole dollar for that little *cake*? With a rose that looks like that one?"

"I wish you wouldn't talk about money all the time," Tollie said to Les.

"If I had more, I wouldn't," Les said, watching Janice's hand shake a little when she began to light the candles on the cake.

"Let's get along," Janice said. "It's our girl's birthday."

"You want me to light them, Mamma?"

"Thank you, Sweetie." Janice handed the matches to Tollie.

"I still want to know why you gave her a Russian name before I die," Les said.

"Me too," Tollie said.

"Play your cards right and I might tell you," Janice said, grinning a little, then looking down.

Les began to feel good inside, in spite of the dollar she'd got god-knows-where and wasted on a single cake. In spite of knowing exactly where she must have got a dollar. He wasn't going to bring that up. It was the first time in about three years she'd smiled and teased him. God, he loved her! It was the only thing inside himself, through and through, that seemed to make up for all he wasn't on the outside, out in the world.

"Hang on a minute," Les said, getting up. "I got a couple things out in the car I need to bring in before we blow out any candles."

"Hurry up," Tollie said. "Wax is going to drip on my cake."

Les brought the champagne in and set it on the table. He'd pawned the binoculars to get it, and it was just New York State, not French. But she was just a kid. She wouldn't know the difference. Hell, he wouldn't know the difference.

"I thought we could put ice in it," he said. "No way to get it home cold in this weather."

"Thank god the summer is almost over," Janice said. "That's another thing to celebrate."

"I can't believe I'm going to drink champagne," Tollie said. She had a fascinated look on her face, Janice thought. This is turning out to be so good. . . .

"Thanks, Les," Tollie said. "The champagne is a nice idea."

"All the way from New York State," Les said.

"Wait till I tell Lily," Tollie said.

"Let me the get the ice." Janice got up and got an ice tray out of the refrigerator. She felt better, for the first time since it happened. She felt a little hope for them. It made her relax inside a little; she almost didn't need any champagne.

"Close your eyes and blow out the candles!" Les exhorted Tollie. "Let's get the show on the road."

Tollie closed her eyes.

"Well?" Les said. "Has she gone to sleep or what?"

"Sh," Janice said. "Let her wish as long as she wants to."

Tollie opened her eyes. "Okay. I'm ready." She blew as hard as she could and all the candles died. "Every last one," she said.

"Hey," Les said, raising one of the cold aluminum tea glasses Janice had put the champagne in, each a different, dazzling color. "Here's to Tollie-Tanya Ramsey, and her Mamma, the two prettiest women in Hopeless Mills."

"Women!" Tollie said, smiling at Janice. Janice winked at her. They all drank the champagne.

"Whew," Tollie said. "I never thought I'd come this far in life—champagne!"

"Wait till you taste the cake," Janice said, beginning to section it off. "It's a special cake that comes from New York. Well, this particular one didn't come from New York, but the recipe did. You're going to love it, both of you."

"I want a big piece," Tollie said.

"Everybody is getting a big piece," Janice said, cutting the cake into thirds.

Look at that, Les thought. I think she's coming around. He took the plate holding his piece of cake and set it in his dinner plate.

"Now," he said, standing up and reaching in the pocket of his loose pants. He brought out a small package, wrapped in gift wrap, tied with a piece of grosgrain ribbon. They'd wrapped it at the store, but he'd had to give them a dime. "It's not what I wanted to get you," he told Tollie.

"That's all right," Tollie said. "The champagne was enough." She unwrapped the package: two Eveready batteries. She looked at Les.

"I'm going to get you one of them battery-radios when I get some money together," Les said. "At least you'll have the batteries. Keep them in the refrigerator and they'll still be good."

"Thanks," Tollie said. "I think that's real nice. It gives me something to look forward to."

"Dig in," Janice said. "I know you're going to love this." She took a bite of the cake. Oh, no, she thought. It got too hot. I know it did. That's what I get for not coming right home that day, that and Les being so sweet for a change. She held her mouth closed and let the cake melt on her tongue and swallowed. God. Will it kill us?

119

"It's good, Mamma," Tollie said, a thoughtful look on her face. She nodded and took another small piece on her fork. "Yes, it's very good. Exotic."

"Good," Les said. "I think so." Can I eat the rest of this without puking my guts out, he thought. I reckon.

"It's not bad," Janice said. Maybe it's not bad, she thought. Maybe it's just the way they make New York cheesecake in Hope Mills.

The three of them sat at the table a long time. Slowly, bite by awkward bite, lifting out the candles as they needed to, they finished the pungent slices of cake, carried their plates to the sink, and went to sit under the Water-Fan to finish the bottle of champagne.

2: THE FALL OF THE YEAR

"Are we going to have a good time tonight or not?" Lily said. "You're acting as nervous as a pregnant cat!"

Don't I have enough to make me nervous? Tollie thought. With all you know, not to mention all you don't know?

She said, "I heard you could get brain damage from drinking grain alcohol."

"You probably can," Lily said, taking a swig from the bottle of spiked Grapette. As usual, she'd brought along the ingredients for Purple Jesus in her tote bag—a glass jar of grain, a plastic lemon full of lemon juice—just in case something got her down. She'd bought the bottle of Grapette at the food stand. She didn't want to be depressed one minute during the last dance of the summer at Rolando's Beach.

Already it was September. They were back in school. It was a hazard, all the way around, pretending that it was still high summer, just for this Saturday night. But I'm up to it, Lily thought. She said, "You can probably damage your stomach, kidneys, liver, eyes and heart, too. But not us. We're too young to get damaged."

They were sitting in the parking lot, in the Oldsmobile, the radio on low, waiting for it to get dark. They'd spent the whole day on the beach. Tollie felt sunburned, and she *was* nervous. Besides all else she had on her mind, she had to sweat the immediate future: Would she be able to dance right, or would she make a fool of herself?

Some people were already dancing in the pavilion, but not many, and not with much enthusiasm. Nothing much would get going before nine, nine-thirty, Lily had said.

If then, Tollie thought. The season was over. This was something else—a gesture of hope and belief in a summer to come, or something else altogether.

Tollie had had her shower in the ladies shower room, washed her hair, put on her dress, Straw Hat perfume, lipstick, flats, nylons fastened onto her garter belt. She felt as ready as she'd ever be.

Lily had taken her shower in her bathing suit. She'd made herself up and fixed her hair and was still sitting in the damp checkerboard-cutout bathing suit, a folded beach towel underneath her. She was resting her head on the steering wheel.

Tollie wished Lily would put on her clothes.

Tollie thought about her own dress. That was the one thing she was confident about for tonight, the sundress Janice had got her for her birthday. Using her secret money, hidden under the ironing board cover—What else? She hoped her mother hadn't spent too much of it. Secret money was a good thing. Money that men didn't know you had.

The dress was so soft you didn't even have to iron it. Its colors were fast and true, intentionally muted, so that even when it faded, years from now, it wouldn't look faded. She'd love her mother always for this dress—as well as for the natural reasons, of course—but the dress was proof of some deep understanding Janice had of things. And it shows she really wants to ease my way, Tollie was thinking, half-tuned out to "Love Letters in the Sand." Even if she has to make it hard too.

Tollie conjured the whole dress in her mind, let it float in blank space like a dress in a paper-doll book before you cut it out. She'd never had anything this nice to wear. Nothing else in her whole life that she'd felt like she wouldn't need to apologize for in some situation or other. That was what real, undeniable quality meant.

"Have a drink," Lily said, sitting up straight. "It'll loosen you up. You just about *smell* like nerves. It won't give you brain damage!"

"I don't want any, even if I can't get damaged," Tollie said. "I'm never going to drink hard-liquor. At least not until I'm eighteen. We always said we'd wait till then."

"We said we'd wait on a lot of stuff," Lily said. "We said we'd never smoke, curse, cut school, let anybody feel us up unless we really wanted to, and only through our clothes then. Not screw till we got married. Keep going to church, and improve on our souls. Remember church?"

"Remember souls?" Tollie said glumly.

"Every Sunday morning in white anklets and white maryjanes, little white bibles with crosses dangling off the zippers? Jesus!"

"Fans with pictures of snow on them," Tollie said. "Put out by the funeral home." Actually, she felt a little lonesome for those days.

"Prissy little dresses, white gloves, *Easter* bonnets."

"Sunrise service. . . . "

"I can still see us standing out there in the goddam dew with Daddy, the Fanatic, and his Child Bride," Lily said. "Daddy was holding you up so you could see the sun rising behind a plastic cross as big as a tree, decorated with kleenex-flowers, like a float."

"*Glo*-rie," Tollie intoned. That's what the preacher at Lily's church had always said every few sentences, *Glo*-rie.

"Daddy still prides himself on saving your little heathern soul," Lily said. "He always says you never would have got the Word of God, if he hadn't stepped in, never mind that you turned into a back-slider. He thinks you and I'll both reform when we get out of this 'teenage mess.'" She took another swig of the Purple Jesus. "Sometimes I can hardly believe we survived to tell the tale."

"I kind of liked church, and the sunrise service," Tollie said. "Back then."

"Forbidden fruit," Lily said. "If Janice had taken you to church you'd have hated it like I did. At least she had the sense to not let some old holy-roller dunk you in a river swimming with cottonmouths, giving you about ten years' worth of nightmares, like my mother let happen to me. Of course your mother was more than fourteen years old when you were born."

"Mamma was a Presbyterian," Tollie said. "In Whiteville, a long time ago."

"Mine says she's 'agnostic' now—a person with an open mind, or was that half a mind? Daddy's still a Primitive Baptist. *So* primitive I think he's liable to start his own church before he dies. The Primitive Primitive-Baptists. The closer he gets to losing his job, the more extreme he gets."

"He bought that coastal property," Tollie allowed.

"I wouldn't be surprised if he joined up with the snake handlers or the pig-gut readers."

"Like Madame Lucretia." Tollie didn't know if Madame Lucretia read pig-guts along with palms or not, but it seemed possible. Arlene said Madame Lucretia knew ways to find the answer to anything you wanted to know. Maybe she'd be someone worth consulting.

"Is she a church?" Lily asked. "I thought she was just an old con-woman."

"She might be. Les says he'll never go to church again until they carry him into one in a box."

"I'm glad that's one promise we didn't keep," Lily said. "Going to church. The last few times I went, all I could do was cry. I went Easter a year ago, mainly because Daddy bribed me with a sack dress. They kept singing those old idiot songs, and all of a sudden I was crying my eyes out. "Just As I Am"—you know how they'll sing that thing, and sing it, and sing it? Till the preacher's satisfied that enough people have crawled up to the altar like dogs and confessed that they're no better than a sinning dog—twenty, thirty times? It's quarter till one and everybody's starving. Then I was crying and Daddy was *so* happy. He kept trying to push me out into the aisle to crawl up and say I was a sinner and rededicate myself to Jesus. Which I never would have done, after the other time when the preacher took hold of me and started babbling a new sermon—'Behold our Lily of the Field, tore up by her roots! She's come to profess the sordidness of her sinning life! Sisters, she didn't *toil!* She just waited for the Grace of Gawd to come into her heart and propel her forward like a bi-sickle or a air-o-plane. . . . ' Jesus of Bethlehem, Nazareth, and Galilee!"

"Your preacher did have a way about him," Tollie said.

"Oh, here's a good one," Lily said, turning up the radio. It was "Rockin' Pneumonia and the Boogie-Woogie Flu." Lily rocked and boogie-woogied in her seat till the song was over. Tollie watched her. She herself knew that was a good song—she could feel how it stirred you up inside and made you want to move around—but she couldn't even snap her fingers to it, just in front of Lily. She was never going to be able to rock herself through this dance tonight. That depressed her. How could you feel something so strong inside you and not give in and let it . . . well, *propel* you, "like a bi-sickle" inside you? I must be inhibited, Tollie thought. It was a word she knew from biology, a reference to stunted life. I must have serious inhibitions. It's probably all these years of having to worry about my reputation. It's probably ruined me for life, and rock 'n' roll.

Lily turned the radio down again. "Anyway, they were Just-as-I-Am-ing and I was crying and Daddy kept whispering 'Go on down Lily, Go on down Lily.' I felt like I was going to die from . . . something. *Stupid.*"

"It's emotional," Tollie agreed. "No matter what you know in your head. They count on it."

"Finally, I got bored and calmed down. But it took the longest time. On the way home, Daddy fuming at the wheel, I said to myself, no more: I'm never going near a church again, at least not till I'm old, when there might be something in it for me. He's just going to have to bribe Marie or go by himself. And I haven't gone. That's one promise I've kept."

Lily took a drink. "They give you grape juice for communion! I think that's about the tackiest, holy-roller thing I've ever heard of. If I ever, in some weak moment when I'm about 89 years old, decide to go back to church, just in case, it's going to be a church where they give you real wine."

"You going to want real human flesh instead of a cracker too?" Tollie smoothed her dress with her sweaty hands. She wished she were home in bed.

"Smartass," Lily said.

"I still wish we'd kept some of our old promises," Tollie said. "I can't believe we're always doing ourselves a favor. Especially the way you're chugging that stuff."

"Don't get on a high horse. You drank out there in the woods with Speedy Gonzalez."

"Just beer," Tollie said. "Why don't you go get into your dress. The sun's going down."

"Yep, it is," Lily said, looking out on the lake where Rolando was sailing around alone in his boat, everybody else shooed out of the water and off the beach. The sky was the color of blood, she noted, with a little yellow in it. The pines framed it in black jagged lines. If you squinted, you couldn't see the boat very well, just the sail; it looked like a big shark-fin cutting through the water.

"I wish you'd stop drinking that stuff and get into your dress," Tollie said again, after five minutes of silence while Lily looked out at the sunset. Lily was going to irritate her to death one of these days. Tollie settled her back against the door and looked at Lily in the rose-colored light. Lily was looking more and more like a grown woman. She was looking more like a movie star, or somebody who could walk across the stage in a Miss Universe contest. Getting high, looking like she was getting ready to rock 'n' roll all night in her bathing suit, she looked a little dangerous—wild, foreign, strong and weak at once. What would happen to them before midnight, if they were starting off like this?

"You're going to get an irritation if you keep sitting around in that wet suit," Tollie said.

"You sound about a hundred years old. Like some old prune faced mamma-mouse—'You're going to get an irritation,'" Lily mimicked. "I've got an irritation. I'm irritated with just about everything that falls on my eyes and ears. Let's get something else on this radio, too. That asshole will be up in his asshole Kastle in the Air in five minutes." Lily turned the dials on the radio, moving from static to static.

"See if you can get Memphis," Tollie said.

"It's too early. . . . Hey! What do you know."

They sat for a while longer, listening to the Memphis station, to a disk jockey who was comforting, who just played the music and didn't try too hard.

"I heard they make this stuff in bathtubs down at the Azalea Festival," Lily said, regarding her diminishing Purple Jesus. "With lemon halves in it. Let's go this year, you want to? I'm this old and I've never been to *one* Azalea Festival."

"I don't even know when it is," Tollie said nervously. She felt breathless, like Lily had suggested they take a trip to the moon.

"It's when the azaleas bloom, Bashful, Sleepy, and Dopey! Don't act like I'm doing something *against* you in inviting you to go with me down to the beach for a weekend, a hundred miles from home!" Lily looked sharply at Tollie. "You are about the least adventurous person I believe I've ever known. I can't imagine what kind of life you're going to have."

"Let's drop it," Tollie said, turning so she could look Lily halfway in the eye. "You ride herd on me, Lily. Day after miserable day, lately. I don't know how much more I can take."

Lily started to say something, seemed to think better of it and looked out at the lake. Tollie did too, burning with shock and shame. What did it mean that she was afraid to go a hundred miles from home?

They could see Rolando's sail coming toward the shore.

"It reminds me of 'Red Sails in the Sunset,'" Lily said. Tollie could tell she was trying to make peace. "Eighth grade. Pat Boone. Can you believe we ever were dumb enough to like Pat Boone?"

128

"I think you're shitfaced," Tollie said, disgusted. The scene reminded her of "Somewhere Beyond the Sea." She'd hardly been aware of Rolando's boat, just the sky going on and on, to Outer Space, the sun blazing down and heading for a whole other world. "That was Tab Hunter. *I* was in the seventh grade and I didn't like Pat Boone a bit. Besides, that sail is white."

"Well, I can see *that*," Lily said. "What in the world has got you so touchy now? You're acting *so* touchy these days. Like you've been riding the great white horse for about a month."

Rolando brought his boat in and folded up the sail. Tollie watched the last red of sunset disappear over the horizon. Her sunburn was beginning to hurt a little and she could feel sand inside her nylons and flats, though she'd been careful to wash her feet well in the shower. Now she'd dance worse than she would have. I should have stayed at home, she thought. I'm not cut out for this. What's it going to matter, anyway, if I can rock 'n' roll or not? What difference is it going to make in the long run?

"I guess we might as well go on up," Lily said when it was almost dark, turning off the radio. The parking lot had filled up with cars after all. The music from the pavilion's juke box had been turned up very loud.

"Not yet," Tollie said. "Let it get more crowded."

"*Jesus*," Lily said.

They sat in the car, listening to the juke box: Lloyd Price, The Drifters, Jackie Wilson, Huey 'Piano' Smith. Between songs you could hear the sounds of shoe-soles on the gravel, and people laughing and talking as they walked from their cars.

"Are you really going to go up there like that?" Tollie said wearily. "Aren't you just asking for it."

"Maybe I am," Lily said, finishing the drink and shoving the bottle under the seat. "Maybe I'm a glutton for punishment."

Standing at the juke box, wishing she had a quarter, Tollie pretended to study the red and white labels. Nobody looked like he might ask her to dance. Lily was dancing. Up on her toes in her bare feet, the only one in a bathing suit. She danced in a slow, sensual way, smiling a cryptic half-smile, sort of looking into the face of her partner, but sort of remote too.

Other people were watching Lily, like they had on the beach. Some of the girls were smiling and whispering to each other, or to the boys they were with.

Doesn't she know how she looks to everybody? Tollie wondered. Her naval framed like a snapshot in a locket?

On the other hand, that was an interesting notion. . . .

"Can you dance?"

Tollie turned. He was already holding out his hand. Raeford Faircloth.

Then he had her wrist and, with a slight pressure on it, he was urging her toward the floor. Before she could answer him, he had his arm under her arm, his firm hand on her back. He had pulled her tight up against him, onto her toes.

He was wearing a soft blue shirt, chambray maybe, with the sleeves rolled, and blue jeans, which nobody else was wearing. He might be the best-looking male I've ever seen this close up, Tollie thought, amazed that she was already out on the floor with him. It had less to do with his looks than his attitude, she realized. He wasn't nervous. Anybody could see that, just the way he was smiling, kind of a half-smile, his eyes amused, but interested. She could tell he just rolled along with things. He was one of those people.

At least it's a slow dance, Tollie thought gratefully. "What a Difference a Day Makes." A good song to dance to. Nobody was tired of it yet, though you heard it every day, and the floor was packed. They wouldn't have room for him to try anything fancy. Dinah Washington's voice was soothing, and thrilling, at the same time. She was one of those singers who'd go on and on.

Raeford danced lazily. Already he'd put his cheek against hers. It felt full of sun. She could smell his aftershave, Bay Rum, which she knew from having smelled it on certain boys at school. Boys who didn't know she was alive, she thought with a stab of nerves. What was going on here?

Raeford pulled back to look into her face.

"Tanya," he said, considering her or her name, she couldn't tell which. He pulled her close again and put his cheek back against hers. His loafer scraped her foot when she missed a step. Was he shitfaced too? But then they were back in step, and he was propelling her skillfully, wrapping her in his tropical scent.

"Where did you get a name like Tanya," he asked when they were dancing a few minutes later to The Platters, "Twilight Time."

"It's Russian," Tollie said.

Raeford leaned back and looked at her wryly. "Are you a Communist? Spying on things out at the Base?"

"Of course not!" Tollie said, feeling obliged to defend her sudden Russian self. "I . . . My real father's family was from Russia. Before they were from New York City."

Well? It *could* be true. "I'm sure they weren't Communists. Where did you get a name like Raeford? It's the name of a town."

"It is," he acknowledged.

"What's the rest of it?" she asked, hoping for ammunition, if she had to counter attack. "I know about Faircloth. What's your middle name?"

"McLaurin."

"Hmmph," Tollie said. "Any relation to Roland-o?"

Raeford shrugged. "Common name."

"I'll say," Tollie said.

That seemed to be all he was going to say on the subject. Tollie wanted to say something amusing, to counter her cynical remark. People couldn't help who they were kin to. But nothing occurred to her. "Everybody calls me Tollie," she confessed. "You could call me that."

132

He smiled. His teeth are beautiful, Tollie thought. He could be on tv, on a toothpaste commercial.

"Oh, I think I'll call you Tanya," he said. He dipped her a little.

Tollie frowned. "I feel like you're making fun of me and I can't figure out exactly how."

He didn't say anything. He's mad, Tollie thought. The only person who's asked me to dance all night and I can't get along with him for five minutes.

When the song was over, Tollie stepped back from him. She was afraid he'd keep dancing her around the floor. He didn't seem like somebody who'd stop dancing if he wanted to dance just because the song had ended.

The music came back, a cha-cha. Tollie could see Lily begin to dance, a boy trailing her, both of them dancing backwards for a few steps, then Lily twirling, the boy following behind her again. Tollie didn't know how to cha-cha, but Raeford had already taken her hand. "Let's dance some more," he said. "Or would you rather go out to my car and have a drink?"

Tollie hesitated. She didn't want to do either one, and she wanted to do both. She ought to say she wanted to go to the restroom and then sneak out a window and head for the hills. Somebody with as much confidence as he had could probably get somebody like her to agree to anything he could come up with. She didn't need even one more trouble than she already had.

"The car, I guess," she said. She'd never be able to cha-cha without some lessons, and she sure didn't want to get them from him. "But I don't want to get *in* your car."

"All right," he said.

At the edge of the parking lot, several spaces down from Lily's daddy's Oldsmobile, Raeford opened the door to his little car. It gave off a slight smell of motor oil, which she'd been too nervous to notice the time she'd ridden in it. It smelled good. Maybe she could get in, just for a minute.

"What kind of car is this?" she asked, sitting back in one of the leather seats.

"It's a red car," Raeford said, opening the glove compartment. He took out a silver flask. "Just like you're a Red girl. I think I might be entering a new phase of life."

He took a swig out of the flask and passed it to Tollie. "Sorry it's not vodka," he said.

"No thanks," she said primly. "I should have asked for a drink out of the machine."

"You got a bathing suit?"

"In my girlfriend's car. But I don't think Rolando lets people swim this late."

"You want to get it? I'm going to take you to swim somewhere else."

Tollie didn't say anything.

"Which car is it?" he asked.

"That white Oldsmobile," she said. "Wait a minute." She found a pencil and some kind of ticket in the glove compartment. "Can I use this?"

"I hope so," he said, his voice teasing her—which she *didn't* appreciate.

She scrawled a note to Lily, telling her that she'd be back, to wait for her. Raeford got out of the car and walked into the dark with the note, then emerged with her bathing suit rolled up in one of the beach towels. He seemed to have an automatic sense of where things were and how to get to them.

"I know where you can sit and get drinks out of the machine all night for free," he said.

He'd already started the car and its loud noise defeated Tollie. She didn't say anything. She'd just see what happened. He didn't seem like the type who'd cut your throat out on a lonely country road and leave you for the buzzards.

At the Flamingo Motor Inn and New York Restaurant, one of the many unpatronized businesses left behind on the old four-lane, Tollie lay on a lounger in her bathing suit, a thick white towel around her shoulders, and watched the underwater lights play against the aquamarine of the swimming pool. An empty yellow raft bobbed slightly in a breeze that had come up a few minutes before. In the distance, the sky lit up fitfully with heat lightning. There were two or three large wet marks on the lounger's cushion where the few seconds' rain had splatted before it stopped, one hot drop on her thigh. She balanced a Grapette on her belly and listened to Big Mack on very low volume coming from the portable radio Raeford had set on an umbrella table nearby. Old Mackie said a storm was on the way, but not to worry because he wasn't going anywhere, "Just comin' atcha for three more hours, leading off with Earl Bostic, to L. from M., who hopes she still thinks about him Once in a While. . . . "

"Here," Raeford said, setting a club sandwich down on the concrete near Tollie's hand and taking a seat a couple feet away on a footstool made out of plastic strips. "I put Russian dressing on it, just for you."

"How do you get to go in the kitchen after the restaurant is closed?" Tollie asked, picking up the sandwich. She felt good. While he was gone she'd gone swimming in the big swimming pool with yucca plants growing all around it. There were no occupants of The Motor Inn that she could detect, and there were almost no cars on the old highway. She'd been able to pretend she was on private property, swimming—Lily-like—in her own private pool, high in the hills above Hollywood, or in Florida, the scraggly yuccas hallucinated tall as palms.

Then she'd taken an outdoor shower and helped herself to a clean, plush towel and a free Grapette. She'd settled back into a comfortable lounge chair to listen to music and observe the decor of the Motor Inn, which was very pleasing to her. A large Flamingo outlined in pink neon rose next to the motel's sign out near the road. The line of rooms was sided in a turquoise material that looked like opaque glass, and there were huge boulders all around, grounded in small, smooth stones. Everything was lit up by ground lighting, in spite of there being no customers.

It was the life of Riley, she guessed. The best-looking male she'd ever seen in her life had brought her an enormous sandwich on a tray, for her to eat as she lounged around an enormous pool, an enormous cotton towel around her shoulders, an enormous supply of soft drinks waiting in a machine you didn't even have to put money into. This must be how Her Grace, the Princess of Monaco, lived.

"My uncle and aunt own it," Raeford said. "They're building a new place nearer the Interstate. Meantime, I'm keeping an eye on this one. The restaurant still gets the business people at lunch."

"So . . . is this your job?"

"You could say that. It is for now, until they close it up."

"Then what will you do?"

"I don't know." He didn't seem particularly concerned.

"I don't know what I'm going to do either," Tollie said. "Not exactly. Just that I want to do it out of Hopeless Mills."

Tollie felt a moment's queasiness, remembering how nervous she'd felt about the idea of going to Wilmington to the Azalea Festival—a Lily idea, which made it about 99% sure not to become a reality, and it had scared her anyway. The fact that it had scared her, scared her even worse.

"I bet you want to go to Hollywood," Raeford said lazily.

"That's my girlfriend Lily," Tollie said, offended. "I was thinking more along the lines of Cuba, or Jamaica." She wasn't going to mention Puerto Rico!

"That's a little different," Raeford conceded.

"I don't know," Tollie said thoughtfully. "I think maybe it's just the original of Hollywood. You know, like a model? It sort of embarrasses me. I wish I just wanted to go to Raleigh, or Charlotte, or Richmond, with something specific in mind to *do,* instead of just fixing on a place.

I'll probably never get to go anywhere, anyway. Let's change the subject. This sandwich is good." She ate it slowly, assessing it. It had swiss cheese, turkey, lettuce, tomato, an unfamiliar and very spicy cold-cut. Raeford had put pickle spears and potato salad on the plate too.

"Don't you want some?" she asked.

"No, I like my turkey wild." He smiled at her and she smiled back. Wild Turkey was the name of the liquor he was drinking, pouring it from the bottle into a coca-cola glass full of crushed ice. He sure was nice. He'd given her a room to change in, shown her to the outdoor shower and the towels, dug up a radio, got her food when he'd heard her stomach growl—without embarrassing her any more than the sound had already embarrassed her. He seemed delicately tuned to things, like the Clear Channels were.

"What kind of cold-cut is this?" Tollie asked.

"Pastrami," Raeford said. "Uncle Alton hired the cook to come down from New York twenty years ago, since most of the traffic was going from New York to Florida and back, and not real receptive to grits and okra. He's made a mint out of this business."

"Why doesn't he retire and move to some place like Florida?" Tollie thought most everybody would move to Florida, if they could. As close as you could get to Paradise in the U.S.A.

"He can't stop himself. He was the youngest boy. Grandaddy left the farm to the oldest boy, which was Daddy. It's called primogeniture and people stopped doing it about two hundred years ago, but that didn't stop Grandaddy. Alton took whatever little bit it was that he got left and turned it into more money than Daddy and my brother will ever see in their lives out there on the farm. This place is just a little of it. He's got all ten fingers in ten separate pies."

They must be related to Roland-o, Tollie observed, chewing slowly.

"Not to mention that Daddy getting the farm probably ruined my brother's life."

Tollie perked up. "How?"

"Rowen never wanted to be a farmer. He just does it for the family."

"Oh," Tollie said. That was interesting.

"Alton made money for spite, and I guess he'll probably keep doing it for spite."

"Spite is a powerful emotion," Tollie acknowledged, almost happily. It was nice to have a real conversation with a boy. She and Ramírez had almost never talked. Just like Janice and Les.

137

It was the first time in a long time she'd been inclined to be really happy, even counting her birthday. She felt like she was getting an evening in paradise—a pool the color of the Caribbean Sea, the palmish yuccas, even the neon flamingo, fake as it was, was a happy illusion. Were there really birds like that walking the face of the earth on their long stork-legs? She didn't know. She had seen so many drawings of them, so many fake flamingos in yards, so many printed on men's shirts and beach towels that she didn't know if they were real, or something like Mickey Mouse, made up but having a huge reality.

Tonight *had* been magical. Food had swum right up to her, and she had survived the dance at Rolando's, even if she hadn't proved she could rock 'n' roll.

Then she felt her mood begin to fall.

Even at the dance—listening to energizing, happy music—every few minutes she had remembered that life was troubled, that Janice was lying back in her bedroom drugged by belladonna, the heat lightning illuminating her wrists, where X marked the spot; that Les was going to be out of a job; that Lily was probably going to ruin her life. That life was sad and hard all over the planet for most people, and that she, Tollie, had troubles specific to herself. The unfamiliar happy feeling that sometimes took off on its own whenever she mysteriously forgot to be sad infused her with hope, but it hardly ever lasted a minute. Before a minute was up, the other thing would creep in like a fog of sulphur and oppress everything beneath its sickening thickness, weighing her down.

She wondered if this was what her biology teacher called "conditioning," this easy relinquishing of happiness to depression and sorrow. She didn't know whether she was doing it to herself or whether it was something she was caught in and couldn't help herself out of, like a biological system that took little accounting of eccentricity, writing it off, in the teacher's word, as "aberration." Were happiness and hopefulness aberrations? They sure didn't feel natural, not to her. She felt it was likely that she'd turn out to be someone whose *every* teeny surge of happiness and hope would be instantly subdued by a swift black depression, cut through by grief and unease, so that the good things would seem unnatural, and vice versa, and that this would become her nature, and her character.

She chewed her sandwich pensively. She thought that she believed in ideas like conditioning, though nobody else, much, in Hope Mills seemed to. They liked to pin the blame on a person, as if she'd perverted herself all alone, from inside. But the word "perverted" sounded like it *had* to mean something that came from the outside. You could almost hear the wrestling in its syllables, someone strong redirecting someone weaker.

She felt like her life was determined already: How could happiness lift you from the sulfur and carry you away, after something had made you nip at every sign of its spreading wings for all this time?

Tollie finished her sandwich. "That was good," she told Raeford, who was pouring himself another drink out of the bottle with the unnaturally brilliant turkey.

"All of a sudden you don't look like it's so good," he said.

"I had a long day in the sun," she said. "What else have you been doing since high school besides working here?"

"I was in the army," he said. "Then I travelled around, following some book I'd read, about being on the road. I was still a kid."

"Really?" Tollie said. She needed to get on the road. "Who wrote it?"

"A Beatnik."

"A Beatnik! You don't look like one."

"That's good," Raeford said. "What do you know about Beatniks?"

"I saw one on Perry Mason, or one of those shows, maybe The Thin Man. He was a poet, *and* the murderer. You don't have a beard. Or sandals."

"I'm not one. I found being on the road to be a pain in the can."

"Did you ever go to Green-wich Village," Tollie asked. "In New York? I read in the paper that most of them live there, the real ones."

"Yes, I did," Raeford said.

"What was it like?"

"Like a lot of other places, underneath."

"You sound like my Mamma. She used to live in New York."

Raeford gave her a look. "Really? That's what you sort of said once before. But I never heard that."

Tollie gave him a sharp look. "Do you know my Mamma, then?"

Raeford looked away and took a drink. "Then I came back home and went up to Chapel Hill for a couple of years, like Daddy wanted. But I was wasting my G.I. Bill and the old man's money. So I thought I'd drop out a while."

"Drop out," Tollie said, tasting the words, and the concept, letting Raeford Faircloth off the hook. When kids at Hope Mills High dropped out, it sounded like they were dead. But a guy who'd been "on the road," and to New York—"I wish I could drop out," she said. "Not out of school. Just . . . drop out."

"Out of what?" Raeford said, raising an eyebrow.

Grinning at her like she was ten years old! "You don't have to act superior," Tollie said. "I'm not as old as you—so what?"

"How old are you?" Raeford said. He scooted his chair forward and leaned up, bending over her. He looked into her eyes and ran the back of his index finger along her cheek. It reminded Tollie of a movie she'd seen when she was little, with Janice. "Magnificent Obsession." A doctor bending over his patient, his lover, and checking her welfare and progress.

"Miss Tanya," Raeford said softly.

"I wish you'd call me Tollie," Tollie said.

"Oh you're going to be a Tanya," he said. "You'd better get used to it. Tollie's not going to be enough of a name for you."

"What do you mean?" Tollie said.

"I mean that I see something in you." He let his lips graze her cheek. Adrenalin shot through Tollie's stomach—his closeness, the whiskey, the Bay Rum.

He kissed her on the mouth.

"Eighteen," Tollie lied. "I'm eighteen."

He kissed her again.

"You're too old for me," she said.

"No I'm not," Raeford said, kissing her shoulder. "I'm just eighteen myself."

"That's not true," Tollie whispered. "I've got to go. I'm at the dance with my girlfriend. She'll be worried."

"All right," Raeford said. He kissed her again on the lips and touched the front of her bathing suit, lightly, with his hand. "By the way, did I tell you I thought you were wearing about the softest, prettiest dress I've ever seen?"

Tollie could feel her heart thumping hard.

"Now go put it on," he said.

"I could shoot you," Lily said, once Tollie was in the Oldsmobile and Raeford had driven out of Rolando's parking lot.

"I'm sorry," Tollie said. "I misjudged the time."

Lily ground the key in the ignition, started over, did it right. "I'll be lucky if Daddy lets me have this car again before Christmas. It's one a goddam clock in the morning!"

"I'll tell your Daddy it's my fault." Tollie felt sick. She'd just had the best night of her life, and already her problems were worse than ever because of it.

"Shit," Lily said. She gunned the car and sped across the gravel of the parking lot. The wind had picked up, Tollie noticed. The black pine branches lurched in the air above the car. Suddenly rain began to fall, hard, on the windshield.

"At last," Tollie said. It was the first real rain they'd had since last spring. She'd even stopped expecting rain, she realized. A real rain had begun to seem a thing of the past. Even the worst thunderstorms had turned out to be mostly thunder and lightning. Lily turned on the windshield wipers, but otherwise didn't acknowledge it. She was fuming, beyond noticing.

"While you were out with a cute boy, I was fighting off 'Rolando'—that creep! His name is Roland Wiggins McLaurin, which everybody knows. What is this 'Ro-lahn-do' crap?"

"Somebody said he was in the black market in the Panama Canal, when he was in the service," Tollie said, seizing the chance to be

141

helpful. Lily was *really* mad this time. "I think they use Spanish down there. Maybe it's something Spanish he brought back with him."

"Like V.D.!" Lily said. "He tried to pull my bathing suit off in front of a couple of his asshole buddies—can you believe that? He thought I was too drunk to count. Well, I showed him. I could drink a gallon of Purple Jesus and still get away from that creep. It's your fault. If you'd been there, I could have gone home. But no, I had to sit here and take their shit, with the doors locked and the windows rolled up, in all this heat. He tore my bathing suit too."

They were on the highway, passing the Flamingo Motor Inn. Tollie could see the little red car parked in front of the office, Raeford out in the rain, skimming the pool with a net on a long pole. Oh, Jesus . . . Jesus. . . . She started crying.

"I could shoot you," Lily said again. They drove a few minutes in silence. "Oh, come on, Tollie. Stop crying. Crocodile tears! Daddy's going to skin me."

They got off the highway and started toward the Mill.

Lily pulled over into the Mill's parking lot and cut off the motor. She reached into the seat behind her. "I better get on my dress or Daddy will have my hide. If he'd ever see this suit. . . . Would you stop that crying? I feel bad enough." Lily looked at Tollie in the parking lot's light. Tollie was looking down on her lap. Her face was running with tears and spotted with the shadows of the raindrops, some of them running down the windshield, tears on top of tears.

"What in the world is wrong with you?" Lily demanded. "I'm the one in trouble."

"I missed my period," Tollie said miserably. "Six weeks ago."

Les has a dog.

He got it from Billy Sutt, when Billy got laid off and headed for Detroit—"Or maybe California or maybe the brand-new state of Hawaii," Billy said, "before it's all over, no shit." Before Billy lit out, Les watched him give away everything but his car and the shirt on his back. The shirt was a bright nylon Hawaiian shirt full of palm trees and suns. He told Les that the dog was part-Golden retriever, part-something-else.

"I reckon," Les said skeptically. By then, the dog was already in the backseat of Les's Ford, panting, looking around with bright eyes, its ears laid back in bliss. Billy was in his own car, an old Studebaker (Billy called it the Stupid-Fucker; he said he was getting a new El Dorado the minute he got situated). He was revving the motor, grinning beneath his shades and raising two fingers in parting. Then he was out of the Mill parking lot in a cloud of dust. A dusty red sun on the sleeve of his shirt was the last Les saw of him, the roar through the Stupid-Fucker's broken muffler the last he heard.

Billy was like a lot of old boys in Hope Mills these days, Les has noticed: getting out of Hope Mills.

The dog is big, blond, and happy-looking, with enormous feet. Les isn't exactly sure how he let Billy talk him into taking it, but he is glad he did: it is like he has a little bit of new purpose now. The dog looks like it is smiling all the time. Its name is Lucky.

Les and Lucky are in the backyard, where Lucky had been tethered to the clothesline pole all day. But now it is evening, the dog is free, roaming near the uncertain borderline where Les's weeds begin to turn into Arlene's scraggly bluegrass. Lucky's nostrils are quivering several inches above the ground, and he has just planted one of his big feet on Arlene's fall-blooming asters, which are already weak from the drought, barely blooming at all. Even the marigolds are droopy and pale, and the row of collards that Arlene planted optimistically in the middle of a drought are so skimpy they'll never be ready for New Year's Day. You want collards that look like palm trees by then, Les thinks disdainfully. Bursting with sugar to sweeten your life in the present and bring luck for the future. Those things look hopeless.

"Come on, Boy," Les says, holding a stick at his hip. "Let's see if you're a retriever or not."

"Not," Arlene says on her way up the outside steps from her basement with a laundry basket full of rumpled clean clothes. "If that thing breaks many more of my flowers, he's going to be the little shepherd of Kingdom Come. I'll pop him, Les. I'm not kidding."

Arlene pauses on the stairs and looks sternly at Les with her big green eyes. Les can't quite see their color because it is almost dark, but he can never think of Arlene without thinking of her eyes: dusty-green, the exact color of money. Les thinks her haircut looks like a helmet, like something one of those old Roman soldiers might have worn. She's a wiry little thing to begin with. Now that she's had all her hair cut off, she looks more like a boy than ever. Les likes a woman to have long hair, like Nature intended.

"Don't worry about it," Les says, coughing a little into the first air that's been crisp enough to seem like fall. He looks away from Arlene and fixes on Lucky—trotting along the side of Arlene's pitiful collards and skinny flowers, sniffing and smiling like he is in Paradise itself, though Les knows the flowers can't smell like much, puny as they look. But then, it doesn't take much to please a dog, he thinks. But then, again, Arlene doesn't want Lucky to have even that little bit. It ticks Les off.

"He ain't in your yard good yet," Les says to Arlene. "I believe your flowers might be over in *my* yard, now that you brought it up."

"Maybe you want to get the surveyor out here," Arlene says.

"I didn't say that." Les can feel the stick weighing his arm down. Why is everybody on the face of the earth struggling against him nowadays? Bosses, old boys at work, young boys that pump his gas. His own kid. Women. "But then again, maybe I do want to see a survey, if you want to make something out of nothing."

"Maybe you want to pay the fifty dollars too," Arlene says, steadying the basket on her hip and going up the last steps and into her kitchen, letting the door bang behind her.

"Come on, Boy," Les says to Lucky. "Come on over on your Master's own property. Let's see what you can do."

Les throws the stick for the dog, but each time Lucky just stands there, like a rooted tree. "I'm the goddam retriever," Les mumbles when he's gone after the stick himself several times. Lucky is interested, though, Les believes. The dog has stood out a few feet toward where the stick was going to go, every time. Lucky has watched him throw the stick, every time. Alert. Wagging his tail, smiling and showing his tongue. Every time, his ears have cocked up. Every time, his eyes have lit up like the stars in the sky.

Finally, there are stars in the sky. "I'm going to tie you up for the night now," Les tells Lucky. "You're kind of a disappointment as a retriever, Boy."

Les can hear the dog panting happily, full of hope in spite of the chain waiting for him out on the clothesline pole. Maybe he's not smart enough to figure out that it's waiting for him, Les thinks. Maybe that's the key to the general happiness of dogs.

"Well, come on." Les throws the stick away, hard, and moves to take Lucky by his collar and lead him to where he has to go, but before he can get a good grip, the dog bounds away.

It is dark for real now. The only light is from the streetlight down the block. The stars are no good at all. Jesus, Les thinks. I can't even hold onto a dog for a week.

"Lucky?" He sends his voice out a little bit into the night, but he doesn't have much hope. Things have been getting away from him pretty good lately.

Suddenly the dog comes bounding back, not much more than a shadow, into the little bit of space where Les can see anything. Lucky is wagging his shadowy tail, his coat just a patch of dim light. He rubs his muzzle against Les's hand. Lucky has the stick—or at least *a* stick—gripped in his teeth.

Les doesn't want to examine it too closely. He can use whatever kind of good news he can get.

145

He moves his hand to the dog's head.

"Good dawg," he says. He feels the animal's soft hair, knows it is gold-colored, even in the dark.

"Good dawgy," he says, with more conviction. "Good old dawgy-dawg."

For the first time in her life, Tollie thought she knew what people felt when they said they were in love. It was about time, she guessed.

She was dating Raeford now, on a regular basis. Not every night, like with Ramírez, and not always at night. Raeford had taken her out twice on Sunday afternoon, to the movies and for a ride. Not a word had been said about going steady, but that was all right. He didn't seem the type. Besides, what kind of girl could go steady with one boy while they were incubating the baby of another one?

The whole thing was worrisome. On the one hand, she hoped and would have prayed, if she prayed on a regular basis, that Raeford would never know. On the other, she felt like the fair thing was to tell him before he spent any more money on her. He'd spent money on movies and gas, and he always bought her a nice snack or real meal when they went out. How many more trips to the Miracle Theatre could she let him pay for? They'd already seen "Imitation of Life," "Suddenly, Last Summer," and "Anatomy of a Murder," though the only one she'd picked herself had been "Imitation of Life," which Raeford had pronounced a soap opera, making her feel foolish, especially since she'd cried her eyes out when Mahalia Jackson had sung at the Negro mother's funeral. After that, she'd let him pick. He probably did have better taste than she did, if he'd been paying attention to things in the world, which she knew he had. After all, he was paying, period.

She wished she could offer to pay sometimes, but she had to save every dime she could accidentally get her hands on, even her lunch money—when she could stand it—in the interest of solving her "problem," somehow. At least she could let him kiss her and touch her breasts, but she knew she probably liked that better than he did, so it didn't settle her debts. How many more chicken baskets and pizza-burgers and barbeque plates could she consume and still be able to deny she was taking advantage of Raeford Faircloth, whether or not he was rich? (Even if his brother might be taking advantage of her mother?) And yet, when he pulled into a drive-in or wanted to go to The Palm Court or Hanes Soda Shoppe, she could never say she wasn't hungry. Nowadays, she was hungry every minute.

Not to mention all the liquor he bought them. He drank most of it, though. Most of the time, she'd rather just have a Coca Cola or a Tru-ade. Raeford seemed to drink all the time, but it never affected him that she could tell. She wasn't sure why he bothered.

Yes, they were dating, but only on the weekends. Raeford thought she ought to stay home and study on school nights. She liked that he seemed responsible that way.

Now, night hours were used more industriously than they used to be. She tried to tune out all the junk in her house, all the junk in her life, and do her schoolwork. Study her Spanish. Memorize poems. Build her vocabulary. She liked feeling that she had work to do, after a lifetime of drifting in junk, toward junk. She knew she'd better improve herself or she'd never be able to hold onto a boy like Raeford Faircloth—or do anything else worth doing. Being in love had given her work to do, and it had also given her hope. Considering her circumstances, hope against hope.

It was early on a Saturday afternoon, almost Halloween. Tollie had put in a whole morning on her schoolwork before she'd done a little wash and hung it on the line, then made lunch for herself and Janice. It was sunny outside, a mild day like October days used to be before the funny weather of 1959, just a little windy. Janice was reading *McCalls* on her bed, or lying there with *McCalls*. Her Mother's eyes were getting that zombie look again, Tollie had observed. It was like Janice might be getting ready to leave the planet. Tollie was worried, about that and everything else, but couldn't she just have one afternoon without her troubles weighing down her mind? If she just didn't think about Janice, would things stay the same? Or would they collapse in the absence of her worry?

Sometimes, lately, she believed that her own worry was necessary to her mother's stability, that if she moved her mind too far away from the problem, trouble would come down on them like the leaves from a tree after a sudden frost. That was an awful way to go through life.

The grilled cheese sandwich she had made her mother was cold on its plate by Janice's bed, untouched. Les had gone out in his "drinking shirt," taking his dog with him. Tollie guessed he'd be out in the bars half the night. He'd sold his gun rack, bought a few groceries, and now the extra money was burning a hole in his pocket. Janice said he was going to get in a fight with a soldier one of these days and end up in a hospital, or dead. That was always happening to somebody in the paper, but usually the soldiers kept it among themselves. Still, hanging out in the bars with soldiers was just asking for it. Even Tollie knew that. She knew, now, that hanging out with soldiers in any way, anywhere, could ruin your life, not just your reputation. It had all turned out worse than even Les had predicted.

I can't think about that stuff any more right now, Tollie thought, wrapping herself in her robe. She went to the bathroom and closed herself in, then started her bathwater. I've got to save my strength for the things I can do something about, she thought. She had to memorize 1000 lines of poetry and recite them to Mrs. Wiggins for English class before the end of the school year. Also for Mrs. Wiggins, she had to keep a list of new words and a record of how she had used each one at least once in a conversation or letter. She carried a little pocket notebook in her purse and put down every new word that passed by her ear, each on its own page, with room left to record the situation in which she'd found it useful. She'd already filled one notebook and had started on a new one. That was one thing she'd never outgrown: her curiosity about new words. You could live your life and never learn them all—all that possibility in just 26 letters of the alphabet. It was almost as mysterious as music, all those songs and so few notes. Words and music: just two of the expansive mysteries in life, amazing in their variety, given all the limitations that seemed to operate generally on human beings themselves. At least the humans I know, Tollie thought, adjusting the faucets.

Now she was learning new Spanish words too, making her feel like she was expanding her horizons, even when she was trapped in her traitor-body which was itself trapped in her tight house in Hopeless Mills, a house entangled with other people's problems, like vines had overrun it, keeping out the light and fresh air. But words, at least, were something that she could still talk to her mother about. That was something.

"What did you mean when you said I was 'impressionable,' " she'd asked Janice only yesterday—*months* after her mother had used the word. But all that time it had been hanging in Tollie's mind like a sleeping bat. A clue to her deep character or just her mother's . . . impression? She couldn't tell.

"I mean that things make an easy impression on you."

"I looked it up," Tollie said thoughtfully.

"So? Doesn't it mean what I said."

"It could. It also said 'sensitive.' Which I *don't* want to be, by the way: I'll get eaten alive."

"You are sensitive." Janice smiled a little. She looks so tired, Tollie thought. Why don't I just leave her be?

"But in a nice way," Janice said. "Not like hot-house-flower sensitive."

"But when you called me 'impressionable,' " Tollie said, unable to leave it alone, "It sounded like you were criticizing."

"I just meant that maybe you're affected too easily by things."

"Like I'm not stable?" Tollie said. "I like that."

Janice closed her eyes.

"I didn't mean anything by that," Tollie said quickly. Everything was so delicate these days that sometimes she wished she didn't have a tongue, like the woman in the myth. On the other hand, she felt bound to defending her impressionable Self.

"The dictionary said it meant you were capable of being affected 'intellectually, emotionally, and morally.' If that's so, I think being 'impressionable' is a good thing."

"I didn't mean anything by it," Janice said wearily, her eyes still closed.

"I mean, if you weren't going to be affected by things 'intellectually, emotionally, and morally,' why would you bother to get out of bed in the morning? *I* intend to be affected until the day I die!"

"Just forget it, Tollie."

"No, I won't. I can't believe it would be a virtue to be like an unaffected rock for all your days."

"You're the girl with two summer skirts just alike, wearing them every day. I don't see you as so receptive. I haven't got the energy for this."

"Well, which is it, Mamma? Am I impressionable or not so *receptive*."

"You figure it out," Janice had said. "I'm going to take a pill."

Tollie filled the White Rain bottle's cap with shampoo and held it under the bathtub tap. She'd take a bubble bath and try to get her mind clear. She began to brush her teeth while the water ran. The water pressure was so low in their neighborhood, it took forever to fill a tub. She wished she could just not think while she waited, and not think while she bathed, either. It seemed like everything she thought about led her back to her troubled mind, except for the clean subjects of schoolwork—but not school itself, Good-God no! Maybe she was impressionable in the bad sense. Maybe if she had a more stable character, things wouldn't affect her in the troubling way they did. Still, she wouldn't want to be an old hard rock.

She'd just keep her mind on her schoolwork more, until things straightened out, if they did. Learn a little algebra, even if she couldn't see a good use for it in the world. Perfect her Spanish. Not that she thought she'd ever see Puerto Rico or even Ramírez again. She liked it, though. *Mañana. Hoy. Nunca más.* She'd been shocked to realize *Negro* meant black, literally: Not so polite after all. Everybody she knew used "black" when they wanted to be really insulting to the Negroes. She was struck anew with the vast injustice that seemed loose in the world like ether. The Negroes, hoping to get respect by getting people to use a Spanish word that they didn't even know the hidden meaning of. She was glad she wasn't rich enough or poor enough to know any Negroes personally, since she wouldn't know which word to use with them, now that she knew Spanish.

She rinsed her mouth and put her toothbrush back in the holder. She eyed the feeble bubbles in her bathwater critically. Raeford had several Negroes working right in his house, cooking and cleaning, others doing yardwork; three whole families of them tenanted on his brother's farm in gray old shacks, still plowing with mules, some of them. She poured a little more White Rain into the tub, noting the name and wondering whether she'd noted it earlier without knowing she'd noted it, sending her thoughts in the direction of "racial problems." They were using that phrase in the news now, all the time. People were scared they were going to integrate the schools here. And the restaurants. People wrote letters to the editor of the paper saying they wouldn't sit down and eat off the same plates as the Negroes in a restaurant, if it came to that. Which was stupid. Negroes cooked all the food in the restaurants anyway. Patted out the biscuits with their

151

hands, cut up the chickens, tasted the seasonings in the vegetables with the cooking spoon. You knew they ate off the plates back in the kitchen and always had, so what was the big deal?

She bent over the tub and moved her hands rapidly in the water, watching the shampoo foam up in a more satisfying way. There wasn't any profit in this line of thought. The subject was too big for it to matter what she thought about it. She'd better return her thoughts to more neutral school subjects. She had a natural interest in World History. And World Geography. Civics, which had grown out of her natural interest in Current Events, learned back in the good ol' *Weekly Reader* days. Health.

Of course she had a more specific reason than usual to be interested in Health this year. She was following the discussion of Reproduction in her textbook with a breaking heart. She guessed she'd studied that chapter more than anything in all her school days, reading it over and over and over, seeing if she could get a clue as to how to make her body do the unnatural thing, how to get Nature not to take its course.

So far, there hadn't been any clues. Once a thing was set in motion inside your body, it was hard to interrupt. Like it was answering to higher laws, secrets kept from you yourself.

That was life. Fragile and uneasy, yet so hard to reverse once it got going. Violence was about the only way. It almost made her sick to think about it. Sicker. She felt sick a lot of the time these days.

She'd listened hard the day that the Health class had split up for Questions and Answers. The school nurse had come into class to answer the questions of the girls, and the boys had gone off with the football coach. The nurse seemed okay. She was a yankee, probably a soldier's wife, dark and wild-haired. She made a joke about having come to answer that burning question Who Wrote the Book of Love? but nobody had laughed. Tollie had smiled. It was pretty funny.

The girls in her class were abyssmal. They had asked the dumbest questions—? "Is there any way to be married without having to do it?" (When you knew they were dying to do it, or were already doing it but wanted to throw you off by wasting precious time with a question like that, self-centered!) "Do you have to do it on your Wedding Night or can you put it off?" "Can't you break it riding a horse?" "Will it grow back if you're careful?" "How do you get your husband to believe it happened while you were riding a horse?" "Can a doctor tell when it was a horse?" "Can a doctor give you a note certifying it was a horse?"—Jesus: how many girls in Hope Mills had a horse?—"Any way to make sure you have a boy first when you have babies?" "Is it true that white people can get V.D.?"

The whole thing was useless, but she hadn't had the nerve to ask about anything she needed to know about. How could she? They'd just expel her from school forever, make her parents pack her off to the Florence Crittendon Home, put the baby up for adoption, and then she'd be on her own, uneducated, her reputation ruined. Her own Health was in danger, and it was like everything else: When things got crucial, there wasn't much help to be had.

She couldn't imagine what the boys had talked about with the Coach. Their minds were always in the gutter anyway, and they all tried to act *so* knowledgeable. Snickering, pushing each other when they made their "innuendos," a useful word for her notebook. Claiming this girl and that girl would "put out," whether or not they'd ever said two words to her. She'd bet they'd all pretended they didn't have question one.

Tollie pulled her hair up in a rubberband so it wouldn't get wet while she bathed. She hated that junk. Generally, though, she felt like she was rising above it a little. All that running around at night last year, just to get out of the house, had been exhausting. She liked her new way of being—*trying* to tune out as much as she could of what she couldn't do anything about and refocusing herself on something that might do her some good. That had to be better than just running out the door and getting on the road with some guy who didn't have one single interest of yours on his mind. She'd be glad she went to that dance at Rolando's Beach for the rest of her life, whatever happened with her and Raeford. She was getting some good habits, at last.

That Raeford had gone to Chapel Hill for a while, and had said he was thinking of going back, had set her to thinking too. If she ever got out of the situation she was in and got her own body back, a little peace of mind, maybe she could go to Chapel Hill. After all, it wasn't like nobody in her family had experience with college. Her Aunt Gracie had gone to college, a long time ago.

Tollie swished the bubbles around with her hand again, inflating them for the moment when she would step in and sink down into their iridescent foam like Lily Jones or a movie star. She smiled, in spite of her troubles. Neither Lily Jones nor a movie star would have to depend on White Rain, unnaturally whipped up by their own agitating.

But then she wasn't Lily Jones or a movie star. She was resourceful Tollie Ramsey.

Instantly her smile dropped from her face. Resourceful, up to a point only. How in the world was she going to get out of this mess?

She touched her belly through her robe. Was it unnaturally hard, or was that her imagination? Just some 'impression?'

She wasn't going to think about that today! She was going to think about a bright and shining future, if it killed her. Chapel Hill, Aunt Gracie. You never knew about a thing like that. Just when you were down on your luck, somebody could step out of the shadows, like Michael Anthony, and give you a break that would change your life for good, for the better. Her aunt sent her a birthday card every year, a little something for Christmas. Maybe Aunt Gracie could advise her.

Tollie had been thinking that maybe she could apply for the DAR scholarship that went to one girl at school every year, when she was a senior. Last year it had gone to Molly Wiggins. Like she needed it, Tollie thought, plucking at her eyebrows over the bathroom sink. You had to dress up and go have tea with the DAR, by yourself, and then eventually they'd decide your fate, based on how you conducted yourself. Could she do that? Could she find somebody to lend her pearls, a sweater set, nice hose, like the Wiggins' girls had? You probably had to wear gloves too.

Finally the tub was full. She tested the water with her hand, noting that the bubbles had all disintegrated. Well, so what? It had been a logical idea to use White Rain. She'd probably have some real bubble bath before she died. She watched her hand grow ghostly pale in the water, then return to its normal color as she withdrew it and dried it off on her robe. In the last year or so, it seemed everybody had stopped wearing gloves except in cold weather. You could look out on Sunday in warm weather and see women walking to church without the white shorty cotton gloves that everybody used to wear, without even a hat. At first, you noticed women bareheaded, with bare hands, but carrying their hats and gloves. Now women and girls, both, just went. Now, almost nobody used the gloves for anything but to put on their stockings so they wouldn't get a run, or else they wore them over Vaseline at night to soften their hands. Nobody had worn them downtown to shop since a few years after the War, Janice said.

The world was changing, every day, Tollie acknowledged. Did she like it or did she not? Janice was right. There was a part of her that was 'impressionable' and a part of her that resisted. It seemed like that would be a hard kind of character to see you down the road of life.

She looked at her hand again. Only yesterday, she'd had to stand up in class and address her own hand, along with all the other girls in turn, as if they were Lady MacBeth. The boys had all had to stand up in their turn and recite Lord MacBeth's words from his moment of deepest despair: Life is a tale . . . told by an idiot. . . .

Tollie could believe it. She held her hand out from her body and thought of it as a disembodied thing, about to do what it was about to do, once she could figure out how. Then, could even all the perfumes of Arabia sweeten this little hand? Once it had her own blood on it?

Her own blood. Suddenly she wondered if killing the baby-to-be, however a thing like that could be done, wouldn't be something like Janice's x-marks. Were they both, mother and daughter, bound for Hell on Earth and Hell in the Hereafter too? Unless they could escape to another planet? Forbidden Planet. Dix Hill or Chapel Hill. Both other planets, both forbidden, but in different ways.

Tollie rubbed the hand against her robe. Then she took the robe off and stepped into the tub. She turned the hot water back on and let it run some more, till the water was as hot as she could take it, then she cut it off. She had started taking baths instead of showers because she'd read, in a woman's magazine that Arlene had brought over to Janice, how it was bad for pregnant women to take baths. She wasn't sure why. Maybe something in the temperature of the water, if you could take it hot enough, would cause the baby to let go and float away. She wished it could be that easy: that the baby would just decide to loosen its little claw from her insides and drift away. Maybe it would be smiling and waving and glad to go, leaving her body free and unweighted, hers again.

She looked down thoughtfully on her belly as she soaped herself with the last sliver of the Straw Hat soap. So far, nothing was showing there, but her breasts were bigger. Boys had started to notice her more at school. She'd started wearing looser tops. The last thing she wanted was people paying more attention to her body. The more she could blend in, the longer it would take people to notice her troubles. And she needed to buy time, get information. Lily had given her all her sack dresses and chemise dresses. Even though they were going out of style, too much out of style for Lily Jones—or Lili Lorene, as she'd started calling herself some of the time—you could still get away with wearing them. Which Tollie guessed she would.

She stretched her arm out in front of her and soaped it, and then lathered her fateful hands until they were white with soap foam. She had heard that the DAR didn't like change, so she thought you'd definitely want to wear white gloves to tea with them. Not a sack dress, though, nothing that was—or had been—a fad. She wouldn't have to have tea with the DAR until she was a senior. Maybe she could save up for a suit, a nice pair of calfskin pumps, kid gloves. Tollie dipped her hands in the water and let the soapsuds slip away. That was depressing: the skin of baby animals on your feet, your hands. Maybe the tea would be in the summertime, and she could wear cotton gloves, straw pumps. A nice dress in voile or a little suit of linen or polished cotton or soft cotton like her sundress was made from. If there was still such a thing as cotton by 1961. Before then, could she get a summer job, somewhere? A Christmas job, back at Kresge's where she'd worked last year?

She lay back in the water, fatigued. She probably ought to look into a real job, not just pick-up work like babysitting and picking crops and Christmas work. It would cost her money just to apply to a college. She ought to go down to Pandora's Box, like she'd intended to. She could work Saturdays and after school, every day.

She'd copied down the address of the University from a poster the librarian had made for the bulletin board at school and had written for information, but it hadn't come yet. She had picked up from somewhere in the osmosis of high school that they had scholarships up there. Maybe she could get a job, once she got in. Maybe a bank would make her a loan, if she promised to pay it back when she graduated.

She stretched her hands up and wiped them on the towel swinging above her head on the towel rack and then reached for her "facial." She smeared Miracle Whip on her face and settled back to let it dry. She'd read that it was a good facial substance—well, actually that mayonnaise was, but they didn't have any, one of Les's new economies at the Winn-Dixie. Miracle Whip, as a name, sounded more like a facial anyway. She wanted to look pretty today, because this afternoon, like something materializing out of a dream, against all your disbelief, Raeford was taking her up to Chapel Hill. They were going to have dinner, see Raeford's friend Randy, and go to a foreign movie. It was like something out of a movie itself. Or something out of thin air: something she wouldn't have even known how to want a month ago.

Stop! she thought. Don't you dare think about it till he's here.

She realized that was what she'd been doing all day, not daring to think about it, lest the Fates step in to teach her humility, putting some obstacle in her way.

Every time she couldn't help letting it cross her mind, her heart leapt up, like the poet's when he saw daffodils. But she wasn't about to tempt Fate too much.

The water felt good. She drifted, imagining herself living in a dormitory, like the girls in the stories in *Seventeen* and *Co-ed*, which she read during library period, or bought sometimes, if she had the money. She liked thinking of Raeford picking her up in his little car at her dormitory, which she imagined as a castle-like building in a big grove of trees. It would be a bright sunny day just about this time of year. The sky would be Carolina Blue, the leaves red and gold. Not a cloud. It would be right before a football game and he would pin a big chrysanthemum, set on a Carolina Blue ribbon, to her new cashmere suit jacket. She knew about this because, only last Monday, Cindy Wiggins had worn such a corsage to school. Her daddy had bought it for her at a football game in Chapel Hill on the weekend, and one for her mother too, Cindy had told another girl as the two of them chatted at the table in front of Tollie's in the lunchroom. Everybody at school had something to say about it. That wasn't the kind of thing a person from Hope Mills did every day.

Tollie kept her eyes closed, the better to dream. She liked thinking that Raeford might join a fraternity, like boys in the *Seventeen* stories sometimes did, though Raeford didn't seem like the type that would join much. He was like her in that respect. But she liked to imagine him putting his fraternity pin on her new cashmere sweater, right over her heart. That had happened in *Seventeen* too, and it had already happened to Molly Wiggins up at Peace College, Tollie had heard: some boy at State. It was like being engaged.

"Tollie?"

"What?" Tollie said instantly, sitting up straight in the tub and listening hard. "Are you okay, Mamma?"

"Yes. I was just wondering if you were okay."

"I'm okay."

"You don't have the radio in there do you?"

"No, Mamma. Go back on your bed. I'm okay."

"Okay."

Tollie knew Janice was still standing outside the door.

157

"I'm really okay, Mamma." Could Janice tell she wasn't? With that sixth-sense that mentally disturbed people sometimes had? "Go back on your bed."

"Okay," Janice said doubtfully.

Straining, Tollie could hear the soft shuffle of her mother's bedroom shoes, moving down the hall. She let out the breath she'd been holding and then settled back down into the tub and closed her eyes.

In her deepest dreams, she imagined herself and Raeford married, going to classes by day, studying together in a little apartment at night. That had happened in a story in a *Redbook* that Arlene had dropped off.

Football, fraternities. Fancy little cars, soft sweaters. It was sure a different view of men than you got in *True* and *Man's Adventure*. That kind of life wouldn't appeal to somebody like Les one bit. Or Ramírez. Or even Tyson Wiggins, juvenile delinquent cousin of Molly and Cindy, still on the wrong side of the tracks. And on the wrong side of the law too: it was just a matter of time.

Tollie tested her facial. It felt gooey. The magazine where she'd got the idea said it would tighten up. Well, maybe it would. She forced herself to relax again and drifted, happy for a change in her thinking ahead. She was glad to have a place to think about that wasn't Hope Mills or Puerto Rico. Chapel Hill. Even the name suggested it was a sort of place of resurrection. Or something. Not as grand as what the preachers called the New Jerusalem, but something in that direction.

Yes, she definitely had to change her ways. Study more. Get serious. Logic told her that Raeford had had at least some experience with smart girls. But it was hard to find out much about that part of his life. She had tried, by asking subtle questions, but she hadn't found out anything yet. She didn't even know if he dated other girls or not. She hoped not. On the other hand, what would he have been doing on the twenty-one days and nights this month that he hadn't taken her out? She'd better be a little on guard. She didn't like to think about being on guard, not when she was in love. And she hated thinking about Raeford Faircloth out with another girl, smart or dumb as lye soap!

That he wouldn't tell her anything let her know, at least, that he was discreet. That was something.

Tollie tested her facial again. It was still gooey. She gave up and wiped it off with a washcloth. She'd be waterlogged if she stayed in the tub any longer. Who needed a tub anyway? When she could put her worries off for a minute, she felt herself to be in the deep warm pool of Love. It was as if she were floating there, among exotic flowers, breathing their perfume and looking up at palm trees full of happy monkeys. She didn't feel stupid about it at all, as she had felt when she used to imagine herself in faraway Puerto Rico with Ramírez. That was just a pipedream, from the outside. Something from inside was warming the pool of Love.

She stepped out of the bathtub and began to dry herself off. She had an hour and a half to fix herself up. Raeford was coming at 2:30. She couldn't wait to see Chapel Hill. She was interested in the new foreign movie they were going to see, too, "Hiroshima Mon Amour." The only foreign movies that ever came to Hope Mills were Brigitte Bardot, mostly for the soldiers. They had titles that were easy to figure out: "Love Is My Profession," "And God Created Woman." She didn't know what to think about a title like "Hiroshima Mon Amour." It reminded her of "Chanson d'Amour," but at the same time The Bomb.

It would be interesting to see what it was all about.

Raeford himself sure was interesting.

Lying in bed, waiting for sleep to rise like a widening mist from the belladonna that Arlene has obtained illegally from a palmist (with careful description of the optimum dosage for a deep sleep that stops short of fatal), Janice thinks of Rowen Faircloth, the one thing in life that can still give her hope.

It is not a large hope, and she is not sure whether it comes from Rowen himself or her thinking about him, just that she is grateful now for the smallest, most fleeting blessings in her life. But it is a gratitude felt vaguely, as every good thing is felt now, muted by a raw grief that fatigues her in advance of everything else.

Sometimes when she thinks about him with certain feats of attention, she later dreams about him, though it is hard for her to think of this as cause and effect. The particulars of transportation to and within the land of dreams seem unknowable, and dreams of Rowen, which keep her from other dreams, she attributes neither to herself nor to the drug but entirely to grace. The dreaming, by no means a sure thing, she takes as proof of grace and of blessing, loose and senseless in the universe, occurring randomly, accounting for the unequal distribution. She does not need to believe there is intelligence behind all this, nor intent, nor even that grace and blessing will surely come to everyone in time. If they never come to her again, she will have had more than her share. When things are random there is no share, and that she has had any kind of tiny miracle at all is a miracle itself, if a person can think that way, which she can.

If there were anything that could be called a share, perhaps it is just that small, or smaller, or nothing at all.

In the darkened room, illuminated only by the knifelines of fall light around the blind, Janice is listening to the locusts and sourwoods outside, singing their dying song as their limbs rub against each other in the wind. She tries to concentrate, to remember in vivid if not particularly accurate detail her first meeting with Rowen. It is the intensity of vision she can bring to the scene that seems to count. She tries to roll it out like a movie, but already listing subtly toward sleep, she settles for a freeze-frame. Seen from behind, she stands with the naked baby on her hip, approaching (in purpose, but of course frozen) the produce tent he is in the process of setting up on a grassless patch of shade near the Mill. But of course he is frozen too, up on the bed of his truck, bent down to grab a bushel basket of okra by its wire handles. A teenage boy is frozen in his advance toward the truck.

In the still, her hair is tucked neatly behind her ears and she is wearing a fluent dress in a flowery print. The flowers are yellow and purple-throated, exotic, like the blooms on palm-like okra plants. On the truck, he is wearing work clothes, with rolled sleeves that display the small, neat muscles in his arms. The muscles and the contours of his face are treated to a heroic stylistics of line and shadow, like something public she remembers from youth, a newspaper reproduction of a painting by Thomas Hart Benton or certain scenes from the movie-lives of heroic farm laborers.

She doesn't know why the image has risen in this particular style. Sometimes the figures are in close-up, but softly filmed, looking straight at the camera, the tops of their heads tilted toward each other, Jean Harlow and Clark Gable, though in person she and Rowen look nothing like the two actors. On those nights the truck, the produce, the tree, the tent, the ground and the boy are all obliterated, all but the baby who rests at her waist, raising one of his hands to grab at some invisible fruit on some invisible tree, smiling his open-mouthed smile.

Suddenly she, with the baby on her hip again, looms in front of the rest of it: tent, truck, man, and boy. The lighting is the kind she knows from cinematic daybreaks in black and white, and there is a large swelling music. Things seem propitious for dreaming. . . .

But she loses it without warning, like a picture on tv that has gone to snow. When, after some effort, she has vision again, she and the baby have metamorphosed closer to him, and to the boy who has taken

162

the bushel of okra in his hands and turned toward the tent. It is no longer a freeze-frame, but a photograph of one, so that she is at once closer up and more remote. This makes her anxious, and besides, by now she is realizing the limited usefulness of the frozen images, whatever their degree of immediacy. Too many of the questions unasked of these artful arrangements have already been answered by her, shifting the terms of her effort. She is hurrying to move faster than she had dared only moments before. She knows that the boy is getting just this one hour's instruction about how to man the stand for his brother, who is already impatient to be off to his usual, more important business of running their large enterprise. Now galloping toward sleep, nervous, as always when she remarks how close they came to missing each other, Janice gives herself over to the sharp reality of memory, or memory remembered, but sharp as a razor even so: a sudden and fortuitous wipe, wiping away all she'd been trying to invent with her eye and leaving her in sound alone. The music is changing, becoming speech, which she strains to hear as precisely as if listening to the fragmented calls of birds with an ear toward naming their names.

"Hey, little fella . . . Little-piggy went to market . . . little-piggy stayed home—ba-a-a-d piggy! We like them all to go to market!" (This is Rowen.)

"Ah-ah-ah—" (This is baby.)

"He's a happy fella. Here, I'll hold him while you pick out what you want. Rae, help this lady. Come on, young-folks, let's sit over here and wait for your Mamma. . . ."

"Just a peck of new potatoes. I haven't got any place to store a bushel of anything at a time. . . ." (This is me.)

"Go to sleep you little baby." (Who is this? Is it Rowen? Or God?)

" . . . look good. I'd buy some, but I can't carry it all and him too. . . ." (This is me . . . complaining?)

" . . . whatever you want. I'll drop you off . . . got to get off from here anyway. . . ." (Sir Galahad.)

" . . . about half a bushel . . . I put up a lot of pickles just to give away . . . sweet ones." (Lady Bountiful.)

" . . . weeee-weeee!" (Rowen. . . .)

"Thanks again for taking him. . . ."

"It gives me a chance to try it out, without trying it out. . . ."

"What do you think?"

"I think I like it."

It is the dream.

163

Her bath over, wrapped in her bathrobe in her bedroom, Tollie bent over and began to brush her hair, distributing the oils, like they said you should do in *Seventeen*. Then she felt guilty and stopped, re-membering her mother's dry, flyaway hair. Youth had flown from Jan-ice, there was no doubt about that. Rowen Faircloth had flown from her too, or was getting ready to. Raeford said Rowen was thinking of selling the farm, putting Wiggie in a home, and "moving on down the line."

Moving where?" she'd asked.

Raeford had laughed. "Probably nowhere. But he's talking about India."

"India?" Tollie had never heard of such a thing. "What would he do there?"

"He said he'd just think. Think till the end of time."

"I never heard of such a thing," Tollie said, fearful for the effects of this news on her mother, as well as genuinely surprised at the notion of India.

"He always was philosophical," Raeford said. He seemed amused, in his unruffled way. "He's about as likely to do it as I am."

Was he just saying that? Tollie wondered. (And how likely are you to go to India, Raeford Faircloth? I know you're going to move on down the line somewhere, know it in my bones.) Was he saying Rowen wouldn't leave because he didn't want her to worry about her mother? She wished she didn't know about that, whatever it was. And how long

165

would it be until Janice knew her, Tollie's, secret? What would her mother think of history repeating itself?

Tollie put her hairbrush back in her straw basket with her combs and lipstick and what was left of the perfume Janice had given her, which she'd used liberally since she started going out with Raeford. Sometimes she didn't know how she could think about all she had to think about in this world. School, Raeford, history and the future, Janice, Les's job, Lili Lorene, her own looks, her own special "problem at hand." Her heart sure didn't leap up for long.

She looked at herself in the mirror of what had been her vanity, now a desk. She wished she looked older, more dried-up, just so she wouldn't have to feel guilty about looking so much younger than Janice. That must be one of the worst feelings in the world, guilt, and she felt it every day of her life.

She leaned forward over her blotter and the neatly piled schoolbooks and peered into her own eyes. How in the world did you manage to go so wrong in fifteen years, girl?

She took off her robe and tossed it over the mirror. She didn't even want to look at herself, never mind all the work she had to do on her face and hair before 2:30. She liked it that she didn't have a vanity in her room anymore, too. That seemed one less thing to feel guilty about—Vanity, a major sin. Also, the room was more serious without toilet items spread out, leading her into the temptation of just plopping down, any time, and primping. She was sure it was bad for your brain to concentrate on your looks too much, not to mention your conscience, if you lived in the house with a fading professional Beauty.

Even if her vanity mirror did still loom over her desk, she never would primp there again. She'd made enough mistakes out of spending too much time looking in the mirror, she guessed, even if she hadn't been anywhere near as bad as Lily. She'd learned to smoke there, for instance—sitting in front of her mirror and observing herself: french-inhaling, blowing smoke rings by popping herself in the cheek with her forefinger, exhaling smoke in the languid way of movie stars. Junk. She'd spent more time than she liked to remember with cut-out eyebrow and lip shapes in front of that mirror. Holding up the plastic sheets and working their geometrics onto her features with her eyebrow pencil and lipstick. She'd tried on cardboard "hairdos" ordered from an ad in Lily's *Modern Romances* once upon a time, squandered money. She'd spent precious time observing herself as several

166

species of blond, as a redhead (she'd looked a little like Jeanne Crain). She'd tried on the blue-black picture of curls that were the hair color of Wonder Woman, Veronica, Nancy's Aunt Fritzi and other cartoon characters. All the cardboard-hair had setting instructions on the back, telling you which sections to roll this way, which that, what to do up in bobby pins. When you ordered the set of cardboard hair, you checked the form as to the natural shape of your face: oval, oblong, round, heart, or square. Your package of hairdos would show how to make the most of your "perfect oval," if you had one. Otherwise, they would show you how to camouflage your face's natural shape so that you'd seem to have some kind of an oval. She'd never thought about the shape of her face before that. But then she'd studied it for a long time at her vanity, pulling her hair back from her forehead and cheeks, scrutinizing the contours of her cheeks and chin. She had a small widow's peak, but neither really high cheekbones nor a really pointy chin. Still, she'd finally decided that she was closest to a "heart" anyway. The little dip in her hairline in the middle of her forehead gave way to a jawline descending from the tips of her ears into a *slight* point; her cheekbones weren't prominent, but they were *sort of* high, which she could emphasize with rouge (made out of lipstick), if she wanted to. She understood from everywhere that high cheekbones were a desirable feature. She'd learned how to make the most of her cleavage by putting a little rouge there, but she'd never had an occasion to show it out in public yet, and wouldn't: not under the present circumstances. She'd learned how to make a dimple in her chin by a subtle trick of her eyebrow pencil. She'd bought a Roux rinse in "Amber" to give her hair highlights, but it hadn't worked. She'd spent her lunch money on "Gold" and it hadn't worked either. And she'd never dared take any of these changes out of the privacy of her room.

Junk, junk, junk.

If Raeford Faircloth had a chance of finding out some of these things about her, she'd probably just crawl on in a hole and die.

Tollie stepped into the nicest of the sack dresses Lily had given her. She wondered if it would be okay to wear. She wished she had some shetland sweaters like Raeford himself wore, maybe a kilt, kneesocks, Cindy Wiggins' style. She uncovered the mirror and surveyed herself in sections, bending down, then getting up on tiptoe. Yep, a lot hadn't worked from the perspective of the vanity as a vanity. She was glad to have it transformed. Who wanted to look like some of the women in

167

magazines looked anyway? (Who but Lily Jones, and she ought to be having second thoughts, the way people were treating her.)

Tollie opened the door of her room and ran smack into Arlene, who she hadn't even known was in the house.

"Tollie, are you going out for long?" Arlene asked, a worried look on her face. She stepped forward, forcing Tollie to back up until they both stood back inside her bedroom, the door partly closed.

"I . . . yes. I probably am."

"I don't think it's a good idea," Arlene whispered. "Things are going wrong for her again, I think. God knows where Les is, or when he might get home."

"Could you stay with her?" Tollie asked, embarrassed. It wasn't like it recommended you to want to go on a date instead of taking care of your sick mother.

"I can't, honey. I've got in-laws coming. I've got cooking to do."

"I know I ought to stay," Tollie said. "But today is just special."

"And you have to go."

Tollie and Arlene turned. In the gap of doorway, Tollie could see her mother's stark face within the dull halo of her hair, her pained eyes.

"Mamma . . . ," Tollie said.

"I don't want you missing a trip to Chapel Hill because of me," Janice said, not even looking at Arlene. "I'm all right."

"Janice, Honey," Arlene said helplessly.

"I mean it," Janice said, keeping her eyes on Tollie. "I will *not* be that kind of mother. Now I'm going back to lie down on my bed. I won't move till you get back, I promise. You just go on and enjoy yourself."

"I'm going to be gone for several hours," Tollie said uncertainly. "If I go." Her heart felt heavy as lead. "I shouldn't go."

"I won't move," Janice said, turning to go to her bedroom. "And you won't stay here. I won't allow it."

Tollie and Arlene looked at each other.

"I guess I'll go," Tollie said, half-sick with the idea. She searched Arlene's face. It seemed to register a hint of disapproval, but when Arlene spoke Tollie couldn't tell whether there was disapproval or encouragement, in spite of the words.

"I'll check in on her when I can," Arlene said. "You go on. You have a good time. You've had enough on your mind lately."

"I think you look real cute today," Raeford said. They were speeding along with the top down on the winding two-lane road toward Chapel Hill, an hour away. A world away, Tollie thought happily, then sadly, then happily again, beginning to enjoy the whip of her hair in the wind. She expected the town to loom up on the distant landscape at some point, like those cathedral-towns in Europe that were pictured in her world history book.

"Thanks," she said to Raeford, smiling at him. You do too, she wanted to say. You look real cute. Today, and every day. He was wearing his uniform, the blue chambray shirt and jeans, but also a tan corduroy jacket, which looked soft with wear, comfortable, like he was.

The car was noisy, close to the ground. It felt funny to be travelling so fast, so close to the road that every bump and stray piece of rock or gravel registered the fact of itself in your progress. She couldn't help thinking that maybe the vigorous ride would help toward solving her problem. Women did seem to lose babies from riding the ever-helpful horse in the movies. Riding a horse couldn't be much rougher than this.

She could feel herself turning sorrowful again, but she steeled herself and stopped it. Sometimes you just had to forget about things in the interest of saving your life. She was going to have this afternoon and night, whatever waited for her later on.

It was hard to hear over the car's noise, so she and Raeford didn't talk. She leaned her head back and let the sun fall on her cheeks, squinting up at the Carolina Blue sky. Now and then she could see golden leaves overhead, from tree-branches that hung out over the road. There was a small line of broken and unthreatening cloud, wispy as old sky-writing whose message had disintegrated beyond meaning.

The radio was on. It was hard to hear beneath the car's noise, but if she strained, she could hear it—"Back in the USA" by Chuck Berry and his *relentless* guitar, which a person couldn't resist, she didn't think, whether they rock 'n' rolled or not.

He was singing about looking for a drive-in, searching for a café. . . .

Where they'd let a Negro sit down and eat, she realized with a little shock. Did anybody else hear that? She looked over at Raeford, who was watching the road with a relaxed look on his face, tapping the steering wheel a little.

Probably no one did, she concluded. Or it wouldn't be allowed on the airwaves, at least not in the South. And yet there it was, and people just thought they were rock 'n' rolling to a beat. Subversive.

I'm not going to think about Negroes anymore today either, Tollie thought, fixing her eyes on the clear blue heavens and letting Chuck Berry become part of the general noise of the ride.

Nor that, she thought a few minutes later when she vaguely heard The Drifters, "There Goes My Baby."

When they got near Chapel Hill, Raeford switched to the station at the University, classical music. Tollie didn't have much experience with classical music. No station in Hope Mills ever played it. Music class at school was endless rounds of "Row-Row-Row Your Boat," year after year. She sort of liked how the music on the radio sounded, at least as much of it as she could hear if she strained her ears. You could tell it was subtle, even if you didn't understand it. Also, that you were supposed to like it . . . if you were a refined person on your way to Chapel Hill. But it was a foreign language to her. Even if it *said* something in its codes, she'd probably never know what it was.

Soothing, maybe, if you could listen to it without competition from a car's motor and gravel flying up against metal like hail from below.

No troubling messages. Just pure, sequenced notes.

Sort of boring.

Roll Over, Beethoven. Chuck Berry had said that too.

170

Chapel Hill didn't loom up. They just drove into it, a small gold-leafed town built around big, square brick buildings, a line of main street with all the businesses on one side. Tollie felt disappointed. She'd expected more.

Groggy from her dream, Janice sits under the moon in her night-gown on the back steps of her house. It's not too cold yet. Arlene's kitchen window is open, its light cast in a gold square on the ground. She can hear Arlene moving pots and pans around, talking with her in-laws. She can smell chicken frying, splattering in its grease.

The belladonna has worn off. She has taken a Miltown and is wait-ing for its effects. Sleep had done her no good at all. Neither sleep nor dream, this time. Everybody knows Rowen Faircloth is done with her, don't they? She knows it. She knows what she looks like. She knows she deserves it, too.

When she was pregnant in New York, her Daddy had died in Whiteville. She hadn't even been able to come home for the funeral. When she'd come home later, with Tollie, Gracie was back too, in the house of Mamma-the-Widow. The House of Women, in a town of women, all the men off fighting. Everybody fighting in the House of Women, too. And then, in the summer, not a week before the War was over, she spied on her sister Gracie down in the garden behind their mother's house—Gracie with the only man left in town, the pharma-cist, both of them gleaming in their white clothes before they disap-peared behind the dark pyracantha. The next day, a man had come with the news about their brother Buddy, in the South Pacific. How long had it taken after Rowen Faircloth till her own little boy was dead in his crib? Not long at all. You almost had to conclude that the deaths of males, and maybe bad luck of every kind, were tied to the sexual practices of women. Or maybe it was just plain old sin and retribution.

If that's what it is with Rowen, sin or sex-practice.

Rowen is . . . ascetic. More or less. Which probably explains why he's put up with her this long. Maybe he will go to India, as he's said he might, become a Holy Man. Take his little brother with him, before Tollie does something with him and Les dies on them, cause and effect. Then where will mother-and-daughter be?

She can see Arlene in the window that is over her sink, her head with its Italian boy haircut bent down. Arlene keeps saying, You'll get used to it. Lots of women lose babies and it's awful, I'm not saying it's not, but they get used to it. There's nothing wrong with that. It saves their lives.

Janice doesn't think she will get used to it. But what if she does? That's scary in itself. As scary as having become a weirdo, which could lead anywhere.

Nut. Cracked. Cracked nut.

She thinks of all the years she was clear and normal in other people's eyes, how when she'd see the weirdos, she'd think, Poor old things, and go on about her business, like anybody else would.

The sharp white moonlight silhouettes Arlene's scrubby trees and the big black screen of loblolly pines way down where the golf course starts. Janice sees that she needs to shave her legs. Les hides her razor and will only lend it to her, to use while he stands outside the bathroom door. Poor Les. She never meant him any harm.

He threw out all the knives except the butter knives. A person couldn't cook a decent meal in their kitchen now, even if she had the energy.

So what. Les is never home, Tollie either. She can't blame them. On the other hand, she'd like to be somewhere else too. They want to be away from her, in her hour of need. Let them eat cheesecake.

Does she have an hour of need? She can't help things, *ergo*, as Arlene would say, she has no need. Okay. Les and Tollie: Go, with my blessing.

The pines look like a line of hands raised against the sky. Somebody at the undertaker's wrapped his little fist around the stem of a rosebud. She wouldn't have thought to do that herself, but once it was done, she thought it was okay. They were always putting something in the hands of dead people. Probably because their hands, empty, looked so stiff. There couldn't be much that's sadder than the empty hands of dead people. Sitting there under the undertaker's tent at the end, trying to see into the box after they'd already closed it up, there was a little comfort in the rose. Until she tried to see whether there were thorns on the stem, cutting into his hand, deciding there were. Then Les was half-carrying her away, and when she looked over his shoulder she could see Tollie standing with her back toward the box, watching her mother and Les.

The steam is coming out of Arlene's window. The chicken must be on a platter now, the empty pan in the sink. Janice can hear chairs being scraped up to the table. A moment of silence. Some murmuring. She knows she's responsible for Arlene's getting supper on the table so late, and she's sorry for it, like she's sorry for everything.

She looks at her wrists in the moonlight, her own crosses to bear. She looks at her hands, their lines darkly sketching her fate, which is also dark, must be.

Once, when Tollie was supposed to be minding him, he crawled back into the bedroom, got hold of a razorblade. When they heard him crying and got to him, he had it in his fist, squeezing it tighter with the pain. His little arm was running with blood, dripping on the floor, soaking into his t-shirt. That was the only time she ever slapped Tollie in the face. Tollie's face turned white as a sheet, not red. She didn't cry a bit, just waited till Janice got the razorblade out of his hand and took him to the bathroom, then Tollie got a towel and wiped up the floor. They never said a word about it, ever. Poor Tollie.

I'm ruining her life, Janice thinks. I can't help anything.

Poor Tollie.

That's what Les had said, that August day when she was lying with Tollie on a blanket in her mother's backyard, sunbathing, anything to warm up after the news about Buddy. Her mother in her dark bedroom, a husband and a son lost in not much more than a year's time. Gracie hysterical, not just about Buddy but the pharmacist, who suddenly had other fish to fry. Everybody acting like she, Janice, was the cause of it all, with her bastard child. A curse on the House of Women.

"Where's her Daddy?" asked Les, who'd come to see Janice's own Daddy on cotton business, not knowing he was dead—asking about Tollie, but giving Janice "the look."

"Dead in the War," Janice said, looking at little Tollie and beginning to see a light. "Her Daddy's a War Hero."

"Pore little thing," Les said with a sympathetic cough. "Seems like she'd need a daddy."

Janice looked at him. The hat and sunglasses were in the way, but he didn't look too bad. He had a vehicle idling in the alleyway behind him, that was the main thing.

Her mother didn't have time to make her a cake, or the energy. She didn't have time to make herself a dress. After he'd come around a few times—discreetly, since her house was in mourning—she'd made up her mind. It didn't look like the War was ever going to be over anyway, no guarantee that any men at all would come home alive. She just packed up the baby's few things and went to the courthouse, settled for Les.

She didn't mean him any harm, then, and she especially doesn't now. He's suffered too. And he's tried to take some kind of care of them all these years. She didn't know she'd meet someone like Rowen.

Is it even Rowen? Was it?

Maybe it was just her life. Her not being able to go on, thinking that what it was was what it was.

Mamma, when she was dying, in her bed for months, wearing a diaper, said, "I feel like all I can do now is live in sweet memory. I make myself forget all about this. I make myself forget the memories that weren't sweet too. I make myself. Time is short."

Poor Mamma.

Poor Les. Poor Tollie. Poor Baby.

Poor Daddy. Poor Buddy. Poor Mamma again.

Poor little things, one and all.

Several hours later, Tollie and Raeford and Randy's girlfriend, Bennett, were finishing up their dinners in the Rathskellar, an underground restaurant lit with candles and pungent with the smells of sizzling steaks. Tollie was enjoying her meal—she'd been starving, all through the movie—but mostly she was miserable. At Randy's apartment, Raeford had introduced her as "Tanya," as if her regular name wasn't good enough to use with his friends. (As if he felt about her, in front of them, like she'd felt about herself in front of him, back when they'd first met. . . .) Then, she'd been stuck for an hour in one of those butterfly chairs that you couldn't get out of without tipping it over (which she'd done in the end), while Raeford and Randy and Bennett had talked around her, making jokes that were too subtle for her to catch, hinting about past experiences that she couldn't know a thing about, drinking like fish. She didn't know when she'd seen Raeford Faircloth drink so much in so little time, and that was saying something. She'd had a drink too, rum and coke, which Randy had stirred—with his *finger*. The finger of an obstetrician-gynecologist in training, no telling where it had been! They sure were *refined* in Chapel Hill, was all she could think, stuck in that chair, stuck in Lily's castoff sackdress and a ratty old cardigan while a girl wearing an expensive camel-hair blazer and a nice flannel skirt flirted with Raeford right under her nose, like Tollie Ramsey counted for nothing. A girl with the most perfect haircut Tollie had ever seen, while she herself had hair cut by Lily's mother, with sewing scissors.

Then, insult to injury, Bennett had invited herself to go to the movies and out to dinner with them, since Randy had to work at the hospital all night. That gave a person food for thought too: somebody as crude as Randy, working in a hospital. And on top of that, he'd had more to drink than Raeford had. No wonder sick people couldn't get help in this world.

Tollie tried to put it all out of her mind. She wanted to enjoy something about this trip, after all it had cost her. (Mamma! How was she?)

Tollie shook her thoughts from her head and took a big bite of her Beef Stroganoff, which she guessed Raeford would tease her about on the way home, if he had the *nerve* to remind her, ever again, about "Tanya." He and Bennett had ordered steaks, which had come to the table on flat iron griddles, surrounded by french fries and garnished with a perseved crabapple on a lettuce leaf. They looked good, but Tollie wasn't sorry about the Beef Stroganoff. She hadn't been able to resist the way it was described on the menu, and it was delicious, as good as anything she'd ever put in her mouth.

"*Are* you Russian?" Bennett asked suddenly, seeming half-aware of Tollie at last.

"Part," Tollie said. She wished she'd never told that lie to Raeford. Now she had to keep it up, when she looked about as exotic as an old feedsack stuck in a cardigan.

"That's . . . unusual," Bennett said, scrutinizing Tollie for a minute before picking up a piece of steak-trimming with her fingers and chewing at the last bit of edible meat clinging to it. Then she picked up the bone and began to pick the meat off of it.

That's what you could do if you were a girl of Bennett's class of people, Tollie thought: eat with your fingers in public, gnaw on a bone like an animal, and never give it a thought.

"I thought that movie was pretentious," Bennett said, throwing the bone on her plate and wiping her hands and patting her mouth with the big wine-colored cloth napkin.

"I thought it was kind of sexy," Raeford said.

"I was about to go to sleep," Bennett said.

Tollie had liked the movie, though parts of it puzzled her. She hadn't found it sexy. She thought that part of the point might be that the fact of the Bomb dropping on Japan could interfere with people's love lives, but she wasn't sure. It certainly hadn't bored her. If nothing else, reading the subtitles ought to keep a person awake.

178

She was getting bored with Bennett, though. Whiner. Intruder. Flirt. She doesn't know what to do with an education, Tollie thought. I would. I'd know, and yet I'll never get the chance. She's had every chance in the world, you can just tell, and she always will have.

"What are you studying?" Tollie said to Bennett, feeling more aggressive now that her sack dress and home-cut hair were less visible in the dark restaurant. She'd had a glass of wine, too, out of a bottle wrapped in a straw-basket. Such bottles were all around the restaurant, with candles in them, candlewax obscuring the straw.

"French," Bennett said yawning behind her hand. "Just the merest thought of it makes me yawn, as you can see," she said, looking at Raeford. "I hate it."

"Could you understand the movie?" Tollie said.

Bennett looked away from Raeford and back to Tollie, as if she'd been disturbed. Good, Tollie thought.

"Without the subtitles?" Tollie persisted.

"That's another thing," Bennett said irritably, looking at Raeford again. "The sound track was awful. Or they slurred the words or something."

"What grade are you in?" Tollie asked.

Bennett looked at her. "What *grade* am I in?"

"In college, you say 'What year are you,' " Raeford said with equanimity, pouring more of the wine into his glass.

"Don't you go to school?" Bennett said to Tollie.

"I go to high school," Tollie said. Her face was flaming, she could feel it. She was glad again for the candlelight, this shadowy dungeon of a restaurant. "I'm taking Spanish," she said, trying to make up lost ground.

"I wouldn't bother with that, if I were you," Bennett said, lighting a Salem. "When you get to school, Spanish doesn't count. It's for boneheads."

"Why did you go into French?" Tollie asked, hoping her voice didn't register how mad she felt. Why didn't you just go out and drown yourself before you got to be so stupid and rude?

"Daddy," Bennett said. "Mamma. Mamma thinks, if all else fails, I can fall back on teaching school, which I'd rather kill myself than do. Daddy thinks, if nothing else, I can go with them to France when they're old and help them tour around. I don't know what Mamma thinks is going to fail. I'm going to marry Randy, have a couple of babies, and watch him make money. I'm going to decorate the house, join the Junior League, get a place at the beach, study antiques, wait bliss-fully for my patrimony, and Randy's, and be generally and specifically happy, every day of my life, all the rest of my life. What could fail? I want some cheesecake."

Raeford signaled a waiter. "Do you want some dessert?" he asked Tollie.

"No," Tollie said.

"You'll be sorry," Bennett said. "It's *très . . . bien.*" Bennett smiled a huge smile. Raeford laughed cheerfully. Tollie could see he didn't re-sent Bennett a bit. Maybe Raeford did live in too-different a world from hers for her feelings for him to come to much. Lily had been say-ing that all along.

"I guess I'll have some," Tollie said.

The cake was delicious when it came. Better than my birthday cake by a mile, Tollie thought, then felt guilty. Her mother had been so proud of that cake. She felt more guilty. She realized she hadn't thought about Janice for half an hour. She hoped Arlene was check-ing on her.

"Where are you going to go to school?" Bennett asked Tollie, look-ing half-interested, once she seemed to have run out of conversation to have with Raeford, who was drinking a brandy and settling up the bill.

"Here," Tollie said. "Maybe."

"Are you going to be a dental hygienist?"

"No," Tollie said. "Why? Why would I?"

"Well, what else? They don't take freshman girls here, or sopho-mores. They only take about two juniors a year. All they generally take girls into is that old dental hygienist program. Most of them never look inside a mouth, once they're out of here. They just marry dentists and forget it ever happened."

"Don't you go here?" Tollie said.

"I'm at Women's College, with everybody else," Bennett said placidly. "I couldn't even transfer here in my junior year, with my grades." She looked at Tollie. "You don't seem to know a whole lot."

"I'm only in the tenth grade," Tollie said, biting her tongue the minute it was out of her mouth. Raeford had just turned back toward them. Now the cat was out of the bag.

"She's very precocious for her age," Raeford said, giving her hand a little squeeze.

180

"She must be," Bennett said, winking at Raeford. She laughed a low, suggestive laugh.

"I need to get back to Hope Mills," Tollie said to Raeford, ignoring Bennett. "It's getting near my curfew." She gave Bennett an undisguised look of dislike.

Raeford laughed again. "I expect we'd better," he said. "You ladies got everything?"

Tollie felt angry that he hadn't said anything to put a rein on Bennett. But then what could he say? 'She's not precocious *that* way?' What a lie that would be, even if he didn't know it.

"Got everything *I* need," Bennett said, scooting out of the booth. "I don't know about y'all though. Got everything you need, Tanya? Yes, it looks to me like you do. Got everything, Raeford?" She gave Raeford a wink.

I hate her, Tollie thought. I hate her rich-bitch guts.

"If you were ashamed of me, you shouldn't have taken me up there," she said to Raeford once they'd driven out of Chapel Hill. The top was up on the car now, muting the engine's noise a little.

"I wasn't," Raeford said, his face looking surprised in the dim lights of the dashboard. "I'm not."

"You sure did ignore me, once we were with your friends," Tollie said. She still had to strain her voice to be heard over the motor.

Raeford reached out and took her hand and kissed it. "I'm sorry," he said. "Randy and I probably know each other too well. We tend to act like we alone invented the world when we get together."

"Is he from Hope Mills?"

"No, I met him in military school, then followed him to Chapel Hill. He's sort of like a big brother. Or a big brother I prefer to the one I've got."

"What's wrong with your own?" Tollie asked, curious for several reasons. She needed to know more about Rowen Faircloth, whether or not he might end up being her stepfather, which she felt pretty sure he wouldn't. Still: he could sure affect her life

"I don't know. You can't know Rowen very well. It's like he's self-contained, living in another world."

"I don't think Randy's a good person for you to model yourself after," Tollie said. "You're miles ahead of him. And that Bennett—"

Raeford laughed and squeezed her hand. "They're all right."

"Why do you take me out?" Tollie asked after a little while. "I can't figure it out. I am just a high school girl. I don't have the looks or the clothes. You could go out with lots of girls."

Raeford hesitated. "I do," he said finally. "You probably should know that. I go out with several girls. Women."

Tollie felt cold. "I figured as much," she said, half-lying. She didn't think she had figured as much, not really. "Are some of them college girls?"

"Yes," Raeford said. "Some of them are drop-outs too. I sort of play the field."

"It sounds it," Tollie said

"I wouldn't want to hurt you, Tollie," Raeford said. "That's why I don't force myself on you, too much."

"You couldn't force yourself on me!" Tollie said, indignant. "I wouldn't let you."

"There are different kinds of force," Raeford said. He put his arm out and pulled her toward him a little. It was uncomfortable, with the gearshift sticking up between their separate seats. Tollie's back hurt, but she didn't move.

"Why do you go out with me?" she persisted. "What's in it for you?"

Raeford looked into her face. "What's in it for you?" he asked. He looked back at the road. So did Tollie. It was dark.

"I like you," Tollie said. "You make me feel hopeful."

"That's how I feel," Raeford said. "I like you. I'm hopeful for you."

"I appreciate your interest in me," Tollie said stiffly.

"You're an uncommon person, Tollie," he said. She could barely hear him over the noise of the car.

"Why did you call me 'Tanya' up there?" Suddenly Tollie didn't trust anything he was saying. She extricated herself from his arm and sat back in her own seat. "I think you were ashamed of me."

"No," Raeford said. "I wanted them to hesitate, and take a good look at you. Not that they did. Or could, maybe. They're limited people, in some ways. I'm not proud of how they act sometimes."

"Maybe limited in a lot of ways," Tollie said, still hurt.

"Maybe. I wish they were different."

"I don't know why you tolerate them," Tollie said.

"Probably because they're just like I used to be. I'm not proud of that, either. I'm trying pretty hard to be different, but I keep ending up some sort of type. A Beatnik or whatever."

"I. . . ." Tollie clammed up. She felt a little sorry for Raeford, for all his advantages, and the bad lot he'd fallen in with. He seemed younger than he'd seemed when she woke up that morning thinking about him.

"It's frustrating," he said. "That's why I'll probably just go on back and finish school and see what happens then."

"Are they the best friends you've got?" Tollie asked after a minute.

"They probably are," Raeford conceded.

"Let's try to listen to the radio," Tollie said. "My throat hurts from trying to talk over the motor."

It was only a little after ten o'clock when they pulled into Tollie's driveway, but Arlene was pacing in the yard. Like she's been waiting and watching for Cinderella, Tollie thought, watching Arlene hurry toward the car the minute they bumped into the driveway from the street.

"What is it?" Raeford said.

"My mother's crazy," Tollie said flatly, so weary she wasn't sure she could pull herself up out of the car's low seat. "You ought to know some of the truth about me too."

Tollie and Lily were eating lunch in the high school cafeteria, wearing their winter coats. That the school didn't have lockers was one of Lily's constant complaints. You had to wear your coat or struggle to carry it, along with every one of your books, from class to class to class. You had to sit on it at your desk, or if the weather was warm enough for you to get away with just a jacket, you had to try to cram that into the book place under your desk and sit on the books themselves. Unless you wanted to put your coat or jacket in the cloak room and risk somebody ripping out your hem for meanness, or sticking a french tickler in your pocket so they could follow you around all day, knocking elbows and grinning in their pimples, waiting for you to reach for a kleenex and pull that thing out. That had happened to her. She couldn't understand what made high school kids so mean to each other. They were all in the same boat, in some ways, boys and girls, rich kids and Mill Rats. They all were busting with hormones, worried sick about how they seemed to everybody else every day of their lives. Wanting to be liked, concerned about the future. You'd think they'd stick together.

We're together today, Lily thought, looking around the somber cafeteria. Nobody was doing much—not eating, not talking. A few girls were snivelling. Lunch period had been moved forward so that everyone could get fed, have half of their fifth-period class and then go to the auditorium. At one-thirty, a preacher was coming and there was going to be a memorial service for Eva Bledsoe, a senior, who'd been killed Friday night when her daddy's little white Valiant had crossed the center line and gone head-on into a big Virginia-Carolina truck that was hauling a load of chemicals somewhere or other. Eva was the first student to die since they'd all been in high school together. A girl had died in junior high when her radio had fallen into the bathtub, but she'd been new in town, a soldier's kid, and nobody had known her very well. Everybody had known Eva, or known of Eva. Everybody was down at the mouth. The flag was half-mast. It was worse than last year when Buddy Holly and the Big Bopper had got killed. At the next table a couple of Catholics, soldiers' kids too, were wearing black armbands, a practice Lily had been unfamiliar with, but she liked it: it had the proper touch of seriousness. She might get herself one.

After the service, school would be out for the day so that whoever wanted to could go to Eva's funeral at the Rockfish Creek Baptist Church, which was way out in the country, where Eva's parents probably came from, Lily surmised. A lot of people in Hope Mills, especially the Mill Rats, had parents who came from even farther out in the Boonies. She herself had that kind of parents, though once they'd come to the "big city" of Hope Mills, they'd never looked back—! She wouldn't know her own remaining grandparents if she met them on the street, which was kind of sad, if you thought about it. Which she didn't, much.

"Do you think we should go?" Tollie asked for about the tenth time. Lily hadn't answered her before, and didn't now. Tollie was just thinking outloud, trying to decide. Lily hadn't decided herself whether she wanted to drive the Oldsmobile out to Rockfish Creek or not. She guessed she'd see how the memorial service went. She didn't want her or Tollie to get any more depressed than they had to, with all they had to figure out about Tollie's bun in the oven. They needed clear minds, not too much emotion. It had been a big mistake for them to go to the visitation at the funeral home last night.

Lily didn't know how she felt about Eva. She'd known her all her life, but she felt like she'd never known her at all. That's how everybody seemed to feel. She was different.

"Prominent," Tollie-of-the-64-thousand-dollar-vocabulary had said when they'd discussed it on the school bus yesterday morning, shrunk down in a seat near the back like two old women, whispering if they said anything at all, like everybody else. People who didn't follow the newspaper were just hearing about Eva as they got on the bus, and you could watch them change as they walked down the aisle. By the time they took a seat, they were in a state of shock. You just knew what was going on in their minds: If somebody like Eva Bledsoe, a breed apart, could die—at seventeen years old, in an instant—what in the world is waiting out there for me?

"But not . . . accessible," Tollie had whispered, taking a little notebook and a stubby pencil out of her coat pocket. "She wasn't what you could ever think of as a . . . peer." She scribbled something down in the notebook and put it away.

Tollie was going on and keeping that old vocabulary list, Lily reckoned, though Wiggins would never look at it. You couldn't tell Tollie much. Lily herself had kept a list in 10th grade, 42 words, and that old bitch had never looked at it, or tracked her down to recite "The Soul Selects Its Own Society," "She Walks in Beauty," or any of the poems and bits of poems she'd learned by heart. Nor to recite her dozen Quotable Quotes. You just knew that Mrs. Randall Wiggins didn't give a shit whether a Mill Rat learned anything or not.

Lily felt that what Tollie said about Eva was probably true, though normally she didn't believe in that breed-apart stuff, except as it applied to her own self: Lily Jones sure as Hell wasn't like anybody else in Hope Mills. But neither was Eva. The difference was that everybody knew it about Eva and let her be. They must just suspect it about Lily Jones, and so that's why they had to torment her: to try to wear her down to their own level.

Lily Jones was a well-kept secret that would burst out on the world and rub everybody's nose in their past behavior one of these days, Lily vowed. But everybody had been aware, all along, of Eva as something large, in the scheme of high school and beyond. Eva Bledsoe never had seemed like their " . . . peer." But she didn't seem like somebody that they'd all agreed to put on a pedestal, either, like "Most Popular" or Homecoming Queen or Miss Hope Mills High. People on a pedestal weren't a breed apart. They were all part of the same ignorant breed, which ordered everything in life out of their ignorant lack of imagination. Otherwise, Lily Jones would have been on a pedestal, wearing a crown, all her born-days.

Lily took a little bite of collards, chewed thoughtfully, then fiddled with her pork barbeque with her fork. Eva had been kind of otherworldly before she was even in the Other World, she thought. Who could eat this mess, bitter greens, dead meat right before a funeral? She pushed her plate a couple of inches away from her.

189

Eva had been pretty, she'd grant her that. But in an unusual way. Her skin was a natural tan color, and her hair was a subtle blond that Lily almost envied, "sandy" but with natural sunstreaks, summer and winter. That was because Eva was a real athlete, Lily figured, out in the sunshine most days, not just somebody who hopped around in a burlap sack once a year at Field Day. Eva ran track, swam for speed. She'd had to do it on her own. Their high school didn't even have a basketball team for girls, like other high schools in little bitty towns in the middle of Nowhere. That hadn't slowed Eva down. She played basketball for a church team out in the county. She looked graceful and feminine, but strong: tall, well-proportioned, clear eyes and skin, fingernails with no ridges or white spots. She knew Modern Dance and Jazz Dancing from going out to the Base every Saturday morning and taking lessons at the Teen Club from a German woman who was married to a soldier and who'd let Eva in, in spite of her father not being a soldier himself. She'd even danced in several plays at the Base theatre, which Lily wished she'd thought of in time to prepare her dance-talent. You had to have good sense about those kind of things early in life, or the opportunity would just slip away.

Yes, Eva was resourceful, you had to give her that.

Lily opened her milk carton and stuck a straw in, but she didn't drink. She felt like if anything much passed her lips today, she'd most likely vomit. Eva had imagination. Versatility. She would have probably got Most Versatile in the Yearbook, if she'd stayed in her own lane.

Across the cafeteria, Lily could see the gym teacher, Julia Pappas, sitting in a chair against the wall, pulling cafeteria duty with red and swollen eyes. Pappas' thick black hair was too curly to do much with. It stood out around her head like one of those net curler-bonnets. She had her hands stuck down in the pockets of her wool topper, mouse-colored. Lily watched as the teacher balled up her fists inside her pockets and pushed them together, like she was balancing two rocks in her lap. Her lips stuck out slightly, in a tight little pouch, no lipstick. She looked half-dead. Eva had been her favorite student. Probably her only real student, Lily realized, feeling a little pang of sympathy. That must be something: to spend your whole life in a job that was impossible to do long before you ever got near it. Who ever cared about gym? Miss Pappas would have done better to have worked in her father's restaurant, The Palm Court, it seemed to Lily, or to have married another Greek and settled down to family life like all the other

190

daughters of the town's restaurant-owners, settled down to prepare sweeter-than-sweet desserts for the annual Greek Orthodox Church's Bake Sale, one of the few exotic events to take place in Hope Mills.

Seeing the gym teacher reminded Lily that Eva had had focus, as well as versatility: mainly on gymnastics, a sport Lily had never even heard of until a few weeks ago, when Miss Pappas had tried to make the gym class come to attention and watch Eva in action on a bunch of mats strung together to cover almost the whole length of the gym floor. Something like monkey bars had been set up at each end. Everybody was kind of sleepy—it was the last class of the day—so they couldn't get too excited, even though Pappas was down there making noise and waving her arms around, as bad as Old Tinsley, the band teacher. The college-track girls had moved toward her, but slowly, like grazing animals. The others stayed up high in the bleachers at the far ends of the gym, sort of looking at the activity, sleepy-eyed. But then they went back to filing at their nails or fixing each other's spit curls with scotch tape.

Most of the time, Pappas gave slenderizing exercises to the college-track girls, since she couldn't talk them into basketball or softball, except about once a year. She'd just let the Mill Rats do what they were going to do anyway: sit in the bleachers and make up their faces and read *True Romance*. But that day, she wouldn't give up. She'd wanted to display Eva, who had come out onto the floor in a black leotard, her hair pulled back in a knot, like ballerinas wore in magazine pictures. Pappas' hair was flying, wild as a thistle in the wind. She kept trying to corral them: she wanted their undivided attention.

Why did teachers *always* put it that way—"undivided attention," "not one iota." Jesus. Lily picked the cherries out of her cobbler and allowed herself to go on and feel sick at heart, like school was always threatening to make her feel. Wasn't that the worst thing: that somebody like Eva Bledsoe had spent just about every year of her life listening to that stuff, and now she was dead and gone? No undivided attention to give to anything, not one iota of life left in her.

Eva had stood at one end of the line of mats that afternoon, as straight as a bullet, her hands down rigid at her sides. She was looking ahead like nobody was there in the gym but her. Pappas was blowing her whistle like a maniac, her face red as a rose. All of sudden the teacher looked alive and interesting to Lily. You could tell that she could be a pretty little mouse, if she tried. Which she didn't, not one iota. She ought to go blond, put on some lipstick, wear tighter clothes.

"Get on down here, girls," Miss Pappas called. Wheet! Wheet! Wheeeeeeet! "Or I'm going to jerk a knot in your tails. This is something special."

She finally got the class to come down to one section of the bleachers and take a seat, put away their magazines and rat-tail combs and compacts. All the girls in the school were filing in, let out of class to watch Eva. Nobody seemed to know what was going on. It was too late in the day to care. Then Pappas announced that Eva was going to do gymnastics, which nobody had ever heard of. She said that in the summer Eva was going to go all the way to Europe, paid for by the government, to do the same thing in a competition.

She, Pappas, might just as well have been talking Greek, Lily recollected now, looking away from Julia Pappas slumped against the lunchroom wall. Like in that old play, Greek to me—that was everybody's attitude about Eva and gymnastics, but it was only twenty minutes till time to load the buses, so why not?

"World Class," Pappas kept saying, almost a pleading sound, like it would sink into their rock-brains what they had in their midst if she just made enough effort.

How could it? Lily thought. None of them had any experience with anything like that: not just a girl going out for sports and nobody saying she was a morphodite, but a girl going all the way from Hope Mills to Europe to compete in a sport. How did a thing like that happen? How did a girl see *how* to do a thing like that?

It was kind of weird: Eva out in front of half a gym of girls in a skimpy leotard that almost showed her crack and that would get her arrested if she wore it on any beach in the Southeast United States. Some of the girls *were* giggling, a few looked excited, maybe taking a cue from Pappas. But most of them seemed to be orbiting the moon. Lily could only half-concentrate herself. Eva herself looked like she was in another world.

Then there was music from a record player, and Eva was moving. Pappas sat down on the bleachers. She was watching Eva and smiling, her dumb whistle still in her lips.

Eva tumbled around on the mats and flipped herself in the air on the bars, like a monkey . . . except she looked like Wonder Woman's little sister, whatever-her-name-was—Diana?

It was like we weren't even there, Lily thought now, remembering Eva tumbling around to "Cherry Pink and Apple Blossom White."

Suddenly cartwheeling up onto her hands and pulling her long tanned legs together, pointing her strong toes toward heaven.

Lily felt sadder. She and Eva had been little Mill Rats together, back to the Year One. She could still remember Eva as a shy little girl in leggings and maryjanes, standing pigeon-toed in the front row in a primary school photograph, squinting at the sun. Her hair had been pulled up into two short pony tails on the sides of her head, like alert ears. Who would have thought she'd turn out to have such unusual good looks, and do such unusual things.

"Do you think we ought to go?" Tollie asked again.

"I don't know!" Lily said irritably. "Stop asking me. Make up your own mind for a change. Ever since you got in this 'condition' you act like you can't go to the bathroom without me."

Tollie didn't say anything. She was eating her pork barbeque with an appetite that Lily found inappropriate to the occasion. Nobody else was eating, just chopping up their cornbread with their forks and mashing it back into meal, maybe taking a half-hearted sip of milk. Tollie Ramsey looked like she was going to eat the legs off the table.

"You're going to have people gossiping about you 'eating for two' if you don't slow down," Lily said spitefully.

Tollie suspended her fork and looked into Lily's eyes, hurt. She put her fork down and finished chewing what she had in her mouth slowly. But a few minutes later, her eyes were back on her plate. Then she was at it again. Shoveling it in, Lily thought in disgust. Stoking that furnace within a furnace. For what? That little pea was going to be popped out of the pod as soon as they could figure out how to do it. You'd think it would make a person sick, feeding something they were going to kill off, with not even the excuse you'd have to feed and then kill off a chicken or a pig.

"It's not going to get up and run off your plate," she said. "At least slow down."

"I can't help it," Tollie whispered, teary-eyed. "It seems like I'm so hungry I'm going to faint if I don't get food into me quick. But it makes me sick to eat, and to think about eating. I feel like I'm feeding dead meat to dead meat."

Lily was surprised to hear Tollie thinking so close to how she was thinking. Sometimes they seemed to be from different planets, Venus and Pluto.

"I guess you'll let me cry in peace," Tollie said, wiping her eyes with her coatsleeve. "Nobody'll think anything, today, if I cry all day long."

"You haven't got time to worry about this Eva stuff," Lily said.

"I've got the same right to worry about it as you do," Tollie said.

"No you don't," Lily said. "Eva and I go back to the Year One. We were down the street from each other while you were just light swirling around out in the Universe, not even a solid thing."

Tollie looked at her. "Is that what you think we come out of? Light?"

"How the Hell do I know," Lily said viciously. "Eat your goddam dead pig and let's go. We don't have the lee-way to worry philosophy!"

Tollie's eyes teared up again. "I'm under a lot of strain these days," she said accusingly. "You ought to take that into account."

Lily watched as Tollie resumed her lunch with her eyes on her plate, her face tight with hurt. It could be Tollie, Lily suddenly realized. Tollie, not Eva, lying dead in a box over at Barefoot's right this minute. It could be any one of them. Lily looked around the room at her schoolmates. Any one.

Her eyes came back to Tollie. She felt soft and queasy. "Here," she said. "Take my milk and cornbread." She put the milk carton on Tollie's tray, the cornbread on her divided plate. "Take these old collards too."

"Thanks," Tollie said.

After a few minutes she said, "Lily?"

"What?"

"Do you think we ought to go or not?"

Last night, in her coffin, in the pinkish light of Barefoot's Mortuary, Eva had looked more available than in life. It had taken Lily a while to figure it out: for the first time, after knowing Eva all her days, it looked like you could touch her. Because that was it: now you could touch her. You could put out your hand and touch her hand, or her face, or kiss her on the forehead, smooth the pale gold hairs on her dead arm with your fingertip. You could take whatever liberties you could pass off as natural acts of sorrow and grief, and she couldn't stop you. She was not herself anymore. She was anybody's who was looking on.

And nobody *would* try to stop you. Lily noticed that. She and Tollie had to wait till Marie got through talking to Eva's parents before they could get out of there, so she was able to watch how people acted, from a chair back against the wall. Kids from school would stand by the coffin a while and then they'd put out a finger and touch Eva's hand or arm real quick, or her shoulder, which was bare in the wide scooped neck of a blue Easy-Care dress trimmed with an artificial-looking lace collar, like something that might show up on a Valentine candy box in a drug store.

"Eva wouldn't have worn that dress on the last day of her life," Lily whispered to Tollie. Eva had been a simple dresser.

Tollie shrugged. Lily could tell she'd like to get out of the viewing room. She should have had the good sense to stay home, given her 'condition.' Marie was going to take forever. She was still down on her knees beside Mr. and Mrs. Bledsoe's chairs, her hand closed over Mrs.

Bledsoe's fist, which was balled up around a kleenex. Eva's mamma and daddy looked like they were in Outer Space. Marie had on her funeral suit, a dusty-looking black faille, which she'd had since her mother died back in the Forties. She'd take up the hem and let it out, take out the shoulder pads and stick them back in, depending on the style whenever somebody died. It gave Lily the creeps every time she was rooting around in her mother's closet looking for something to borrow and she came across that ugly thing, hanging there like a ghoul, like it was waiting for a body. She wished Marie would burn it. That's what you ought to do with funeral clothes, burn them after every time. It'd be worth the expense.

Now she was going to have her own black dress, hanging in her own closet. Marie said she was too old now to go to a funeral in a regular Sunday School dress. Lily guessed that was so. Marie had been sewing all day and had just finished a black wool jumper out of Simplicity. Tonight she was going to stitch up an unlined black jacket from a jiffy pattern. The jumper and the jacket together were supposed to give the impression of a suit for the funeral. "Then I thought you could wear the jumper to school, with different blouses," Marie had said hopefully, trying to bring Lily out of her sulk. "The jacket would be good to wear for dress-up at night, with a pin or corsage on it."

"I might burn it all," Lily had said furiously. She might. For *two* reasons. When was Marie ever going to learn how to sew right? "And I haven't even decided to go to a funeral!"

Lily looked away from Marie and the Bledsoes and observed the viewing room. Barefoot's was about the worst funeral home in town. Fold-out cafeteria chairs. Painted cinder-block walls, inside and out. Cheap sheetrock on the ceiling, not even painted. Why did people put up with that? Concrete floor, with just a patch of that artificial grass that they put around graves before they closed them up, spread out under Eva's coffin. She guessed that it was what the Bledsoes could afford, but she'd bet her life they were paying plenty, just to get more depressed than ever with the style of things. When she and Tollie and Marie had come in, it had been right from the dirt parking lot into the viewing room, through a cheap door that was so thin and hollow you could almost step through it, like stepping through a ghost. How did they keep perverts from coming in and mauling bodies at night? How did they keep ordinary thieves from stealing wedding bands and class rings and the valuable keepsakes that people liked to tuck into coffins like in the days of the Pharaohs of Egypt?

It seemed like the Barefoots could have built a room in front of the viewing room so you could prepare yourself. But they just had an office over to the side. It was a real shock to your system to walk in out of the glare of the setting sun and have a dead person, resting inside a set of big white satin jaws and lit up with a spotlight, jump onto your eyeball before you'd even got your vision adjusted to the gloom.

All around the room pink rays of light shot up without rhyme or reason, Lily observed. Giving the sheetrock ceiling several spots of feverish glow, like it had an infection.

It had been like stepping into "the narrow house," itself, she thought. That was an ugly phrase she'd never forget, from having to memorize and recite that old "Thanatopsis" in the seventh grade, and having to listen to thirty-four other kids recite the same goddam thing, not a one of them with a good idea of what that ghoul-poet had on his mind. If they had, they might have jumped up on old-lady McLaurin's desk and screamed in her face—"Woman, what in the Hell are you trying to do to us? We're twelve goddam years old!"

I'd do that today, if I ever saw her. Lily folded her arms and tried to feel natural, sitting in a funeral home that itself gave you the feeling of being in a pink-lit tomb or pyramid where dead people waited out eternity, holed up together. Old McLaurin was the one with one clay foot in the grave, not us. Why did we have to think about that junk before our time?

She'd believe to her own dying day that kids got morbidly oriented toward life by that stuff, generation after generation. It was worse than the bible. At least people came back from the dead in the bible, on a regular-enough basis to give you hope. Though they must have died again, or they'd still be hanging around. Unless History had lost track of them. If that had happened, somebody like old Lazarus would just have to take it, wouldn't he? If he started going around saying he was Lazarus, back from the dead, and that History had just lost him for a couple thousand years, they'd send him up to Dix Hill and throw away the key.

She looked back at Marie on her knees. Even Marie had memorized "Thanatopsis" before she'd dropped out of school to marry Daddy. Something like that could have depressed her so much with the hopelessness of it all that it could have made her drop out and get married

197

and have a baby before she was fourteen years old. School had a lot to answer for in this world.

Marie finished consoling the Bledsoes and walked over to where Tollie and Lily were sitting.

"Are we ready?" Tollie said hopefully. She'd already buttoned her coat, Lily noticed.

"I think we ought to take a last look at Eva," Marie said. "To say good-bye. It's going to be a closed-casket tomorrow."

"Well, that's good!" Lily said. Maybe she could go to the funeral. She hated it when you had to sit there for a half-hour or an hour and watch the profile of a person's face sticking up from down in that box. It was all morbid. They ought to just stick people on a fire and float them off down a river, out of sight, like they did in India or China, she couldn't remember which.

The three of them were standing by the coffin for a last look at Eva when a woman nobody seemed to know came up and stood next to Lily. She was middle-aged and she wore her hair pulled back in an old-fashioned bun. Not one of the sleek new chignons people were beginning to wear, which—Lily couldn't help thinking—would have been just as easy to do up as that old bun: it looked pretty complex, making use of a wire doughnut form, which you could see peeking through the woman's thin hair, and a spray of tiny cloth flowers that were half-pinned around it.

Lily was irritated by the way the woman was standing so close to her, and so close up to where the coffin drew its line between Eva and the world outside its satin tufts. The woman wasn't dressed for the occasion. She was wearing just a cotton housedress printed with purplish flowers and a gray sweater, a pouchy old patent leather pocketbook hung on her elbow. The pocketbook kept nudging Lily, who could only move so far away without pushing Tollie and Marie off the funeral grass.

The woman had been in the room when they got there. Lily realized that now. She'd been vaguely aware of her all the time, like you would be half-aware of a gnat. This was the somebody Lily had been half-aware of traveling between the coffin and the row of chairs along the side of the room, making conversation about the weather in a cheerful voice with whoever she ended up next to, Lily half-remembered. The somebody who'd then travelled back up to Eva, and peered down on her. Then backed off, talked to anybody who'd pretend to listen. She tried to talk to Eva's parents, Lily recollected vaguely, but they didn't seem to know who she was. Even in their daze, the Bledsoes were saying a little something to everybody they knew. But not to that woman. Lily had been half-aware of all this, all along.

Suddenly the woman leaned in toward Eva and bent down, smiling a little. Lily thought she was going to kiss Eva's lips. Marie's hand jerked out toward the woman, then stopped and retreated when the woman stopped her advance.

She didn't kiss Eva. She stayed suspended, at least a foot to the side and a foot above, Lily reckoned. The woman reached her hand out. It hovered in the air over Eva's dress, and moved a little, as if in hocus-pocus. Then it seemed to trace the lines of the dress's bodice in the air.

"She had a beautiful bust-line, didn't she?" the woman said in a friendly voice.

Tollie finally broke the silence after they'd pulled out of Barefoot's parking lot onto Mill Street. "That was sure a funny thing to say."

They drove on in silence until they were stopped at a four-way signal, waiting for their turn to go.

"Maybe she was a seamstress," Marie said thoughtfully.

199

"I'm done with this mess," Lily said, balling up her napkin and dropping it in the lunchroom slop on her plate, what Tollie hadn't eaten. "Let's get out of here."

"Just a minute," Tollie said. She was still working on the last of the collard greens and cornbread. Like some old country hick, Lily thought. She could see a piece of fat-back glistening in the greens like an eyeball, with no iris.

"I don't see how in the world you eat that stuff." Lily was burning up in her coat, all of a sudden. They were sitting near the kitchen area with about a ton of steam coming up from the steamtables. The food made her hot and sticky just to look at it, even though it was all cold by now.

She got up and carried her tray to the dishwashers' window and shoved it in. She didn't have to worry that Tollie would be right on her heels. These days, Tollie was on her heels like a puppy-dog, day in, day out, untouched cherry cobbler or not.

Outside, they did what they always did after lunch—the only post-lunchtime activity available to anybody at the high school: walking round and round the building—like ants, Lily often thought. Well, at least by this time of the year, it was fifteen or twenty minutes of not having to tote your books. She and Tollie put their hands in their coat-pockets and struck out for the West. This late in the year, you didn't have to guard your books too closely. Everybody, even the poorest, like the Babel kids, had found some way to get ahold of books by midterm exams, or else they'd just given up and dropped on out.

By then, also, the Vandals had got the annual new-book destruction out of their systems, Lily thought as they passed Tyson Wiggins, Vandal *extraordinaire*, as Miss Sawyer, her French teacher, would have said. She believed it herself. She'd had to catch a ride home with him one day when they both had forged notes to leave early on family business. He'd wanted to drive around and she'd lowered herself to do it for a half an hour, and all he'd done was keep reaching back behind the driver's seat of his Merc for empty Coca-Cola bottles to throw back behind him on the road—speeding away from the spray of glass. He'd driven through Niggertown and yelled out stuff like "You're so black your ass shines," thrown a few more bottles. It was hard to figure out what motivated somebody like Tyson. She watched him light out now for the trees where people parked their cars. The boys could smoke out there. The girls couldn't smoke anywhere, Lily thought in a wave of irritation. She could use a weed today, if ever.

She watched Tyson, sidewise, as he disappeared around the corner of the lunchroom, then turned her attention back to circling the building, trying to enjoy—at least—being without those damn books. By this time of year you could leave them in the desk of your fourth-period class, pick them up for fifth-period before the first bell and be pretty safe, or just take them on to fifth-period before lunch, like she always did. A lot of the teachers took their lunch to their classrooms and graded papers while they ate. It was just in the rush between first and last bell when something could happen to your books.

I don't even know why I'm thinking about books, Lily thought. Poor Eva.

Again, she resurrected the little pigeon-toed girl in grade school, a girl that she—Lily—had been able to dominate for a little while, if she recollected. She did recollect: it shamed her, no-end.

She and Tollie walked in silence, turning South, then East, then North, then West again, under the bare limbs of pecan and oak trees, fanning out way overhead like umbrellas with no cloth on their spokes. She'd never seen the leaves fall this early, never in her life. The pecans hadn't put out one nut for Home-Ec classes to gather up for making pies, like they usually did. Depressing. There wasn't even an evergreen anywhere on the schoolgrounds, except back where people parked their cars. The one stately pine on the actual schoolgrounds was dead from the summer drought, but still standing out in front of the lunchroom, the color of rust. The ground was so bare from people walking on it that it looked like the oaks and pecans were growing in desert sand.

They passed Mike Crane, an odd-looking old boy with a big head and kind of Japanese-looking eyes, except he wasn't Japanese. She'd never forget him raising his hand in Religion class in ninth grade and asking the teacher, "Do you think there's such a thing as luck?"

That had kind of stopped her—mentally—in her tracks, she remembered. That could have been the only philosophical question anybody had ever asked a teacher in the whole time she'd been going to school in Hope Mills. It had shocked her enough that she'd missed the teacher's answer. She didn't know it till this day. And she'd like to know. Even if you had to take it with a grain of salt, you could put it in the hopper, as Daddy liked to say.

Mike Crane!

"They're saying she killed herself," Tollie said in a low voice.

"What in the world are you talking about?"

"Eva. They're saying she drove the car into the truck."

Lily stopped walking, then Tollie stopped.

They started walking again. "That is just low-down mean gossip," Lily said. "Why in the world would somebody who's supposed to go to Europe next summer do a thing like that? They're so full of shit."

"I'm just telling you what they're saying."

They walked without talking. Lily could see the popular girls circling the building slowly, never the same three together, day to day. Miss Congenialities: We *all* get along . . . ! They were so *nice* to everybody, but they didn't care about anybody except their own bunch. They always shifted around to walk with different ones, because they were scared that somebody would think they were like the girls who still were "best friends," girls who were lonely as the day is long, Lily thought. Still stuck back in grade school, two against the world. It *was* pathetic, but probably necessary.

She sped up a little, leaving Tollie a couple of steps behind. She hated these big groups of shifting rich girls. They were worse than the mice. Worse than any two girls still clinging to each other against the world, losers from Day One. Those poor girls were still better than a Cindy Wiggins, or a Molly Wiggins before her, or any of those girls, who—as a group—would get every one of the Senior Superlatives for themselves in the Yearbook, Lily thought adamantly. Anyone of the rich girls at all could get voted what everybody who saw high school as the real world dreamed about, even the mousiest little mouse: Most Popular. Eva might have got Most Versatile, if she'd lived. Most Athletic, maybe. Maybe not, not being in any group at all. They usually gave Most Athletic to one of the cheerleaders. Lily Jones wasn't going to get anything, unless it was the humiliation of First Runner Up, Miss Hope Mills High—nothing but her 2 × 2 black and white picture between the pictures of Jimmy Lee Jones and Varilyn Jones, two mice. Not club one, not secretary-treasurer of anything, no funny nickname in quotation marks underneath her real name. No picture of herself with the boy who got the matching Superlative, above an extra picture of yourself beneath it, in your cap and gown, with your special saying underneath.

Only the Superlatives got to leave their words behind.

Last year Molly Wiggins had been Most Popular, Most Likely to Succeed, Most Friendly, and Best Dressed. About a hundred pictures of her had been in the Yearbook, counting all her Superlatives, her Clubs and Activities, her "saying" repeated again and again as her picture appeared and reappeared: "Oh, World, I Cannot Hold Thee Close Enough."

It made Lily sort of sad for herself, thinking about how little she'd be leaving behind in the Yearbook, just an old 2 × 2, with a tassel distorting her face.

But she was only sad for a minute. *If* you really thought high school was the world, and that picture was all you had in the Yearbook, you might as well be dead. But she didn't think that way. She'd be Lili Lorene in a year and she'd never look back.

"What do you think we ought to do?" Tollie asked, catching up to Lily.

"I told you not to ask me that again!" Lily said. "Do what you want to, I don't give a rat fart."

"No. I meant about. . . ." Tollie pushed the front of her coat out with her hands, from inside her coat pockets.

"Would you stop that! What's wrong with you?"

"I'm sorry . . . I didn't realize I was doing it till too late."

"Jesus." Lily walked on, leaving Tollie a few steps back again.

"Wait," Tollie said.

Jesus.

Lily stopped and let Tollie catch up. They walked on, and she could feel herself calming down, which was really necessary. She needed to concentrate on Tollie, whether she wanted to or not, even if her own life was probably going to Hell in a houseboat while she was distracted from it.

She looked off into where a tilled tobacco field ran into a little line of bare trees. The limbs looked like writing out there on the sky. She wished she could read some kind of message in it.

"I been thinking about it," she said to Tollie. She lowered her voice and leaned in closer. "I heard you could mix cottonseed oil and quinine and drink it."

"I think I've heard that too," Tollie said. "Not the quinine, but the cottonseed oil."

"It might be worth a try," Lily said.

"Do you think it would hurt me?"

"You're hurt already, for the rest of your days, I guess. I can't believe you were so goddamn dumb."

"Don't start that again," Tollie said wearily. "It's not helpful."

"Not helpful," Lily mimicked sourly. "I think, being as how you've dragged me into this mess, when I've got my own life that needs concentration, you ought to take whatever I want to say, as graceful as if you were Molly Wiggins herself. As for the cottonseed and quinine water, I doubt it would kill you. I heard turpentine might work too. And mistletoe. 'Tis the season, *almost!*"

"Where would I get it?" Tollie asked. "The cottonseed. I *know* turpentine and mistletoe would kill me."

"I think that's a problem for that spic soldier to figure out."

"I haven't seen him in almost three months," Tollie said. "Give me some practical advice, for once."

"You haven't had Lily Jones *really* on his tail. Let's go out on Friday night, to the Kastle again. Somebody'll know where he is."

"We already tried that. You just want to flip the bird to Mack."

"I do not! Let's try the Kastle, and if we don't find him, let's try the Base itself."

"Would you?"

"Would you—? Would you stop being so goddam timid? You're driving me to distraction, as old Sawyer says about a hundred times a day. That must be the most distracted woman on god's green earth by now."

"I'd like to be in her class," Tollie said mournfully. "I don't think I'll ever make it to my junior year where I could take French."

"Stop that," Lily said. "Look how long I've been in French class and I still don't know a thing I went in there wanting to know. It's a waste of time. So stop being pitiful. I don't want to have to say I told you so. I can't believe you're taking Spanish, though. Where in the world could that get you *now*? They just put it in for Mill Rats. It's like Shop, or Shorthand."

"It's the only language they'll just *let* you take, regardless of the grade you're in," Tollie said defensively.

"Well, that ought to tell you something right there. They just need warm bodies."

Tollie pulled her coat closer to her body. "Poor Eva," she said glumly.

"Sorry," Lily said, pulling her own coat tighter and folding her arms to keep it there.

They turned South again, ambling along the blind side of the building. They walked slower here, like everybody else. They were out of sight of all eyes of authority for a few hundred feet. The teachers never patroled out here. They had their hands full as it was, Lily guessed. On the south side, you could see couples kissing long slobbery kisses. If anybody was going to try to grab your tit or hit your tit and run, this was where they did it, but only in warm weather when you weren't wearing a coat or you had your arms full of books. Before it had turned cold, some old boy had walked right up to Tollie and said "It looks like you're getting a nice set." Lily couldn't believe it! Not that he wouldn't say that—boys talked like that to your face all the time. She couldn't believe that little old skinny Tollie Ramsey suddenly had a "nice set"—which she did.

Of course it was only temporary. Once that bun was out of the oven, she'd be flat as Olive Oyl again.

Pretty soon that cute Faircloth boy would stop coming around too, if he already hadn't. She'd noticed that Tollie hadn't said anything about him lately. Whereas before it was: Raeford this, Raeford that. Lily hadn't been able to help herself finally. "Do you and him double-date with his brother and your mother?" she'd asked.

She'd felt bad about that about a minute later, but she'd just got sick of hearing about how Tollie Ramsey, a Mill Rat like herself, and knocked-up too, was going out with a rich boy who had a red sports car, while she, Lili Lorene (spending her last days in the body of Lily Jones, before she shed it like it was snakeskin!) was sitting home alone, night after night after night. It made her sick to think of it, not a bit of it her own fault.

They strolled along the south side, glad to be out of the wind that had started up and whipped their hair around before they'd turned the corner. They were safe today. Nobody was in the mood to try anything.

They passed two girls practicing the bop, with serious faces, to the low music from a pocket radio they'd wedged into the branches of a crape myrtle. A tree that, after the leaves fell, looked more naked than other trees, Lily thought. Its limbs were so smooth they looked like they were covered with human skin. She almost hated to come up on that tree without its leaves. It made her almost want to throw her coat over it and cover it up.

The girls were dancing to "The Battle of New Orleans," or trying to. They didn't know how to dance, little mice. Ordinarily, she'd have said something mean and ugly. After all, poor Eva wasn't dancing, and never would again. But she was feeling sentimental. High school was hard on most people, little mice especially. Of course, you *couldn't* bop to that song—!

"Old Wiggins is getting ready to come around that corner," she said as she walked by. She enjoyed, in a half-hearted way, watching the girls break apart and cut off the radio, hide it in a coat and scurry off, mousy-like.

"Why did you lie to them?" Tollie said as they themselves left the blind stretch of their walk and headed East.

"Why not?" Lily said. "They're sorry dancers anyway."

A few minutes before the bell, Tollie and Lily were sneaking a weed with boys back in the parking lot. Tollie was nervous. Girls couldn't smoke at school!

"Nobody'll notice today," Lily had argued as they'd slipped around the building and run, bent-over, among the cars, all of them belonging to boys too: a girl couldn't drive a car to school.

Now they were out of sight of the building, their cigarettes lit. They were leaning up against Tyson Wiggins' inky-colored Merc, with Tyson and Jimmy Barefoot, the son of the man who owned Barefoot's Mortuary.

Lily french-inhaled once, out of habit, then monitored herself. She sure didn't want to give either one of these old boys any ideas. Tyson looked like the worst Teenage Monster: leather jacket, pegged pants, a duck-tail that disappeared into his collar on one end and swooped down onto his forehead on the other where it was greased almost to a point, but in the last inch it curled out into something that looked like a two-sided fish-hook. Jimmy Barefoot wore a crew cut, no-color crew neck sweaters, white shirts and socks, pimple-city. Jesus. High school boys.

"Are y'all going this afternoon?" Tollie asked them.

"Why?" Tyson asked. "For the fun of it?"

"Some people do," Jimmy said, dragging on his Lucky Strike.

Tyson snorted. "I been to one funeral in my life, and that's the last. Anybody can die from now on and get in the ground without my help."

"I'll be there," Jimmy said. "I got to help Daddy, make a little cash for the weekend."

"I think people ought to go off in the woods to die," Tyson said. He held his lips in an O and blew a couple of doughnut shaped rings into the air, then flipped the butt into the pinestraw. "Like a fox would, and save other people the trouble. Blow their own brains out when they feel the time coming. Next time anybody sees them, they're just old bones."

"Then I wouldn't have a pot to piss in," Jimmy said.

"I'd go blow my brains out now, if I was you, Barefoot," Tyson said. "If all I had to look forward to was corking and pumping up dead people for a living."

"I don't think you've got much of anything to look forward to," Jimmy said defensively.

"I didn't mean to *start* anything," Tollie said wearily. "It's time for the bell anyway. Anybody want this?" She held the half-smoked cigarette out a little.

"I'll take it," Tyson said. "I'm running low." He took the cigarette and puffed on it. "Hey," he said, taking it out of his mouth and wiping at it. "You nigger-lipped the damn thing."

"Sorry," Tollie said. "Let's go, Lily. There's the first bell."

"I'd especially think that broad would of gone off somewhere out of sight," Tyson said, still picking at the cigarette. "Since she had the choice."

"Oh, come on!" Lily said hotly. "I'll never believe she killed her own self."

"Frankly, my dear, I don't give a shit," Tyson said. He took a puff and blew a line of O's. "She never gave me any."

"You make me sick," Lily said.

"Let's go," Tollie said, nudging Lily.

"They're saying she was knocked up," Jimmy said. "I'll get Daddy to ask the Coroner. Personally, I blame that piece of shit she was driving."

Tyson bent his legs at the knees and tilted back in a pose—"There goes my ba-aby."

"Asshole," Lily said. "Creep."

Suddenly Tyson was grinning a mean little grin. "Did you see her naked?" he asked Jimmy. Jimmy grinned too and looked down.

"Come on, Lily," Tollie said. "I've got to get my books. The second bell's going to ring any minute."

"Does she have as nice tits as it looked like she did in her clothes?" Tyson said.

Jimmy flicked his cigarette into the pinestraw and put his hands in his pockets, still wearing his grim little grin. "I'm cutting out," he said. "I got to help Daddy with this thing."

"Sure you're not going to cop one last feel?" Tyson asked Jimmy's back as Jimmy started toward his Impala. Tollie could see Jimmy's crewcut standing up against the fall sky like an upside-down shoebrush.

"Naw, I'm driving the hearse," Jimmy said without turning around.

"Was she a real blond?" Tyson called after him.

Then Jimmy was revving up his big white car. When he drove out of the parking lot, Tollie could hear the radio coming through the windows, over the rumble of the adjusted muffler: "What'd I Say," Ray Charles. She watched the car, its lowered rear-end barely off the ground. As she watched it disappear down the road, she realized that the funeral director's son was the only kid in their school who could afford a new car, outside of the managers' kids, whose daddies would just move on to manage something else when the Mill closed, she guessed. Even the Wiggins' kids had slightly used cars, and their relatives sold cars.

Even when Jimmy's car was out of sight, the rude racket of its muffler hung in the air. Take that, it seemed to say.

Tollie watched Lily put out her cigarette with her shoe. Had Jimmy seen Eva naked? He hadn't said no. But maybe that was just some boy-stuff going on with him and Tyson. Weird, but maybe not much weirder than a lot of what went on with guys when they were talking about girls who couldn't help themselves.

"I think you're a disgusting slimy worm, Tyson," Lily said. "I think you're mentally sick."

"And I think you're a whoring little slut, so who cares?"

Tollie saw Lily start at the venom in Tyson's voice. He was giving her a look so dense with hate that you knew it was something that lived in him night and day, every day of the year, that anything else was thin as the veneer on new furniture, thin as frost. Why? Tollie wondered. Because Lily was a girl who didn't pay much attention to boys her own age? Then what *must* he think of poor Eva, whose attention had been so far beyond them all? The second bell had just finished ringing.

"And I think you've most likely got a little bitty wee-wee," Lily said, glaring at Tyson.

"You couldn't take a quarter of it, even in your mouth," Tyson said. His eyes were hard and spiteful.

"Don't make me puke, Ass-breath." Lily drew her coat around her.

"Come on, Lily," Tollie said, starting toward the school.

"And you," Tyson said to Tollie's back. "Your Mamma's crazy, I heard. A certified nut. And whoring around."

Tollie pulled her coat tight and sped up.

"You're probably a whore too," Tyson called after her. "Even if you are skinny as a god-damn pencil. Bony-Maroni."

He hates me too, Tollie thought, shocked. Then, remembering recent, more subtle insults, slights and jokes, from others—she felt a chill of realization: They all hate me. They hate *us*, girls and women. All boys and all men. They do.

Lily caught up. "Don't listen to that Halloween ghoul," she said. "Jesus." She pulled her coat collar up around her neck.

"Let's hurry," Tollie said, shivering. She felt a deep sorrow realizing what Tyson could do in his mind, nobody to stop him: Think of her, skinny and naked. Of Eva, naked and dead as a winter tree. Both of them helpless in the eyes and mind of a person like Tyson Wiggins. Not to mention his thoughts about her mother! The hard word *nut* tacked on her. . . .

"Are you okay?" Lily asked.

"Yeah," Tollie said, feeling mostly dead herself. It was an awful world, once you weren't a kid anymore. You had to think about bodies—and minds—so differently. You had to think of bodies as things people wanted to do stuff to. As dead Things for real. God didn't let you know anything for sure about death, and yet He allowed people to see all kinds of stuff about you, alive or dead, that they just cooked up in their twisted brains. You had to suffer it, deal with it in the dark.

"He doesn't know what a whore is," Lily said disdainfully. "If he did, he'd know we wouldn't do a thing like that for money!"

Tollie wiped her nose on her coatsleeve. "I feel like I've wandered into Hell," she said. "One day it was a normal world, full of games and cookies. And then I was in high school."

"I know what you mean," Lily said.

"Why do they call it high school?" Tollie said. "I've never learned less—from books—in my life. Everything's a distraction! They ought to call it low school. I think we're moving backwards."

"If we quit, we're ruined," Lily said. "Everybody says so. We've just got to tough it out."

"Whores!" Tollie scoffed. "*Ghouls* sneaking to look at dead girls!" She was livid. "It seems like only last week I was bouncing a ball against the side of the house, the thing on my mind whether Mamma would give me a nickel to get a Nutty-Buddy on the way home from grade school!"

"Tempus fuck-it," Lily said.

"I like how you talk!" Tollie complained.

"Me too," Lily said. "Why should boys get to have all the fun? I'm bringing Latin back from the dead."

"Maybe you're right," Tollie conceded. "I sure intend to take up more languages."

She would. Get away from English, Gather Ye Rosebuds, Nobody's an Island. Wrong. Eva Bledsoe had been an island, unto herself. Maybe they'd know a thing like that in other languages.

"It's cold as the grave out here," Lily said, pulling her collar up around her throat. "And we've got to go stand around in a graveyard late in the day. Can you imagine what that's going to feel like? Poor Eva! I remember her in her little plaid jumpers, Oxford shoes. *Plaits.* People called her Skinny-Minnie. Jesus! I feel like I'm going to die myself."

"Let's hurry," Tollie said, speeding up. "We're going to be late, and all because you *insisted* on smoking a weed with those creeps."

"So?" Lily said. "It was sure informative. Have you ever heard anything so sick in your life as that Tyson? And calling us whores and sluts! I'm practically a virgin again, it's been so long. If he only knew—"

"He'd just find something else to call us," Tollie said, walking fast. "They all hate our guts. Think about that." Saying it outloud, she felt another chill, shooting through her belly.

"Would you slow down?" Lily said. "They're not going to be doing one thing in class today. Not that they ever do a whole lot. They should have just cancelled today."

"I can't believe I'm going to miss the last bell," Tollie said frantically, moving faster. "Do you think Jimmy did see Eva? That just about makes me sick to my stomach."

"I don't even want to think about it," Lily panted behind her.

"I'll never be able to look at him the same way," Tollie said. "And Tyson! They ought to lock him up before he robs her grave tonight!"

"Would you stop it? This is morbid."

"I don't care," Tollie said.

She didn't. She thought about a song that had been popular, "Three Bells," by the Browns. One bell for being born, one for getting married, one for dying. If that was a normal life. Was it? Even so, Eva was only getting two bells. If she, Tollie, could just get to class before the last bell rang—

"What is wrong with you?" Lily demanded.

Tollie was almost running. "I can't believe I'm going to have to knock on the door of Miss Barefoot's class and go in there in front of everybody—Miss Barefoot *suspending* the lesson on my account, everybody staring, those two or three *titters* you can depend on—"

"Would you slow down?"

"I can't believe I'm going to have to go in there and get my books. I'd almost rather take the loss."

"If you'll slow down, I'll go in for you. You're making us walk so fast that I'm ruining my flats with the dust we're stirring up."

Tollie stopped and let Lily catch up. "Would you?"

"I like to go into a class that's not my class, after it's already started," Lily said. "It's the closest thing to being on a stage you can find in Hope Mills. Unless you want to dig up some dirt on old Thornton so you can blackmail him into letting you be in 'Our Town.' Why do they put that damn thing on *every* year? You'd think it's the only play anybody ever wrote!"

"I don't see much to it, either," Tollie said, slowing down to keep pace with Lily. "I sure would appreciate it if you'd go in there for me."

Lily stopped and dug a compact out of her coat pocket. She opened it and checked her hair and lipstick, her teeth—in case there was a collard-string; the corners of her eyes for gunk. Looking pret-ty good.

"Do you have French now?" Tollie said. "I must be losing my mind. This is the first year I haven't known your schedule as well as my own."

"Who'd ever believe it, the way you stay on my heels all day."

"Do you have French now or not?"

"Wee-wee. I got to go listen to Sawyer jive-on about hunchbacks and dancing goats, horny priests that try to tell the future by consulting dead people, when everybody knows that dead people are past, not future, then I got to high-tail it to a funeral my own self, maybe. Sometimes I think high school would make a good 3-D movie, Nine Months in Outer Space."

"Don't mention nine months to me," Tollie said irritably. "I can't believe you want to be late to Miss Sawyer's class. I'd love to be in French. Spanish *does* seem like a mistake."

"I find some way to be late just about once a week," Lily said. "To keep in practice. Not that being late for your own class is as good as being late to a class that's not yours—people don't pay half as much attention—but it's the next best thing. Do you think Jimmy did see Eva?"

"Stop."

"If he looked at her, I hope it was something his Daddy made him do, as part of the job, not something he went sneaking around to see."

"Would you shut up? This is morbid," Tollie said. "Let's change the subject. Do you know how lucky you are? I wish I could take French. I feel like I'll never make it to upperclassman, where I could study something more exotic than Spanish, which everybody thinks is for morons. I can't see my future at all, these days."

"Don't you get morbid!" Lily put the compact away. "I wish they'd just teach you how to have a good conversation with somebody in Paris, not all that stuff about some old Hunchback, servant women who run off and stick their legs in a spring and get attacked by a bunch of leeches that about suck them dry. I find that stuff so depressing."

"It sounds it," Tollie agreed. "The last thing I need. I guess I'd better try to be happier with the basics."

"I'd like to know about something in modern French. You know? How to buy clothes at a fashion show, how to get to the Moulin Rouge and the Riviera—remember those movies? How to talk to a movie director and point out . . . your possibilities."

Lily paused at the bottom of the steps to the school and gave her chest a little jut for Tollie's benefit.

"I think you'd make a good 3-D movie yourself," Tollie said as they walked up the steps and went inside. "Poor Eva." There it was, the last bell, *tolling.* . . .

"Yeah, I know," Lily said in a rare mood of contriteness. "I forgot or I wouldn't have stuck mine out."

"I think high school is . . . lurid," Tollie said.

Tollie rested against the faded green of the wall while Lily went into Miss Barefoot's room to get her books.

Tyson Wiggins. He was something else. She'd heard about people like that, but mainly in books or movies. Mostly, she'd thought they were some kind of entertainment device—for weird people who liked to entertain that kind of thing—not real. Now she'd seen one up close, the kind of person you might read about in the paper one day or hear about on the tv news. Like the men that had killed the waitress and left her out in the cornfield.

Across the hall, she could hear Mr. Thornton giving directions to the juniors for the annual production of "Our Town." Normally they rehearsed the play in the auditorium, but today they were in a big storage room where, among other things, the props for "Our Town" were stored year to year: papier-mâché gravestones, fancy trim from old porches, a portable proscenium arch. She guessed that the auditorium was being set up for the memorial service. It was weird. Even with the curtains pulled closed on the stage, everybody would be thinking the same thing this afternoon: that back behind the curtains in the dark was The Coffin. Like something out of the Dark Ages or a horror picture show. Not that anybody admitted to taking it seriously, not in high school. They laughed at it. Mr. Auger, the new Principal, who'd been the old Principal of the grade school before his promotion, had already recognized his mistake in bringing it over with him to his new job. It had been pretty effective in grade school, though, where The Coffin had been the punishment in store for you if you went wrong. If you skipped school, or got into a fight or committed any of about a hundred transgressions, you might have to go back behind the curtain in the auditorium, in the dark, and get in The Coffin and lie there until the Principal himself came to say you could get out. Nobody knew for sure how long that had been going on. For as long as anybody could remember. Mr. Auger had inherited it with his job. It could have been going on since the beginning of time, as far as Tollie knew. It seemed primitive enough for that, as a practice. The Coffin in and of itself was primitive. Old and black, wide for your shoulders. Lined with a ratty old purple cloth. Kids used to speculate that it was a real, used coffin, not one the school had bought new for the purpose, back in the beginning of time. They thought it might have washed up from a grave during a heavy rain and some old ghoul of a Principal had found it, empty or not empty, and then, there it was.

She'd never been in The Coffin herself and, if she thought about it, she couldn't remember but one person, in all of grade school, who had. Johnny Sherman, a boy who'd been in fourth grade with her who couldn't stop peeing his pants. The Coffin hadn't cured him. In fact, it seemed to make him worse. After spending a few hours in The Coffin, it got so he peed every time he walked into the schoolhouse. She could still smell the wool of his pants drying out in a winter school room when all the windows were closed. He'd dropped out in sixth grade and nobody had even sent the truancy people out in the sticks to bring him back. Tollie saw him once, from the window of the school bus, working behind a mule out in the field behind his daddy's old house, like he lived in another century.

Now that The Coffin was at the high school, some of the boys would sneak up on the stage behind the curtain and get in it for fun. There was a rumor that somebody had left a rubber in it, used. There'd been a cartoon about The Coffin in the newspaper. Everybody knew that Mr. Auger was looking for a way to get rid of it without calling anybody's attention to himself. He was a defeated man.

But today, The Coffin would be big and black and real, Tollie thought. Back behind the curtains in everybody's imagination, nothing to laugh at. Unless you were a goon like Tyson Wiggins.

She eavesdropped on Mr. Thornton as he talked to the cast of "Our Town," telling them how to say their lines and move around in relation to each other. She'd probably never know now whether he would have singled her out for a part in her junior year or not. He hadn't singled out Lily, so she guessed he wouldn't have. If not Lily, then not Tollie for sure. Last year Lily had wanted to be in that play so bad she could taste it, but she'd never admit it now. She'd never admitted it then, Tollie remembered. Even when she'd tried out specifically for the main female part—Emily Webb, the dead woman. That was Lily, always aiming beyond herself. Why didn't she just try out for one of the Townspeople? Mr. Thornton himself always played The Stage Manager.

Tollie had read the play in eighth grade and ninth grade, and she'd already seen it once in Assembly. The whole high school saw it free in Assembly every year, the dress rehearsal; and then a lot of kids would have to pay to see it again when they brought their parents at night. It was a mischievious thing to put on in Hope Mills: a mill town with its mill and millworkers located out of sight, not Their Town at all. Lily was right: why not some other play? Why not "The Merchant of Venice?" It gave her the creeps to think that she herself could be dead-in-childbirth by this time next year, like Emily Webb, but real. Haunting Hope Mills and high school, trying to live life over.

What was taking Lily so long? Tollie put her eye close to the frosted glass of Miss Barefoot's classroom door, but she couldn't see anything much, just the shadowy rows of students and Miss Barefoot sitting at her desk, her dress a smear of bright yellow against the big black board. Tollie turned her head to the side and laid her ear against the door's crack. She couldn't hear much sound either, just someone's feet scraping against the wood floor. She leaned back against the wall.

"The dead pity the living," Mr. Thornton was saying. "That's our point here." Tollie couldn't see him, but he swam up in front of her eyes easily. He always looked the same: tall and thin, hair the color of dust. Middle-aged, Ivy League clothes, spit-polished penny loafers. His family used to own Hope Mills' other main business, a furniture factory, before they sold out to a bigger company in High Point. They had a big house out in the country, with Spanish moss growing all over the trees, like in "Gone With the Wind." Mr. Thornton still lived out there with his ancient parents, a bachelor. People said they all dressed up for dinner every night and sat at a long table, just the three of them, under a chandelier, and that they drank wine and had a big Negro woman bring course after course of food when Mrs. Thornton rang a little silver bell. Everybody swore it was true, that the Thorntons never pulled their curtains and you could sneak right up to the window and watch, like a movie, but Tollie never had.

Now the Thorntons' factory building was a damaged wreck sitting on the edge of town with the mortar spilling out of its bricks, a school for retarded Negro kids. It was on a half-day schedule in May and September, like the regular Negro school, so the Negro kids could all work in the fields. Tollie envied them, riding by in their buses at noon, while she and Lily would still be lined up waiting to get into the lunchroom, three hours of school left. She'd rather put in three hours in a tobacco field or a cotton field any day, thinking on her own: That's what she'd decided lately. She'd done some pretty good thinking on her own out in the fields picking crops, when she could get that work. She'd be the only white girl, segregated from the Negro girls, who all seemed to know each other. They spoke their unrecognizable speech among themselves all day as they worked, a foreign language. Tollie could never catch more than a word or two now and then, unless they spoke to her directly, which they rarely did. If they had something to say to her, they enunciated politely, kindly. Patiently, like she was a foreigner. Then they went back to their own talk, excluding her. She'd had nothing to do but think out there, lost to the physical and human world in the shade of her straw hat.

Of course most of the Negro kids stayed home to work all day during planting and harvesting. If they didn't, the people who needed tenant farmers would hire a man who would make his kids stay home. Everybody knew that.

Tollie suddenly felt more depressed than she had been already. There was something hopeless in the whole thing called life, if you asked her. Systems large and small seemed to be in place, everywhere you looked, to keep you from having a chance. Everywhere you couldn't look, too, or could only half-look.

She sagged against the wall, weak with the thought of all that could work against you, little and big things outside yourself and in the mysterious inside too. The inside was as mysterious as the Mysterious East, or Heaven and Hell themselves. Full of cells, any one of which could be warping as you listened to a rehearsal of "Our Town." Full of invisible elements . . . eggs enough for a lifetime of worry . . . motivations that might always be a secret to you yourself. . . . How did people learn to put up with all that?

"The Living, you see, don't know what joy they have in life," Thornton intoned in his famous voice. "That's what we're trying to get across here. Only the Dead know. And they've lost it all already."

Tollie thought about Mr. Thornton, drinking wine with his rich old parents every night under a chandelier blazing with those fat naked baby angels called cherubs, which seemed left over from a different religion—pagan. Even if people did sing about "cherubim and seraphim" in the Christian churches of Hope Mills—she had done it herself—cherubs were something you were more likely to see on a chandelier in a rich person's dining room, she'd bet. She still didn't know what seraphim were, she realized. She took out her pocket notebook and pencil and conjured an image of the word from the recollected page of a hymnal, all drawn out by dashes above the music. She wrote it on its own clean page—Se—ra—phim—then put her notebook and pencil back in her coat pocket. She imagined the old lady lifting her big white napkin to touch her lips with one hand, her silver bell rising in the other—ting-a-ling—and then the Negro woman coming, running, with a cherub-like baby on a silver tray held high in the air. Out in the dark, little pickaninnies had gathered quiet as owls, their eyes on the bright window that was big as a movie screen.

Until somebody up in Raleigh had decided to make the furniture factory a school, the retarded Negro kids had gone to school in another town. Now, not only were Hope Mills' own retarded Negro kids staying in town for school, others were being brought from out in the country. It had a lot of people upset. That's why they were afraid it was only a matter of time till Negroes were in Hope Mills High School itself, they said, never mind what was going on elsewhere in the nation. Then, they worried, it might be the Indians too. So far, the Indians were bused all the way to the nearest Indian school, forty miles away. There'd been an editorial about it in the paper. Some of the Indian kids rode the school bus four hours a day, the paper said and called for a change, but so far nothing had happened that Tollie knew of.

What a mess, Tollie thought wearily. She rolled her body toward Miss Barefoot's door and put her eye back to the obscuring glass, trying to find Lily's bright hair among the shady clumps within that were dark and still as shrubs. Behind her back Thornton was reading somebody's part, the way it ought to be done, according to him. He told everybody he met, the first thing, that he'd gone to a private school in Virginia, then Chapel Hill. Why in the world was he back in Hope Mills, teaching high school, if he was so hot? That's what everybody thought, the first thing, whenever he said it.

Tollie's heart lurched when she thought of Chapel Hill, of Raeford and her stupid dreams about her future in a place that didn't even let girls in, under most circumstances. She wouldn't want to be a dental hygienist, even if she could scare up the money to take the course up there. Not even to be near Raeford Faircloth, if he went back. It was hard to know what he might do. For all she knew, he and his brother were both walking along the River Ganges, wrapped up like Mr. Gandhi, meditating. She hadn't seen Raeford since that night when her mother had slipped away, away to another world. She didn't dare go out now anyway, Janice was so bad off. She raced home from school on the days Les worked, her heart thumping like a tom-tom. Arlene couldn't do more than check in every hour or so. It was a real struggle to try to figure out whether or not to go to Eva Bledsoe's funeral, if Lily would even drive them. It seemed like they should go, but then there was the dangerous situation at home, her mother lying on her bed all day long like she was already in her tomb, unreachable. Sometimes pulling the bedspread up over her face, like she was pronouncing herself dead.

Sometimes Tollie would hear Janice sneak out onto the backsteps early in the morning, before the sun was up. She'd get up herself and tiptoe past Les coughing in his sleep on the sofa, tiptoe to the back door and look out, and there would be her mother, sitting in her night-gown in the cold air. Sometimes the moon would still be in the sky, giving Janice's skin the pallor of marble.

"Y'all have just got to do something!" Arlene kept saying.

What? Tollie wondered. She spent the afternoons by her mother's bed. Sometimes she held her hand. Once, when it was clear that Janice wasn't aware of her at all, she touched one the x-marks on her mother's wrist—her own awful, burdensome sign of the cross. Sometimes she felt anger rise up in her like real fire. And then remorse would push it back down, and she'd be eaten alive by guilt. What good was sympathy if it failed you in the hardest situations? None of this was her mother's fault. She didn't appreciate that old Tyson's remark either.

What can we do, Arlene? But let them send her up to Dix Hill, a fate worse than Hell.

All they could do was hope, hope she'd get okay, out of one of life's mysterious workings. That was all in the world that could help any of them.

Except you, Arlene. Maybe there's something you know. Something that could help me, myself?

Tollie laid her hot cheek against the cool glass of the classroom's door.

"The Living have life, the joy in life, and they don't have the sense to appreciate it," Thornton droned from across the hall.

Old Ichabod, Tollie thought.

"Do you have a pass?"

Tollie leapt back from Miss Barefoot's door and turned into the biology teacher. The one who made everybody who passed through Hope Mills High School slice up a cow's eye, year after year. Where had she got them all?

"My books are in Miss Barefoot's room," Tollie said. The teacher had on a matching sweater set the color of roses. It made her face look like it was flushed. She looked sort of pretty today, Tollie observed, pretty and irritated.

"Well, go on in and get them," the teacher said impatiently. "The service will be starting soon. You're going to miss your whole class."

"Somebody's in there getting them for me," Tollie said.

"Then there are two of you late for class?" The woman checked the tiny face of her wristwatch, holding it about a foot out in front of her face. "I haven't got time to mess with you backsliders today. I've got to do something about the flower sprays that didn't get here yet. Get on to class, without your books." She looked into Tollie's face to make herself clear, which was her habit. She had large round eyes. Tollie could never look back without thinking about cow eyes, even though the teacher's eyes were blue.

She walked away from Tollie. "Now don't be here when I walk back down this hall," she said over her shoulder.

"No, Ma'am," Tollie said. Where in the world was Lily? She didn't want to go through all this *and* lose her books.

She leaned back against the wall. She didn't want to think about going in late to Mrs. Wiggins' class, didn't want to think about the biology teacher coming back down the hall, didn't want to think about Emily Webb coming back to "Our Town" from the Dead, or Eva Bledsoe committing suicide. . . . Didn't want to think about Janice, or about the baby growing inside herself, waiting for her to drink cottonseed oil or turpentine and kill it, or eat juniper berries or snakeroot. The baby—growing at the fantastic rate that babies-to-be grew at, according to what she'd learned in Health, but speeding toward dying, before it ever saw the light of day.

She felt near tears. She had to think about something else.

She tried not to hear old Thornton on joy and life and coming back from the Dead. That man didn't have her problems, and never had. What made him think he had anything to teach anybody, anyway?

She tried to clear out her mind, just to feel the wall holding her up, its cool surface against the back of her head. She wished she had that cigarette back.

She thought about Tyson Wiggins, pushed him away.

He made her think of the three men who'd killed the waitress last summer, pushed them away.

Tyson came back. They came back. She felt sick. Sicker. Failures at sympathy, one and all, herself included.

Nobody had wanted to believe those men had done what they did, but the broomstick had got there somehow. This was what could happen when your sympathetic feelings were undeveloped.

She knew that this case was complicated by the men being men and unable to stop wanting to show off for each other, like Tyson and Jimmy, if you thought about it. It was an overdeveloped sense of your peers that girls didn't have, not like that. Could three girls want to impress each other so much that they'd cut a boy's thing off and leave him dead in a field? She guessed that was the right comparison. She thought girls would be more likely to do something bad to another girl.

That bad? she wondered woozily. No, they'd stop before a thing like that. Only one lone deranged girl might do a thing that bad.

Where was Lily Jones? Tollie didn't want to think anymore today. She didn't want to think about what those men had said to each other out in the dark cornfield that night.

But she found herself thinking about it anyway. It seemed like there was no place she could go in her own mind where there wasn't junk and pain and awful pictures, awful clues to the nature of things.

What had their laughs sounded like? She couldn't quite imagine. But she knew they had laughed. They might have laughed or not laughed when they raped her, and laughed or not laughed when they killed her. But she knew, knew sure as night follows day, that they had laughed when they decided on the broomstick.

Had the broomstick just been out there in the night? Had they put it in the trunk of the car in advance, part of a plan? There wasn't anything in the paper about that.

The whole thing made her feel like those men had come from another planet, Aliens. Yet they were the very same species. So was

224

Tyson, talking about Eva like she'd never had a life to lose. Acting like she had no claim on dignity, now that she was helpless in death.

Tollie stuck her hands in her coat pockets and pulled the coat's bulky fabric closer to her body. She felt like she was growing up at last, getting realistic.

Only last summer she'd thought that everybody had in them a worthwhile "I," hidden from the world, and if you could just get inside them for a minute, you'd find something unanticipated and redeeming. She guessed she still believed that was true of most people. But she also knew that at some point, when she hadn't been giving her thoughts her undivided attention, she'd drawn a line. It was a line as firm and as straight as a broomstick. In this world—where everybody was drawing lines *all* the time even as they were saying everybody was the same, deep inside—she felt like she'd found some moral ground. At last. Some people didn't have a redeeming "I." Some people were beyond the pale.

Tollie Ramsey, Babykiller? Would she be beyond the pale?

Those three men were what you feared, and feared becoming, in your own life, and Tyson Wiggins was in training to be like them: Somebody without even a half a drop of sympathy in his whole system—not for man, woman, child or beast. Somebody who took the scientific view of things to the extreme, she guessed. Able to put themselves at such a distance that everything and everybody was just an arrangement of matter. It had to be something like that. She'd had a little glimpse of that kind of thinking herself, when she'd had to cut up the cow's eye in ninth grade. That teacher had made her do that, wade into that kind of thinking—which had changed her notion of what humans could do, forever—and now she didn't even seem to know Tollie by name. There hadn't been a hint of recognition in her big blue eyes. It didn't seem right. Tollie would *not* think of the teacher by name either!

But she'd never be able to think of what was inside her as just matter, she didn't think. And never *would* think of an actual certified living human or mammal as matter. She guessed she was safe.

"You're out of luck," Lily said, coming out of Miss Barefoot's class and shutting the door. She had a mist of perspiration on her forehead and her face looked pink. "Somebody must of stole your books."

"Oh, no!" Tollie said. "What next? Les doesn't have the money to buy me another set of books."

"Well, don't blame me. I wish I hadn't gone in there for you. The harder I looked, the more those shitheads snickered. I felt like a fool."

"What am I going to do?" Tollie felt the unfairness of everything settle on her like a cape of lead. Was she going to have bad luck her whole life? She wouldn't be surprised if she ended up like Emily Webb, she really wouldn't. Or "nuts," certified.

"I'm going to class," Lily said. "If I don't hurry, somebody will walk out of there with my own books."

Tollie watched Lily stalk off. Down the hall, the biology teacher was coming out of the auditorium. Tollie guessed she'd better face the music. She walked the other way, then upstairs, and entered Mrs. Wiggins' English class.

"Well, the 10 o'clock Scholar," Mrs. Wiggins said, from her desk, stopping the class with a raised hand and turning to look at Tollie. "What makes you come so soon?"

"I lost my books," Tollie said. "I'm sorry I'm late." She could feel everybody looking at her. She was glad she had on her coat.

"You're just in time to do your recitation," Mrs. Wiggins said. "We wouldn't want to penalize you for being late by letting you miss your turn."

"Yes Ma'am," Tollie said, resigned to her teacher's will. She had learned her poem a week ago, but she was hoping to be passed over for reciting in class, as she usually was. Usually Mrs. Wiggins called on the more dramatic students to stand up and recite for everybody. The others could do it privately, between classes, or they could track her down while she was doing cafeteria or bus duty, which Tollie usually did.

"Take off your coat, Tollie."

"I'm kind of cold," Tollie said. She heard that first titter. In-evitable.

"Put it in the cloak room."

"Maybe I'll put it on my desk," Tollie said. "If you don't mind." With her luck today, somebody would mutilate her coat if she put it in the cloak room for the thirty seconds it would take her to recite Emily Dickinson.

She held her stomach in, though she didn't think she was showing yet, and took off her coat, plucking her blouse away from her breasts as she did so. She didn't want anyone to notice her "nice set!" Not looking at anybody, she stepped to the front of the room.

"Now speak out clearly," Mrs. Wiggins said. "Look out at your audience."

Tollie looked out at a place a few inches above the heads of her classmates. She didn't know if they were grinning at her or frowning at her or what. She cleared her throat. Her eyes fell on the face of Brenda Harmon, a new girl, a soldier's daughter from somewhere else. Brenda gave her an encouraging little smile. Tollie smiled back, surprised at the unexpected kindness. She barely knew Brenda.

She kept her eyes on Brenda's face as she got ready to recite, then looked away, not wanting to embarrass her.

"Hope is the thing with feathers," Tollie began. "That perches in the soul . . . And sings the tune without the words . . . And never stops at all. . . ."

The bell rang and everyone got up and began to leave the room.

"That was very nice, Tollie," Mrs. Wiggins said. "A little flat, but if you worked on it and tried to get some emotion into your voice. . . ."

Mrs. Wiggins drifted off, concentrating on locking her desk with an old bent key she kept on a rabbit's foot key-chain.

"Thanks," Tollie said. She put her coat on and left the room. She felt odd, unburdened of her books.

She sat several rows behind Brenda in the auditorium and thought again of her encouraging smile, the rarity of that kind of thing. She didn't want or need to know Brenda any better than she did. It was the fact that a stranger could give you a sign that they wanted you to succeed that meant something. Tollie resolved to take a page from Brenda's book in the future, to encourage others, extend the small kindnesses that could ease a person's way, even if just a little.

She looked around but couldn't find Lily anywhere. Up on the stage, a picture of Eva was set on a table draped in black, two big sprays of white roses fanned out on either side. It wasn't her senior class picture, maybe her junior one. She was wearing a dark sweater and a white clip-on collar big as a pilgrim's but trimmed in lace. They all wore the same collar to have their school pictures made, every year, except the seniors. The photographer brought it with him. It was what they had in common, she realized glumly.

Tollie looked at Eva's picture. She wondered why they hadn't used her senior picture. Then she understood: Showing Eva in the photographer's robe and mortar board would be upsetting, proof of something that hadn't happened yet and would never happen.

A student was moving up each aisle now, handing out something. It looked like a program. Tollie took hers and passed the others on down the row. It was just a piece of mimeograph paper folded in half, but somebody had taken the time to paste a frame of black construction paper around its mimeographic lettering, a job that must have taken all morning. Inside the frame it said Eva Ann Bledsoe, Class of '60.

It could be Lily, Tollie thought with a shock. Lily was Class of '60.

She craned up and looked around. She felt an odd relief when she saw Lily over to the side of a row near the back, looking down, probably at her own sheet of paper. No, she and Lily ought not go to the funeral, Tollie understood. They had too much to contend with already. Let the living bury the dead. She and Lily were in some kind of dangerous twilight themselves.

Tollie turned back around in her seat. Mrs. Bain, the music teacher, took her seat at the piano to one side of the stage. She began to play "In the Sweet Bye and Bye."

Tollie opened the sheet of paper and read the faint purple inscription, faded before it ever got to the page:

More sweet than hopes of paradise,

She being young.

That night, when Tollie lay in her bed listening to the radio, she thought of her little brother Grady. Usually she didn't. She'd put him out of her mind so that her heart wouldn't break, which you had to do with some things, if you could. She thought about his funeral, too, and about Les carrying Janice off from the cemetery, and all the sad afterwards of that little death.

At some point, on the radio, The Browns were singing "Three Bells." It made her sad, the progress of a normal life, uninterrupted by accident: birth, marriage, death. There had to be something important in between. One bell for Eva. An even fainter one for Little Grady.

As Tollie drifted off to sleep, she was half-dreaming about Eva. Eva, in her little white car, driving up into the sky, bound for a place where it wouldn't matter how people thought of her body, which she had claimed for herself in such an unusual way. A place where it wouldn't matter the use those left behind, whatever their needs and mysterious notions, might try to make of her image and her name.

On the Saturday afternoon before Thanksgiving, Lily and Peggy were standing around in their uniforms and sweaters at the Tastee-Freeze, staring out at the empty parking lot. The radio was on low, Dinah Washington. There were still cut-out pumpkins taped on the windows, left from Halloween. Peggy had made them, every one fat-faced and grinning. They were the meanest-looking pumpkins Lily had ever seen. They looked like they had their hands somewhere out of sight, maybe sneaking up your skirt.

Peggy was eating a Banana-Boat boat full of the french fries that hadn't sold at lunch, already turned white from the grease getting cold. She was dipping them into a puddle of the cheap ketchup that Billy, the owner, bought by the ton and then had them pour it into the Del Monte bottles. That wasn't enough: then he thinned it out with vinegar. It didn't seem to bother Peggy. Lily watched while Peggy stuck three or four fries running with catsup-vinegar into her mouth at one time and went to work on them. Lily hated to think what that girl was going to look like *after* teenage skin. Forty miles of bad road. The kind of girl boys are talking about when they say she wouldn't be bad if you put a paper bag over her head. They say that about Peggy now, actually. Though Lily didn't think she looked that bad. Peggy had cute features, big blue eyes and long eyelashes. But you had to look hard to see them. Mostly, you just saw her skin, which looked like it was on fire, before you looked off somewhere else. They called her Pittsburger at school, but that didn't keep the boys from saying she was built like a brick shithouse, whatever that meant. Lily had never seen such a thing. Right after they said that was when the boys mentioned the paper bag.

Lily watched Peggy chawing on those hard greasy potatoes for a few seconds, then looked away. You couldn't tell Peggy a thing. She acted like she lived on the planet Mars. Never had a date, as far as Lily knew. Her old Daddy was waiting for her every night when she got off work. He was the one that looked like a brick shithouse probably looked: big, square, and red. Big old ugly square car. If Peggy was a minute late getting out of here, he'd be tapping the horn. Then they'd drive off in that ugly thing like some old married couple. Which she guessed they were like—Peggy with no dates, Peggy's mamma dead and gone.

"I wouldn't eat that junk you eat if I was starving," Lily said, though she knew it was falling on deaf ears. She was right: Peggy didn't answer, acted like she hadn't heard a thing. It burns me up! Lily thought. I'm cranky today anyway. Worse than Billy's old lady.

Billy's wife came to the Tastee-Freeze about a hundred times a day to check on him, perfumed with Four Roses, hair sticking out like wire, old Raggedy Ann. Billy always told her to go back home in case his mamma had to use the bedpan.

"Do you know how bad that stuff is for you?" Lily persisted. She wasn't cranky enough to say "for your skin," though she might before the day was over. You could tell Peggy was sensitive about her skin because she was always touching her face, even though anybody knew that would make your bad skin worse. She'd touch it real light, like it hurt, which it probably did. But Lily didn't want to get into that with her. It wasn't like they were best friends for life and that she'd have to live with Peggy's post-teenage skin and the failures and heartbreak waiting in the future because that girl was so stubborn now. Peggy ate hot fudge by the dipper, marshmallow creme by the scoop-full, maraschino cherries like they were popcorn. Lily herself only ate the bananas and drank the orange juice, things that would help her keep her good skin, shiny hair, clear eyes, strong bones, teeth, and fingernails. Some days, that was about all she ate. Marie never made a thing at home but tv dinners. She'd told her mother, I'll cook it myself, all you have to do is bring home some decent food. But would she? Marie knew about as much about being a mother as an old stray cat.

They'd been listening to the ne-gro station on the radio, now playing a salute to Billie Holiday, who'd died this year. Listening long

230

enough! "I'm changing the station," she announced. Peggy gnawed on like there was no tomorrow. Lily found Patsy Cline, "Walking After Midnight." Good. She liked her singers alive. It was a kind of lonesome song, though. If you went out walking after midnight around Hopeless Mills, somebody would shove you in his car and drive off to the Woods, like had happened to her the previous week, the one time she was stupid enough not to call her Daddy when she hadn't had a ride home from work. She'd got away from the creep, but she'd had to walk twice as far, sweater stretched out of shape for all time, stockings torn. She guessed she was lucky. She could have ended up in a field of cornstobs, broomsticked to death.

All of a sudden, Lily felt really mean. "That stuff's going to ruin your looks forever," she told Peggy. "Ruin your skin worse than now."

Peggy turned to look at Lily, her blue eyes growing moist. She put the fries in the trashcan beside her, turned away and started wiping the counter.

Oh, shit, Lily thought impatiently. She's making me feel worse! Skinny-Minnie. I don't know how, given her diet. Skinny with real big boobs, that's the kind of figure that drives boys crazy, and she's got it and can't use it to the best advantage. Which is too bad, but her own fault—What, me worry?

Lily turned and stared at the meanest Halloween pumpkin of them all. Sometimes she thought that a girl could be an old biology-class skeleton with big enough boobs and they'd elect you Homecoming Queen, not even bother putting a bag over your head. The less there is of you, the more the boobs stand out. She guessed that was what boys liked best: being able to pretend that you were just boobs and boobs alone.

Billy was always finding some way to get at Peggy's, squeezing in front of her when he could have gone behind—he liked to go *behind* her, Lily, the creep. Or had liked to, until she'd put her foot down. Always getting an elbow in Peggy's boobs, always telling her she's got her "Peggy" pin on wrong and repinning it, brushing his pinky-knuckle against her nipple all the time he's doing it. Of course Peggy just looked like she was orbiting around in Outer Space, ignoring that hairy old finger. Lily herself had finally told him, Billy, you rub your greasy old hand against my ass again, mistake or not, and I'm going to call the sheriff, also tell my Daddy and he's going to beat the shit out of you, then he's going to tell his preacher and you're going to have a bunch of holyrollers walking around outside with signs, like boycotting colored folks. Billy said, It wouldn't be the first time. She hadn't known whether he meant her or him or boycotting, but he'd quit grabbing at her butt. Which probably had made things a littler harder on Peggy, but Lily Jones was not in the charity business.

She guessed Peggy got some revenge by sneaking all that food. Her pockets were always full of shredded coconut, sundae nuts, raisins.

It was getting on toward two o'clock, getting really chilly in the ol' Tastee-Freeze. Billy always cut off the heat after the lunch traffic had eaten their hotdogs and barbeques and plate lunches and didn't cut back on it till right before suppertime. Nobody much came in for custard in the afternoon this time of the year. Lily pulled her sweater around her, wishing she were somewhere else. This job was hardly worth it. Fifty-two cents an hour. Nobody left you tips on frozen custard. Nobody wanted frozen custard in November. Billy ought to be paying her and Peggy seventy-five cents, the legal minimum wage, but nooooo. Families didn't tip, kids by themselves didn't tip, women hardly ever left you more than a nickel. Everybody acted like you were working for the privilege of serving them alone, rude as Hell, a lot of them. But what was she going to do? Go down and work Christmas rush at Kresge's three weeks a year like Tollie Ramsey? *If* she even gets to do it this year, with that bun in the oven. What in the world is she going to do about that? Time was running out! Was she going to drive left of center, like Poor Eva was rumored to have?

We've both had our minds on it night and day, and we can't see what to do, Lily thought, for the hundredth time in a week. That thing is just in there, growing like a cancer, invisible. Except that any minute it's not going to be invisible, and then—

Tollie. Tollie had never had her, Lily's, luck in life. Even she wouldn't trust to luck anymore. It gave her the creeps to think how she used to act, like she was trusting to Jesus, like her Daddy did.

Peggy sidled over to the wet maple-nuts and fished a few out of the syrup and ate them, pretending to be cleaning the area. Billy was in the backroom, doing who-knew-what. Playing pocket pool, Lily guessed. He'd tried to get Peggy to come back there twice. Bring those empty slaw trays back here, Peggy! Peggy, I could use some help with these onions. Lily had taken pity and carried the slaw trays back herself, watched his old dogface drop down to his knees when she'd whipped in, dumped the new slaw over the old hot slaw left from lunch and stirred it all around, ptomaine city, like he liked them to do. Later, she'd gone back there and grabbed a sharp onion-cutting knife, smiled, tested its blade on her thumb, before he'd told her he could take care of it after all.

"Go ahead and eat them all," Lily said to Peggy. Enough charity for one day. "Your skin's going to look like pictures of the moon." She watched another little ruffle of tears accumulate. Predictable! She wasn't going to worry about *Peggy*.

Just then, Tollie came through the door, causing Lily to smile. Billy hated it when you had company at work. She slipped out from behind the counter and led Tollie out of sight of the door to the backroom.

"What's up," Lily asked.

"I tried to call him," she said, looking about hysterical. "I never could get through to the barracks. Somebody told me that company's out on maneuvers for a month. But that could be a lie, they could be on their way to the Suez Canal or Indochina. Or the Dominican Republic and he's AWOL—"

"Would you calm down," Lily said.

Tollie exhaled. "Yes. I can do that. I don't know what he could do anyway."

"Don't think for a minute about marrying him!" That would be just like her.

"Are you crazy, Lily? He wouldn't. Even if *you* put a shotgun up to his head. If we could find him. Which we can't."

"Sometimes they will," Lily said. "They'll marry you and then divorce you when the baby comes. At least it gives it a name."

"I can give it a name my own self," Tollie said indignantly. "A name's not what I need. And he'd never marry me!"

"Count your blessings," Lily said. "He might give you some money, though. They've got a home in Raleigh you could go to, but I wouldn't. Mainly, you need information. I'd like to get that thing out of there like it was a bad meal."

"I'm thinking of talking to Arlene," Tollie said.

"Why?" Lily exclaimed. "I wouldn't tell anybody if I were you. Especially not somebody next door."

"She gets something for Mamma at the palmreader's. I think she could ask if there's not some kind of potion for what's wrong with me."

"Let me put my mind on it a little longer," Lily said.

"Okay. I've got to go."

Tollie didn't move.

"Well?" Lily said. "Spit it out."

"Raeford's coming tonight."

"Hm. I'd thought maybe that was *finis,* as we say."

"I think he's going to do what Ramírez did, just with a little better manners."

"You mean, the Big Nasty?"

"No! God, Lily. He's going to tell me he's not going to take me out anymore. It comes to the very same thing as Ramírez, except he won't be leaving his mark on me. I don't even think I care what Raeford Faircloth does! I've got too much other stuff on my mind."

"I'll say you have," Lily said. "This is just as well. He's been a distraction all along. That's probably why you're still in this mess."

"No, I'm in this mess, still, because Lily Jones was going to really get on Ramírez's tail!" Tollie said defensively.

"I can't live your life for you!" Lily flared. "I got to get back to work here."

"Okay," Tollie sighed. "Let's not fight. I hope Les will be home tonight. I'm so scared about Mamma you'd think I'd have a miscarriage like agitated people are supposed to do. I wouldn't go out, except I want to leave a certain . . . impression. I hate for him to put me out of his mind thinking I've got no class. That I'm just a footstamper and whiner."

"Well, I guess I see the point of that," Lily said.

"I still don't know what I'm going to do after that," Tollie said nervously.

"Just let me put my mind on it a little longer. Don't tell Arlene yet. We're going to get you out of this mess and then we're going to get you one of those college scholarships that they give people when their daddy gets killed in the War, like Wayne Dixon." Might as well give her a little hope. They probably wouldn't give a girl one of those scholarships, though. Even if her daddy had been a Hero.

Tollie looked down, blinking.

"Oh, come on!" Lily said. "And go on. I'll put my mind on all of it. Just don't start crying on me today. You and *Peggy*!"

After Tollie left, Lily cut down the radio—those Chipmunks!—and began to do her side-work, filling salt and peppers, napkins. She was getting really cold by now. Peggy was peeling potatoes for suppertime, not even washing them. Billy's probably going to go out of business soon, Lily concluded. Rolando McLaurin was opening up one of those Burger Quiks right across the road the day after New Year's. Assembly-line food, you put your order in and a line of people slap everything on a burger you can think of, passing it along, and you walk beside it and pay at the end. One minute or your money back. Bye-bye Billy Ray Kinlaw. And then where will I work, Lily wondered with a deeper chill. Rolando as a boss would be worse than Billy. All the good jobs in dress stores and department stores go to old ladies or girls whose Daddies are connected to something more important than the Tabernacle of God's Shining Light!

It was almost four o'clock when the woman came in the door. Still no heat. There wasn't a car in the lot, so Lily deduced the woman must have walked. It must be fifty degrees inside, god knows what outside. Lily was freezing, cranky. But she got ready to meet the customer, by the book, the way Bill had trained them. First, she smiled, keeping her teeth together so they wouldn't chatter, but it was a Pepsodent smile you couldn't fault.

The woman was old. Not old-old, but her hair had already started to go gray. She had wrinkles near her eyes, which were kind of sad eyes, if Lily thought about it. The eyes were checking out pictures of the sundaes and parfaits and cones dipped in chocolate. She looked hungry. Wrinkles around her mouth, like she'd been holding it tight a long time. Mousy old coat, worn on the cuffs. Scarred patent-leather purse, in wintertime. Wrinkled hand, wedding ring on the right hand. Hard to believe a man would marry somebody like that. Lily reminded herself to keep smiling. Good afternoon, Ma'am.

The woman looked at her, blinked.

Hi! How are you? Lily flashed her pearlies. You look like you'd like something sweet, am I right?

It was a simple question. Not even a question, just something you say. You didn't *mean* anything. You didn't even know her, she didn't know you. But all of a sudden, the woman was looking at Lily like she'd asked her something she really wanted to know.

Then the woman was crying, crying like her heart was going to break in two. Looking right into Lily's eyes with the tears running down her face. A stranger!

"I'm sorry," Lily said, getting a handful of napkins and giving them to the woman. "I don't know what I've done here."

235

"I'm sorry," the woman said, taking the napkins and dabbing at her face and eyes. "I'm sorry." Then she hurried out, without buying a thing.

Billy had seen it all, or most of it. He was starting toward Lily like he wanted her to dig up half-a-cent for the napkins, or else. Peggy was looking off into space, like nothing had happened out of the ordinary. Jesus!

It seemed to Lily that every female she knew was breaking down one way or the other these days, even the ones she didn't know. What in the *world* was going on?

"You'd better watch it, girl," Billy said.

"You'd better watch it, slime-ball," Lily said, so cranky she was seeing him lopsided.

He actually took a step back.

"You!" she said, like she was a ghost jumping out of the dark at him, making those mean eyes shift in that rock-hard head. She turned her back on him, and Peggy too. She was shaking. She felt like she was going to fly apart herself.

Or take off like a Sputnik! Rise up out of this cold old place and never come down again!

"I thought you might be going away," Tollie said as she watched herself pick at her steak and baked potato at The Loblolly Inn. Across from her, Raeford was eating a double shrimp cocktail and drinking his bourbon, which flickered in the lamplight whenever he raised and lowered the glass. He'd said he didn't want a dinner. She didn't either. Seeing him made her feel queasy, with their past and with a future where he wouldn't exist for her at all, she just knew it, but he'd insisted she order a big meal. And now he'd told her he was going away.

"I'm wasting your money," Tollie said. "I can't eat this."

"It's too American for you," Raeford said. "You need some beef stroganoff or some caviar." He was trying to tease her in the old way, but Tollie could feel the strain. She wished she could lighten his load. She guessed she'd caused him enough trouble for a guy who just wanted a casual date, maybe a minor protégée of some kind.

"Do you think the day will ever come when you can buy caviar in Hope Mills?" she asked, taking a big bite of baked potato. I'm going to lighten his load, whatever it takes, she thought. He's been a good person for me to know.

"Yep," Raeford said, jiggling his ice and raising his glass a little for the waiter. "I think one place is going to be pretty much like the next, before it's all over."

"Then why do you want to go off?" Tollie said. "You sound like my mother. And what do you mean, before it's all over? You aren't one

237

of those people that think the Russians are going to drop a bomb on us, are you?"

"I don't know why, what, or if. Thank you sir," he said to the waiter. The Loblolly Inn was the only restaurant around that used Negro waiters. They wore tuxedos.

That remark was condescending, Tollie realized. So was the "Sir." She looked at Raeford with new eyes.

"You sound a little sulky," she said. "Underneath. I wouldn't have thought that of you."

"Well, sorry, Sug," Raeford said.

"Sug!" Tollie scoffed. "Aren't you going to call me 'Girl,' too. I swear. You might as well stay in Hope Mills. I think you've been home too long to fit into the outside world."

"And what would you know about that?"

Tollie's face burned. She wasn't acting one bit like she'd planned to act. She began to saw on her steak. Maybe she'd just cut it all up and shift it around and hide it under the big lettuce leaf and pale slice of tomato that garnished her plate. She wasn't going to stuff her craw to please Raeford Faircloth, as rude as he'd suddenly become! He must have given up completely on her too, along with all his kind.

"I guess I don't know anything," she said. "I guess you just wasted your time on me, all the way around."

Raeford didn't say anything. *Jekyll and Hyde,* Tollie thought. I'm leaving my mother to fend for her poor self to be out with the two of you!

"I don't know why you bothered to invite me out to supper," she said, giving up and crossing her knife and fork on her plate and pushing it toward the top-of-the-line plastic poinsettia blooming on their table, looking more real than real. "Neither one of us is enjoying it."

"I'm sorry," Raeford said. He pushed his shrimp cocktail aside and leaned toward her a little. He did look contrite, Tollie thought. "I didn't invite you out to make you feel worse. I just hate to go off without saying good-bye." He picked up his drink. "Actually, I'm trying to make myself feel better. I feel like I took advantage of you."

"Took advantage?" Tollie exclaimed. "I *hope* you don't mean because I let you feel me up!"

"Sh-sh-h," Raeford said. "Maybe I just mean that I think I led you on. I haven't known much about what I'm doing lately."

Tollie looked at him. Again, as in Chapel Hill, she noticed that he seemed younger than he'd seemed back at the end of the summer. He *had* been just knocking around for a long time, like some kid, if you thought about it.

"Don't worry about it," Tollie said. "You gave me a little hope when I needed it. You don't owe me a thing in this world."

She could see Raeford's face relax. She guessed that's all he wanted, to be let off the hook. Well. He was still a step up from Ramírez.

"So where are you going?" she said. "To India with your brother?"

Raeford laughed. "We ought to. Rowen and I ought to go on over to India and go into a monastery, I guess, where we couldn't do any more harm. Dharma Bums."

"Stop flattering yourself," Tollie said, forcing herself to give him a little smile. "The Ramsey women will *survive,* I imagine. Where are you going? And is Rowen going to India? What's Dharma Bums?"

"Rowen's got a new love interest, some girl that works down at one of the banks. Darlene somebody—"

"That's good," Tollie said quickly. "Tell me about you. Are you going back to Chapel Hill?"

"Nope," Raeford said. "I want a change of scenery. I want some new friends—you were right about Randy and Bennett, sort of. Randy's old man pulled a couple of strings. I'm going to finish school, starting in January, up in Minnesota. Then maybe med school."

"Minnesota," Tollie said, testing out the unusual idea. "That's a cold place."

"Most places seem to be," Raeford said.

"That's pretty gloomy," Tollie said. "Is that your new philosophy? I don't see why *you* of all people would feel that way. As many women as you said you were seeing just a couple of weeks ago."

"I'm just talking," Raeford said. "I'm going to get the check." He signaled the waiter.

"Just talking in a self-indulging way," Tollie said. "I'm almost done with gloomy. I don't know what I can do in life. But I don't want to go through it with a raincloud over my head, like that old Joe in the funny papers. I just need to get my life back in my lane."

"You're right," Raeford said. "Come on. Let's get out of here. You ought to be with happy kids your own age."

"Where?" Tollie said. "Where would you find them?"

Raeford gave the waiter some money. When the waiter was gone, he got up and walked around behind Tollie and pulled her chair out.

"Thanks," Tollie said. She felt good when he put his arm on her back as they walked out of the restaurant: a little bit of normal romantic life, the man being gallant and protective. Eating in a place with potted palms in the corners, waiters in tuxedos, lamp light. But she was glad to be going home. She needed to be checking on her mother: first things first.

"You're the first boy I ever thought I loved," she said matter-of-factly to Raeford as they walked across the parking lot in the cold.

"You just thought it," Raeford said, squeezing the back of her neck through her coat.

"Maybe," Tollie said, pulling her coat tighter. "Anyway, I'll survive it. I've had my mind on so much I can't even get my heart broken right, the way you're supposed to do with a first love."

Raeford laughed. "You're something," he said.

"I hope I might be," Tollie said uncertainly, getting in the car. "Before it's all over."

It was mid-December. Tollie was spending the night at Lily's house. She'd brought her things to school in an old overnight case of Janice's, from the 1940s—dusty-looking leather printed to look like tweed, trimmed in leather cracked by time. She'd had to maneuver it all day long, as well as her winter-coat—and the new used books that she'd had to re-buy, ticking Les off. She couldn't blame him. She'd been careless, careless with her books and careless with everything else, and now paying the piper: loaded down more than ever. When she got off the schoolbus in Lily's brand new neighborhood of ranch houses, the neighborhood so new there wasn't a tree in it yet, she was exhausted. The bus let them out at least a quarter of a mile from Lily's house, so the walk there was another obstacle in front of her—as if she were on an obstacle course just to get to this night. This Fateful Night.

"I'll carry your things," Lily said when they were standing on the red clay shoulder of the strip of asphalt that paved Palmetto Drive and all the flat streets of Palisades Estates. Lily arranged her books on her hip, like a boy, and reached out her free hand for the overnight case.

"Thanks," Tollie said, handing it to her. They began to walk toward Lily's neat little house down where Palmetto Drive t-ed into Banyan Drive. The house wasn't even a year old and already clapped in spanking white aluminum. "I'll never have to paint it," Virgil Lee Jones had said proudly when it was done. "Think of that." Tollie remembered him standing out in the tiny yard, which had thickly self-sown sand-spurs instead of grass, regarding his permanently white house with a

241

sort of wondrous look on his face. At all the windows, white aluminum Venetian blinds were tilted against the sun, and there were black aluminum shutters riveted in place forever to the side of every window.

She and Lily walked in silence, each in her own thoughts. Tollie was grateful not to have to talk about tonight. They'd talked it into the ground already. She just wanted to get it over with, not die, and forget it. Or die. Half the time, she felt like she didn't care one way or the other. Life was such a mess.

She was glad Lily had invited her to stay over, though. There'd be no way Les could check up on her easily, even if he were inclined to, which she didn't think he would be. Their phone had given up the ghost almost a week ago. She'd been calling the phone company from Arlene's every day, telling them it was an emergency. It was. Janice was back at Dix Hill. It had to happen, inevitable. But it was awful not to have a phone when Janice or somebody up in Raleigh might need to get ahold of them. Les had called too. Somebody at Southern Bell said they'd be out to fix or replace the phone, every day, but no one ever came. Arlene had been calling up to Raleigh every other day to see if there was any news. Tollie hated to think of Arlene having to spend her money that way. But tonight, it would be good not to have a line running between Les and the Joneses. She just wanted to get this over, then turn her undivided attention to her mother, where it belonged. She could fight for her own life later on, when things straightened out at home. She wished she'd known that a year ago. Then she wouldn't be in this mess.

She and Lily were walking out in the street, but each time a car or pickup came speeding their way, they had to step off onto the wet shoulder, its red clay accumulating on their shoes as they progressed. The street's paving was so narrow that two cars couldn't pass each other without one of them going off onto the clay. The constant traffic on the shoulders of the streets of Palisades Estates kept anything from growing there but the most persistent weeds. Which nobody was responsible for mowing down, Tollie concluded. There were milkweeds and pokeweeds, lamb's quarter that was two feet high, palm-like thistle plants with dangerous spikey blooms the size of tropical fruit—things that could survive the swerving weight of motor vehicles and a summer of drought and even persist toward the beginning of winter.

Tollie surveyed the stand of hardy vegetation as she and Lily walked. Unlike me, she thought. I didn't survive the summer of 1959 very well, and now it's the winter of my discontent, like in one of Mrs. Wiggins' Quotable Quotes for recitation.

"Watch where you're going," Lily said. "You almost stepped on my new flats."

"Sorry," Tollie said. She didn't even have the energy to get mad at Lily. What was the use? A person who would worry about her new flats when her lifelong friend was going through Hell was hopeless. The shoes already had a rim of red clay stain on their suede. Keeping your shoes looking nice for more than a day in a neighborhood like Palisades Estates was hopeless too. It's a wonder Lily didn't give up, on clean flats and more.

I'm not going to brood about her today, Tollie thought. I'm not going to bicker with her either, for one day in my life. All that bickering makes me feel little-bitty.

She stared ahead, down to where Lily's house was set on the flat street like a monopoly piece on a board of monopoly pieces. She put her thoughts elsewhere.

Hath not the potter power over the clay, of the same lump to make one vessel unto honour, and another unto dishonour? That was one of Mrs. Wiggins' Quotable Quotes, appropriate to bickering. *Dear is bought the honey that is licked off the thorn,* was another. *Of all our evils, the worst of the worst is home-made infelicity. . . . It is human nature to hate those that we have injured. . . . Have more than thou showest, Speak less than thou knowest, Lend less than thou owest. . . . The miserable have no other medicine but only hope.*

These were things Tollie could imagine someone quoting, someday. Others were cryptic: *An honest man is always a child. . . . He has no hope who never had a fear.*

Three more Quotes and I'll be ready to recite, Tollie thought. If I live that long.

She scanned the neighborhood as they approached 109 Banyan Drive, Lily's house. No sidewalks, no front porches, nobody in sight in the whole neighborhood but a couple of lumpy dogs snoozing on their chains in a couple of back yards. A couple of little kids in droopy playclothes climbing on a Jungle Gym. All of them, kids and chained dogs, enclosed behind the chain-link fences that everybody had built around their yards, usually front and back both. What were they trying so hard to protect? Tollie wondered as she and Lily walked. Some houses had strung up their Christmas lights: you could see the dark wires and dark bulbs running along the eaves of the houses. There were a couple of plastic Santa Clauses, no reindeer, standing forlornly in a couple of yards near Lily's house, which had its own chain-links, front and back, running right up against the chain-links next door, so that you had two fences without two inches between them.

"Can you get the gate?" Lily said. "I can't, unless I do it with my teeth."

Tollie opened the gate and held it while Lily passed through. She closed it and secured the latch, then she ascended the two concrete steps to the tiny concrete stoop. Lily waited below, loaded down, while Tollie opened the door. Tollie held the screen door with her back, flattening herself up against it so that Lily could get by her without one of them falling off the stoop. Even so, the sharp edge of Lily's load of books poked her in the belly as it passed. "Sorry," Lily murmured as Tollie followed her across the threshold.

"Put your stuff back in my room," Lily said when they were in the house, their shoes sitting on a mat by the door so that they wouldn't mess up the living room's shag carpet with clay or with the sand that had appeared abruptly and mysteriously the moment they'd stepped into the actual yard, like somebody had dumped one inhospitable soil on top of another on purpose. Which maybe they had, Tollie thought, worried about all the stuff that would fall off her loafers in about an hour when they dried. Some of it was bound to get into Marie's rug. That shag was so deep that their vacuum couldn't do much with it. It was in one of the new synthetics, a glittery green, like grass from a different planet.

"Let's don't forget to clean our shoes before they make a mess," Tollie said, almost whispering. She figured Marie was back in her room reading or sleeping, like Mothers tended to do nowadays.

"Would you stop worrying," Lily said loudly. "Put your things back in my room and I'll get us some sweet-tea." She shoved the overnight case into Tollie's hand and let her own schoolbooks crash down on the new coffee table shaped like a wagonwheel covered with an unbreakable ring of clear plastic.

Tollie walked down the hall in her socks and entered Lily's room, a room that didn't look like Lily at all. Marie had done it: a poster bed with an actual canopy in pink ruffles, a vanity with a skirt and stool to match, flounces everywhere, including the curtains that were pulled back over the Venetian blinds. In the middle of the room there was a surreal square of carpet in the same synthetic as the living room rug,

244

but pink, covered with synthetic stardust. Tollie stood a moment in dislocated amazement, as she did every time she entered Lily's room: another world. The new lamp on the white French Provincial night-stand was a Marie-touch: a porcelain ballerina with a leg out behind her and Dying Swan hands, the image of an image that you might have seen on one of the cultural tv shows, back in the old days. It was one of a pair of lamps, the other on the vanity, both pink-shaded and ruffly.

Tollie crossed the twinkling carpet and set her books back against the wall where they'd be out of the way. She set her overnight case near a bookcase that looked like wood but once you got close you could see it was one of the new indestructible materials made to look like wood, knot-holes and all. The bookcase was new since the last time she'd been over here, but already crammed with books, many of them worn—probably passed along by Marie. A few were bright and new. They'd probably been bought especially for Lily, books Marie and Virgil hoped she would read . . . hope against hope, and in vain, Tollie deduced: the books looked pristine.

She glanced at the titles, just in case she wanted to borrow something whenever, if-ever, she surfaced from her problems and could concentrate again. There was *The Diary of a Young Girl* by Anne Frank, which Tollie had read long ago. It was a book that was supposed to give you courage for the worst life had to offer. She remembered that Mrs. Roosevelt had written an introduction. Tollie pulled the book off the shelf. There it was: Mrs. Roosevelt. She said that Anne was "Sustained by her warmth and wit, her intelligence and the rich resources of her inner life." Tollie put the book back. She wouldn't want to read it again. It had made her feel like her heart was breaking with every page, knowing Anne's future. Sustained . . . but for what? Most of the other books she'd never heard of, not that you couldn't predict their contents from the titles . . . *The Presence of Grace* by J. F. Powers . . . *To Live Again* by Catherine Marshall. *Etiquette* by Frances Benton. *Stay Alive All Your Life* by Norman Vincent Peale. *The Day Christ Died* by Jim Bishop. And of course *Twixt Twelve and Twenty* by Pat Boone—! Marie and Virgil Lee Jones didn't know their daughter one bit.

Instructive books, Tollie surmised, scanning the last of them. But with a couple meant for pleasure, she guessed: *Kids Say the Darndest Things!* by Art Linkletter . . . *Hawaii* by James Michener.

She pulled *Hawaii* out of the case, glanced at its palmy cover and slipped it back reluctantly. She wished she had the peace of mind right

245

now to read about Hawaii . . . to be transported to the land of palm trees and coconuts and flowers as big as your hand.

She straightened up. Then she bent back down when she saw that she'd accidentally dislodged the Bible-according-to-Kotex from the shelf: the pamphlet called *What Every Girl Should Know.* They gave you those in seventh grade, along with a belt and sanitary napkin. She picked the pamphlet up from the floor and put it back between *Hawaii* and *The Presence of Grace.* Useless. Every Girl needed to know more. She was living proof of that.

She was standing under the familiar row of pictures Lily had cut from movie magazines, the room's only art: Marilyn Monroe with her white pleated skirt blowing up to show her legs, Terry Moore in her notorious ermine bathing suit.

Tollie slipped off her coat and laid it on the bed. She took her comb out of her purse and bent down toward the vanity mirror to arrange her hair. She looked awful: hair full of static, white face, dark crescents under her eyes. A pale mouth that kept slipping into a grimace every time her mind slipped off keeping it natural-looking. She looked like Hell. Not that she gave a toot.

She stood up. From the wall Anita Ekberg was smiling her wide smile, Brigitte Bardot pouting out her bottom lip . . . Diana Dors. Mamie Van Doren and Monique Van Vooren. Jayne Mansfield from the neck up only, above Lily's uneven scissor-mark: Lily probably hadn't wanted to be reminded of how far she herself was from having a set of boobs like Jayne Mansfield's. Jayne Mansfield's incredible body materialized in Tollie's mind for a minute. Jesus.

She'd read somewhere that Jayne was intelligent. That she read poetry. Was that true, or just something somebody made up to make her seem like more than boobs? And why? With boobs like that, displayed like that, who could get interested in anything that might or might not be in your head?

Tollie touched her own tender and swollen breasts, thankful they were still a normal-enough size, though no-question they had grown. You could almost be missing your head altogether and people wouldn't notice, if you had boobs insinuated out into space in the incredible way of Jayne Mansfield. You'd always be Boobs, wouldn't you? Jayne was trying to have it both ways, boobs and brains, but she'd never be able to, not in this world.

246

Tollie looked into the movie star's dark, slightly pained eyes. Shame on you, Jayne Mansfield. *Especially* if you read poetry!

Then she felt ashamed herself. Who was she, these days, to be moralizing?

Tollie sank wearily onto the edge of Lily's ruffled bed. She was probably cracking up, going nuts herself. Lecturing movie stars was probably a good sign of it. She had so much on her mind she thought her head might explode. She couldn't even tell what her main problem was. Was it that she had to get through whatever Madame Lucretia was going to do to her tonight and try to make peace with life afterwards? Or was it Janice's situation?

Janice locked up like she'd committed a crime, with no one to help her. Dogs at the County Pound had it better. At least somebody might come in and take them home. It wasn't that easy with a human being, Tollie knew. Even if she could get Lily or Les or Raeford, or Rowen Faircloth, even—she'd thought about that—to drive her up to Raleigh and help her find Dix Hill, she couldn't just walk in and say she wanted to take her mother home. Janice was in the power of other people now.

Tollie imagined her mother as imprisoned in a tower, high on a hill. Janice was gazing sadly out a window, down onto a world that went on without her, like several women in fairy tales Tollie remembered from long, long ago. In those stories, a knight eventually rode by and was struck by the woman's beauty and rescued her. But that wasn't likely to happen in Janice's case. Janice hadn't looked beautiful at all when she'd been taken away. Who would save a woman who wasn't beautiful? That never happened in the fairy tales.

Even a daughter, drunk with good intentions and burning with outrage and love, couldn't rescue Janice. The night before, Tollie had dreamed about herself standing at the bottom of Dix Hill, a mountain so tall she couldn't even see the top of it. It rose in front of her like a steep wall. Somewhere up there, but inaccessible, was Janice. Out of sight, out of sound.

Other dreams had been bizarre. Janice walking along the top of the hill, her neck strung with acorns, smiling her terrible removed smile. Or the dreams were obscene: someone accosting Tollie and insisting that her mother was at Dicks Hill, Dicks Hill, Dicks Hill, screaming it right in her face, grinning like a villain on one of Les's Western tv shows. Then a dream-Tollie tried to puzzle out how men's . . . anatomy . . . might have made her mother end up where she was.

247

She'd failed to puzzle it out. In the dream, and back in the world. Her mother had made some mistakes with men, for sure. Who hadn't? That was the way it was. But it didn't seem like a thing like that could drive you "nuts," set you pacing along a ridge, smiling like a zombie.

Les had said it was just for a couple of weeks and then Janice would be home, but it had been almost a couple of weeks already, with no more such talk. He'd said they couldn't go up to see her, that the doctors said it was best not to. Tollie thought about the way he looked across the room when he said it—and said it, and said it again, like he was trying to keep her from asking him to his face if he'd take her up there. He said it with a line of sweat, or mill-dew, on his lip, in cold weather, which told her he was lying. Les didn't want to see Janice up there. He was scared of it.

That was men, Tollie guessed. Men and boys.

Her third-most important problem was Raeford, even though he'd declared himself out of her life, more or less. What did he think of her, now that he knew that her mother was nuts, certified? Or would he use loony? Crazy, off-her-rocker, bananas? Why was it that even the people who'd started to say Negro instead of nigger would use words like that with no second thoughts? Raeford was very careful to say Negro. She had no idea what he'd call her mother. People didn't seem to see the need to be careful with their words in that situation.

I didn't either, Tollie thought. Not till recently. It's hard to see.

She looked down at her hands, stiff against each other in the vicinity of her heart, like Eva Bledsoe's hands at the end. She felt depressed. All those Little Moron jokes when she was a kid. All those words that had come off her tongue as lightly as dandelion fluff drifted off into a breeze: idiot, imbecile, fool. Even the Bible warned you that you'd burn in Hell for using fool, but who'd paid attention?

She hadn't seen Raeford since their dinner, though he'd called when he'd heard, via his brother she guessed, about Janice. Then he'd called a few days later to see if things were better. No, she'd told him. Things are "the same." Not that he'd come running to hold her hand when the phone had gone out! She could tell they were duty calls anyway. Boys. Boys and men.

"Tollie . . . ," Lily called from the kitchen. "Did you die back there or what?"

"Just a minute," Tollie called back softly, hoping she wouldn't disturb Marie. Not that that seemed to be on Lily's mind. Lily had a mother whose brain was getting stronger, not more troubled, and Lily couldn't appreciate it a bit.

Tollie stood up and looked for the best place to put her coat. There were other touches of Lily insinuated into Marie's scheme against her: A big blue hi-fi, the top of its case flung on the floor, and a stack of records reaching for the moon. A big blue hatbox with the plastic bonnet of Lily's new hair dryer spilling out, on a hose that looked like a fat ripply snake or a gut. About a ton of cosmetics on the vanity's glass. Dark bottles of peroxide. A Modess box right out in plain sight, not in the bottom drawer of your chest of drawers where it belonged.

Tollie hung her coat on a hanger and put it on a hook on the back of the door. There wasn't a coat closet anywhere in the house. There was hardly a piece of trim either, no baseboards, nothing around the windows, just a thin frame around the doors. No front hall: You just walked into the main room, like you did at Barefoot's Mortuary.

Tollie was glad to have these signs of modern times to distract her from her age-old problems. She buttoned one button on her coat so it wouldn't slide off the hanger if somebody opened and shut the door. Lily's new house had no pantry, no basement. They must have gone the way of sidewalks and front porches, old-fashioned things that people thought they wouldn't miss when somebody working for a Rolando Wiggins McLaurin tried to sell them the house. But later on, who knew what you'd miss? When you thought about hanging your coat on the back of your bedroom door for forty or fifty years, you'd miss the old conveniences plenty, she'd bet. Tollie's own house was old and not well kept-up, but it was more convenient than this house. More designed for living, as people on tv and in the magazines liked to say. Not that it was Lily's family's fault. They'd just bought what they could afford to buy, hungry for a change and blind to the consequences.

Who knew what you'd miss later on? Tollie touched the front of her skirt lightly, then laid her hand flat against it. She wasn't showing much, even now. When was it half-a-baby? Which half? she sometimes asked, when she wanted to torment herself for her mistakes.

She looked down on the tiny ball of belly covered with her hand. Will I miss you later on? Little boy or little girl? What would we be like, Mother and Child, in the year 2000, if I could just let you grow and come out and grow some more? Even if I couldn't keep you. We'd both be different.

She couldn't think of who the child might grow up to be without crying. Not that she cared whether it would be Somebody, like she'd heard a man on a tv show say—a show in which the man interviewed, without showing her face, a woman who said she'd never forgive herself for what she'd done, no matter that she was married now and had three children, she would never, ever, stop wondering about the one she'd killed. And the man had said gravely, "Yes, he might have been the President of the United States." The woman had hesitated and then said, "Well, yes. That too."

Tollie lifted the hem of her skirt up and wiped her eyes. The rough wool scratched her face in a way she felt she deserved. What did a thing like that mean, that it was wrong to do what the woman had done because the baby might grow up to be somebody important? She rubbed her face a little harder, thinking of the baby inside her. One way you could think was that you were saving it all the pains of life. But she didn't think about it that way. She thought of what she was going to do tonight as denying somebody all the detail of life, happy and sad, even if most of life was sad. She thought of denying somebody the amazing things that could accumulate within a few square inches of your skull. Detail, incident, memory and dream and daydream, all time available, and the space to roam it and gather it back and invent it new again and again. When she thought of that, she wanted to die herself.

And it was not just the baby in there, just a few hours from its fate, its fate in her hands. Not just the little person who, under normal circumstances, would have come into the world in Puerto Rico and thrived along with everything in a place where things thrived in general. Though the baby was that too, she thought sadly, bereft of all that would have been if things had been different. She could feel fresh tears rising, like someone had lifted the locks down inside her somewhere, where an ocean of tears ebbed and flowed. No, the baby was not just itself. Inside it, dotted in already and waiting, were the seeds of some farther future that would never be. She felt like she was changing history. But it didn't make her feel important at all. It made her feel hopeless, hopeless with the sadness of life. But even convinced that life was mostly sad, invented to break your heart over and over and over again, until your heart just gave up, she wouldn't want to deny life to anything. She wouldn't want to deny anything its body, because you weren't anything without a body. But it had come down to that: her body or the baby's body.

I can't do this, Tollie thought. I'm just going to have to find out how to go to Florence Crittendon and have it and give it away.

Except I can't. I've got to do this and get it over. I've got to finish school, and take care of my mother.

"I put a little bit of grain in your tea," Lily said when she and Tollie were sitting down at the table that was crowded into the breakfast nook. "I figured you'd need something."

"Thanks," Tollie said. She did need something. All she had to do was wait till after the others had supper, having figured out a way not to eat much, like Madame Lucretia had advised Arlene that Tollie should do. Tollie could imagine the two of them, Arlene and Madame Lucretia, sitting at a round table in a dark and spooky room, pretending to consult a crystal ball. Or Arlene watching Madame Lucretia pretending to read her magic cards with her wild red eyes, insisting that all the instructions were coming from Beyond.

"She pretended we were just doing business as usual," Arlene had said, amazed. "That's how it seemed. Like she was reading my palm or something."

Tollie understood that: You found a way to think about whatever it was you were doing that let you go on.

"You be sure to get her to read your palm while you're there, too," Arlene had said, giving Tollie a sweet smile. "I already paid for it. My treat."

Tollie stared into her glass, as if somewhere, way down, there might be some helpful tea leaves. Which was silly. She knew everybody used tea bags nowadays, and even if there were leaves, by a miracle, what would she know about reading them? That took a special education, or special powers. Sometimes she felt like she had no powers, except those brewing around in her body's system, as mysterious as tea leaves.

Sometimes she just felt about 100% powerless, like a little old clam or oyster. Pushed around by the tides from the outside. Bound to spending all your days manufacturing tears upon tears, trying to make a pearl out of whatever dumb thing that had drifted in from the outside. Just waiting to be eaten alive, unless you died first on your own.

She sipped her tea and grain alcohol. "You're sure we can have the car?" she asked Lily.

"Do you know how many times you've asked me that today?" Lily said. "Would you just drink that and try to relax? Tomorrow it'll be behind us and I can get back to my own life, praise Jesus and all the angels. This is the biggest mess I've ever had anything to do with."

"Oh, hi, Tollie," Marie said behind their backs. Tollie spun around, almost upsetting the chrome-and-red plastic chair. Had Marie heard?

"I didn't know you were coming home with Lily today," Marie said. Her glasses were hanging around her neck on a gold chain, bobbing near the book Marie held to her body, a finger inserted into its pages to mark her place. Her hair was piled up on her head in a loose knot and she was wearing a fuzzy pink bathrobe like she'd been in bed all day.

"I *told* you last night *and* this morning," Lily said wearily. "She's spending the night."

"Oh," Marie said, sticking a paper napkin from a holder on the counter into her book, then laying it down near the radio. She opened the refrigerator and got out the tea. "Well, that's fine. Tollie's always welcome." She smiled at Tollie. Tollie smiled back. She liked Marie.

"I don't know what in the world we'll have for supper, though," Marie said. "I've been studying all day. I guess I ought to get in my clothes and see what's in the freezer."

She looked vaguely at the refrigerator, then poured herself a glass of tea. Her mind already seemed to be on something else, Tollie noted. Marie was sort of like the absent-minded professor everybody talked about. Or she would have been, if women could be professors, which Tollie didn't think they could.

"I can't eat any supper anyway," Tollie said tentatively. She hated to disturb Marie's thoughts, but she didn't want her to go to any trouble about supper.

Marie's gaze rose from the depths of her tea glass and focused, slowly, on Tollie's face. She gave Tollie another affectionate smile, but Tollie knew she hadn't got through. "I can't have any supper," she repeated.

"She means Miss Pappas told her not to have *much* supper," Lily said, giving Tollie a stern look. "We're going over to the school tonight so Tollie can try out for the Girl's Pep Club. Miss Pappas doesn't want anybody throwing up on the gym floor when they do their jumping around. We'll just get something at the Tastee-Freeze, after."

"Well," Marie said. "That's fine. Your Daddy and I can fend for ourselves." She smiled and turned on the radio, adjusting the tuner. When she settled on a station, she turned down the volume so low you could barely hear it. Tollie was glad: that old Peter Gunn thing.

"What are you studying?" Tollie asked to change the subject. Also, she was interested.

"Oh!" Marie said, finally attentive. "You just wouldn't believe all I learned today." She picked up her book and came over to the table and squeezed in next to Lily. Lily shot Tollie a vicious look and scrunched up against the wall, taking a slug of her tea.

"It's a brand new book called *The Status Seekers*," Marie said. "I just got it from the Book Club." She put her glasses up on her nose and leaned toward Tollie, her eyes brown and enormous behind the lenses, like cows' eyes, but rapt.

Tollie smiled at Marie, in spite of the ache in her leg where Lily had just kicked her under the table.

"Did you know that, according to this man, *the* dividing line between the social classes now isn't money? It isn't how old your family is, though that will probably always count. It's not where you live or what kind of car you drive."

Lily was looking at her mother curiously. "It's what your daddy does for a living," Lily said. "Anybody knows that. Or your husband."

"Nope," Marie said, opening *The Status Seekers* and spreading it on the table.

"What else?" Lily said. "Unless you don't have a daddy or a husband. Of course you always will have a daddy. I bet that follows you all your life. Unless you're a bastard."

Lily gave Tollie a quick I'm-sorry look and bit her bottom lip. Tollie raised her eyebrows a little to say Forget it. She'd finally confessed that there was no War Hero in her past.

"That's exactly why I'm going to be a movie star," Lily said. "I'm going to do something so far away from what everybody else does that I'll be in a class by myself."

"Oh, Lily," Marie said wearily. "Grow up."

"How? It's not like I've had anybody helping me along!"

"That's not true," Marie said, looking wounded. "Your Daddy and I have always loved you. Virgil Lee took you to church, when you'd let him. When he went to an ordinary church. You were right to stop going to that place he goes to now. I taught you how to clean house and put a hem in a skirt. You're so hard on people."

"I'm not hard enough. Do you know we don't have one single Christmas decoration up yet? When are we going to get a tree? If you leave it to Daddy we'll have a bunch of mangers stuck all over the house. When is the last time you made Christmas cookies? I don't think I'm being hard on you at all!"

Marie gave her a calm look. "There's more to life than all that, Lily. That's just stuff. But don't worry. We'll have a tree and I'll get a fruitcake, like I always do. I might even bake some cookies. I guess I can be "Mom" the way you want for a couple of days, covered with cookie-mix, sugar gritted up under my nails." Marie extended her hands and fluttered her pale, clipped nails as if trying to shake them clean. "But I swear I don't know how you came to have so little imagination about things. I'd think you'd have some pride in your mother having something in her head."

"I have got a hew-mong-us imagination!" Lily flared. "You've got something in your head all right." Lily gave Marie a vicious look. "But I don't care about any of this shit. Christmas, or any of it. All I care about is getting out of here. Then nobody is going to ever look down on me again. That's all I care about. I'm going to be looking down on them. From On High."

"Who's looking down on you now?" Marie said. "Your Daddy's a Foreman."

"Once a Mill Rat, always a Mill Rat," Lily said. "In Hope Mills. But where I'm going, none of this shit is going to mean shit."

Tollie noticed that Lily suddenly had a high color and that her lips and eyes had screwed up like morning glories at night.

Marie looked at Lily with her magnified eyes. "I don't want to hear that stuff, Lily. Your Daddy works hard. He doesn't need to know anything about how you feel."

"Or how you feel," Lily muttered.

"What's that supposed to mean?"

"What are you always studying for? You must have something in mind, now that I'm about gone."

"I have improving my mind on my mind," Marie said. "I study because I want to improve myself, not my lot in life. I'm proud of Virgil Lee. I like being a Foreman's wife. You don't know what you're talking about."

Marie's color was high, too, Tollie noticed. Time to change the subject. "What does the book say?" she asked Marie.

"Oh," Marie said, turning to look at Tollie. She ran her hands across the book's open pages. "It says that there's a Diploma Elite emerging. That the real dividing line in the future will be between people that went to college and people who didn't."

"It's going to be between the famous people and the people you never heard of," Lily said, taking a sip of her tea. "If they're not famous, they can do anything they want and it won't amount to doodle."

"I wish I'd gone to college," Marie said wistfully. "As well as I study on my own, I could know about all there is that it's important to know if somebody had pointed me in the right direction. I've had to educate myself. I never even got in one day of high school. Now they let married girls go to school and everything. Though I don't guess they let unmarried and pregnant girls finish school, do they? They'll probably never do that."

"Girls can't go to Chapel Hill," Tollie said to change the subject again. "Except a few when they're juniors."

"Is that right?" Marie said. "I never knew that."

"Girls can take a dental hygienist course, though," Tollie said. "It's accelerated. It doesn't last but a little while. The faster to get them out of there, I guess."

"Jesus," Lily said. "What a life that would be. Dental Hygiene. It makes me want to puke to think about it."

"I heard they usually just marry dentists anyway," Tollie said.

"Why don't they just kill themselves," Lily said, sipping her tea.

"Well, I've been learning lots of other things," Marie said brightly. "Not just from this book. Wait here. I'll show you some other things I've been reading." Marie got up and started back toward her room, the back of her bathrobe trailing behind on the floor, like a bride's train. "I just want to read you something else."

"Jesus Christ, Tollie," Lily said, taking Tollie's tea and grain alcohol out of her hand and dumping it into her own glass.

"Sorry," Tollie said.

On the counter the radio played almost out of hearing, Frank Sinatra's awful voice idling like a badly tuned car . . . *hii-iiiigh hopes* . . . *hii-ii-iigh hopes*. . . .

Then Big Mack came on the air. "Well, that's it for Platters Without Chatter today, folks. Time for the news. Then we'll be coming attcha with a little Christmas music. . . ."

"Shit!" Lily said, jumping up and slapping the radio over on its side before she shut it off.

"What do you *mean* we can't use the Oldsmobile?" Lily demanded of Virgil. Tollie watched nervously. Lily was standing with her fists on her hips like something out of Maggie and Jiggs. "Did I ask you a god-dam week ago or not?"

"Blaspheming will get you no place you want to go, Girl," Virgil said. "I told you I got to go out tonight myself. I never said you could use it for sure, and I never have. You can use it, maybe, when and if I don't have plans myself."

Tollie watched, sidewise, from a chair focused on the new console Magnavox where the News had just given way to Frankie Laine and the music for "Rawhide." So. Virgil was going to let them down. Les was home on the couch—Rollin'-Rollin'-Rollin'. . . . Where was Janice? What was life like up at Dix Hill? I feel so weird, Tollie thought, sick at her stomach in spite of no dinner. I've just got too much on my mind at one time.

"I need the car, Daddy . . . ," Lily said changing her tone. "Please?"

Tollie was touched. She hadn't heard Lily beg anybody for anything since they were little girls.

"I can drop you off at the schoolhouse," Virgil said. "But that's the best I can do. I got places to go, people to see, like they say."

"The schoolhouse!" Lily burst out. "It won't help us one bit to be dropped off way out there."

"Oh?" Virgil said, giving her a shrewd look. "I was just taking your word for where you said you had to go."

259

"That was just for Mamma," Lily said, moving forward and smiling, sitting down on the couch by her daddy. "You *know* how she is. Actually. . . ." Lily looked over toward where the hall disappeared out of the light and ran in the direction of the ears of Marie Jones. Then, as if conspiring with Virgil Lee, she leaned in closer to him. "You know she *always* wants me to be doing something connected to school!"

"I do know *that!*" Virgil conceded.

"I was just trying to keep her happy. Actually, Tollie and I need to go downtown. They're trying to start up a Teen Fellowship down at the YMCA. I think it's a real good idea. But you know Mamma. She's *so* afraid I'm going to end up a 'Holy Roller' . . . That's *her* word, not mine."

"Well," Virgil said. "That puts it in a different light. I still can't let you have the Oldsmobile. Much as I'd like to." He nodded quickly at Tollie, as if to commend her for the YMCA, then he looked back at Lily. "When things pick up at the Mill, I'm going to buy you one of those new little Larks. Then we won't have to fight about transportation. If you play your cards right."

"That's sweet, Daddy," Lily said, giving Tollie a wink. Tollie looked away quickly, back at "Rawhide." Lily!

"I'd still have to put some restrictions on it, though," Virgil said thoughtfully. "Give girls too much freedom, and the Good Lord will get you your reward."

"That's probably true," Lily said. "But until then, there's where we need to go tonight."

"I could drop you off at the YMCA, no trouble. If you could be ready to go in five minutes."

"We're ready now," Lily said.

"How you going to get home?" Virgil asked.

"Oh, somebody'll give us a ride," Lily said. "There'll be a lot of kids there with cars. We might go out for a milkshake or something after, though. We might not be home till later on."

"Where?" Virgil said suspiciously.

"Don't worry, Daddy!" Lily exploded. Tollie knew Lily could be humble just so long. She guessed that was probably her saving grace, in the long run. "Just don't worry," Lily said again. "We're not going to *dance*. Sometimes I can't believe the Primitive Baptists live in the twentieth-century, much less what's almost nineteen-hundred-and-sixty."

"Watch it," Virgil said dangerously.

"We'll be home as early as we can," Tollie said, trying to head off a disaster, which she was already prepared to sustain. At least one, maybe two or three disasters, before it was tomorrow.

"That's right," Lily said, faking a meek tone. Tollie knew she was seething, and again, she herself was touched. Who would have thought Lily Jones would humble herself not once, but twice within five minutes?

"We'll be home as early as we can, Daddy. I'm sorry I lost my temper." Lily gave Virgil a sweet smile. "I'm just so anxious to get to this meeting. With some good wholesome Teens."

God, Tollie thought. She's going to push our luck.

"Primitive Baptists don't live in the twentieth-century," Virgil said, getting to his feet and digging into his pocket for the car-keys. "That's why we call ourselves Primitives. We go back to the Fundamentals. Let's go."

"Let us run to the bathroom first," Lily said.

"I thought y'all were ready."

"It'll just take a minute. Come on, Tollie. They might not even have a girl's bathroom at the YMCA."

"I hadn't thought of that," Virgil said. "Go on."

"Do you know how far we're going to have to walk to get from the YMCA to B Street?" Tollie asked nervously once they were in the bathroom, Lily primping at the mirror. "And how *are* we going to get home?"

"We'll just have to take a cab, I reckon," Lily said.

"I've only got the fifty dollars she wants," Tollie said, beginning to cry. "All I borrowed from Arlene, my piddling money from Kresge's and babysitting, and not a penny extra. I don't see how I'm going to survive this. I can't walk back here after a thing like that."

Lily gave her hair a final smoothing. She opened the narrow linen closet that was built—grudgingly, it seemed to Tollie—into the wall near the bathtub. It was crammed with the Mill's mistakes, towels and washcloths and bathmats: the one thing that everybody who worked at the Mill had in abundance, if they were shrewd at all, which Virgil Lee Jones always had been, about some things. Tollie watched Lily reach back behind the towels and bring out a large Belk's box.

"Everything they don't want their Little Girl to know about is right in here," Lily whispered. She put the toilet-seat cover down, set the box on it and took its top off. Tollie could see the dark rubber of Marie's douche bag, a gray book printed with black letters, "Marital Happiness for Christian Couples." There were other things too, but she couldn't make them out. What was Lily up to?

Lily reached under the douche bag—"Look at that thing," she whispered. "It looks like somebody's diseased internal organ!" She brought up a thick yellowed envelope, peered inside and took out a twenty dollar bill.

"Lily!" Tollie whispered.

"Shut up," Lily said. "It's for the goddam collection plate. It's for me having to collect all his holy-roller shit for a dozen years and carry it around inside, like my head's a septic tank. In fact—" Lily took another twenty out of the envelope. She gave Tollie a look that warned her not to say anything. "Let them think the Holy Ghost has been here, fumbling around in their old secret Belk's box while they were sleeping. I don't care what they think right now. I don't have any faith that they *can* think, either one of them!"

"I just want to get this over, survive, and forget it," Tollie said wearily. "So I can get ready to help Mamma."

Lily looked at her. "Wait here," she said, slipping out of the bathroom with the money hidden in her fist.

She was back in less than a minute, something still in her fist. "Turn around," she said to Tollie. Tollie turned her back toward Lily. "Hold up your hair," Lily said.

"What are you up to now," Tollie said, but she held her hair up off her neck. She felt Lily's hands move under her chin, then back, fastening the clasp.

"Wear my Lonely Teardrop," Lily said. "For luck."

The houses along B Street were low and mean-looking, Tollie thought. Lower and more mean-looking than the houses in her neighborhood. The street itself, red-clay ruts full of dangerous debris, was worse than her street. The night was cold. At least the clay had hardened. Tollie was glad they didn't have to watch out for mud, counting even the smallest blessings as she walked: no mud, she had a warm coat. She'd found out about Madame Lucretia, she'd made some money at Kresge's, Arlene had helped her, she wouldn't have to drop out of school, she wasn't walking down B Street alone.

Somewhere, behind them, she could hear the Cape Fear River moving along in the dark, washing away who knew what from Hope Mills and carrying it to the clean anonymous ocean. For a minute, she tried to think of the thing that was going to happen to her that way. Just something being washed away, invisible and unknowable in the dead of night, toward the clean tides that would take it in without noting it. Then it would be . . . relocated. Changed into something else. It would still be, something, somewhere. But it would have no known history, and in relation to herself it would be: gone. As if it had never been. Could it be?

The houses were dark, with only an occasional window—so low it looked like it was almost on the ground—glowing its oil lamp glow. There were no electricity poles anywhere, just tall trees. Dark pines with no smell and the bare skeletons of sourwoods and hawthorns and other scrub-trees. Scraggly black locusts, the only trees that still had their leaves, soaring into the sky. From time to time, big balls of what had to be mistletoe appeared, far above in the tallest limbs. The sky was unnaturally brilliant: starlight and moonlight so abundant it didn't seem like night at all. But it is, Tollie thought. This is Night, I'm in Negrotown. I'm on B Street, in a B Movie: Tollie and Lily Meet the Creature.

"Do you ever stop and reflect on how we got into a goddam situation like this," Lily grumbled. "Some old dog or Jigaboo is likely to hop right out of the shadows any minute. Making things worse. I could shoot Daddy. How are we going to get a cab from down here? I don't see a phone-pole one."

"First things first," Tollie said.

"My-my, you *are* getting philosophical."

"Don't bicker with me tonight, Lily. For once? I'm just not up to it."

Lily stuffed her hands in her pockets and clammed up. Tollie knew she was contrite. If not, she'd have got in the last word. Story of their lives.

As they walked, the trees loomed directly overhead, and in the distance too, Tollie observed, so that you almost forgot about the houses when you took the long view. The pines grew into their narrow points at the top and disappeared, and the locusts grew the opposite way: they shot up and fanned out irregularly, widest at their tops. They were like African trees. She had seen the African trees in a grainy educational-movie back in grade school, "Light Comes to the Dark Continent." It was all about Dr. Stanley and Dr. Livingstone, Cecil Rhodes of Rhodesia, diamonds and safari hunts, the distribution of medical supplies and Bibles to the tribes, and treasures saved from the Africans for the great museums of the Western World. She remembered the gray skull shape of Africa displayed on the screen. While a deep voice narrated facts and opinions, lines snaked across the skull like veins until it was covered: the Rivers. She'd memorized them all for extra credit.

Tollie moved down the rutted street reciting the names of the Rivers of Africa like a charm: the Congo, the Nile, the Niger, the Orange, the Congo, the Nile. . . . It was on the Serengeti Plain (the Spaghetti Plain, her teacher had joked) that the camera had lingered: on the exotic trees soaring up and angling out at the tops against the white space of the sky: the Light. The Congo, the Nile, the Niger. The Bani.

Her teeth were chattering. Like a Halloween skeleton's, a spook's, she thought. Spooks. A name some people used for Negroes. Others were Coon, Darky. Buck, Wench, and Pickaninny. Black-Ass. Burr-Head. Jigaboo. Weren't there any friendly names? Her mind was blank of them, she was so scared. Spook, Darky. There were Aunt and Uncle. There were Boy and Gal. High Yella. Her fate was going to be in the hands of somebody who'd been battered with names all her life by somebody who looked a lot like Tollie Ramsey. How would Madame Lucretia feel about that? Did she take pride in her work and try to do a good job, no matter what? Or did she want revenge, for "just this once" something to go wrong? And how had she, Tollie Ramsey, a 15-year-old girl who had nothing to do with History that she knew of, find herself answering for History on a cold white night near the end of 1959?

A Negro woman might be her Salvation: She's got the whole world in her hands. Or a Negro woman might be her death, as in You'll be the death of me. You'll be the death of me yet. Catch your death. The White Nile, the Blue Nile, the Niger, the Serengeti Plain.

"Oh," Tollie said, jerking her hands out of her coat pockets and throwing them in front of her, catching herself on them just before the rest of her hit the ground. Her hands were flaming with pain.

"What happened?" Lily said.

Tollie picked herself up and straightened her coat. "I fell. I guess I stepped in one of these ruts."

"It's bright as day out here," Lily said indignantly. "Watch where you're going. Like I do." Lily looked around. "It ought to be somewhere around here. Are you all right?"

"Yes," Tollie said. But she wasn't. She wasn't ever going to be all right again.

She rubbed her hands on the wool of her coat and put them back in her pockets, moving them to rest over where the baby was sleeping, unaware. Unaware that its own mother was hoping, even as she was picking herself up off the ground, that she'd knocked it loose, that it would die any minute and slide down and out, anonymous in a whoosh of blood, gone and to be forgot.

"These houses all look alike," Lily said. "How are you supposed to tell which is which? She's supposed to have a sign out, but I haven't seen it."

Tollie couldn't talk. She might break her chattering teeth.

"How do people live in these things?" Lily said. "They don't look tall enough to stand up in."

It was true. Tollie looked at the houses. They looked like the above-ground tombs of a few rich families in the Hope Mills Cemetery. Some people could wait for eternity, dead, in a house as big as another person or whole family had to live in all their days. There were sheds out back of the tomb-houses of B Street, and slanted toilets, coops which were probably full of sleeping chickens. Which, in turn, were full of eggs, like she herself was. She could think of it that way, maybe: she was going to lay an egg. With some help from a woman of another race, she was going to inhabit, for a while, another species. Not mammal, but fowl. Foul. Foul is fair and fair is Foul. Egg on your face. Lay an egg.

Tollie watched her shadow collect underneath her in the bright blue moonlight, like a puddle. Why couldn't things have been set up that way for girls and women in the first place? Why couldn't female humans just lay an egg and choose whether to sit on it or not sit on it? Why should chickens have it so easy and Tollie Ramsey have it so hard? Nature and History both out to get her. . . . The Lualaba, the Zambezi, the Kwango, the Wami, the Bomokandi.

Actually, the houses looked more like boats than houses or tombs, the rutted street like a river in waves. The houses were like barges on the Blue Nile, she thought, stiffening her lips against her teeth to protect them. Probably one room, no more than two, one right behind the other. They were "narrow houses," Tollie thought, recollecting the piece of a poem which everybody memorized in seventh grade. She was going to a narrow house, maybe "*the* narrow house," too. She couldn't distract herself from it: she could die tonight, with the stars and moon shining brighter than ever to light her way to wherever she was going.

Where would she be going? With a thing like this on her record? She would never, ever believe in Hell. Or a Heavenly Home, like the church promised: you and God hanging around in Greek-looking clothes, with nothing to talk about, now that you'd got Heaven out of him. She might believe in Paradise. A beautiful place with exceptional trees and flowers and water, where she would exist like ether, with no body and no pain. Moving softly through the warm air. Mingling soundlessly with the ether that was her dead brother and her own little blood-streaked egg of a baby. Her Uncle Buddy and all the War Heroes, her rose-scented Grandmother, Buddy Holly and The Big Bopper, Eva Bledsoe. Just drifting along, waiting for . . . her Mother, she realized. Tollie pulled her coat tighter around her. Then all of them would be ether together for eternity, indistinguishable, vapor. Or maybe light. Or maybe not, maybe nothing at all.

"There it is," Lily said.

There it was. The big red hand that you saw on the advertisements out on the road, painted on white. Except now the hand looked black as night. It rose on a column of wrist and then the fingers splayed out wide. Tollie had stopped in the ruts of B Street, her eyes fixed on the hand of Madame Lucretia's sign. It looked sort of like one of the black locust trees. No. It looked like a black palm, the fingers its fronds.

Palm. A tree. A part of your hand.

"Come on," Lily urged softly from a few feet ahead, where she'd stopped to wait for Tollie. "In an hour we'll be back out here, heading the other way. It's only time."

It sure is different from how I imagined it, Tollie thought, looking around Madame Lucretia's tiny parlor in the soft light from the oil-lamps, realizing at the same moment that she *had* been imagining it, in spite of herself. She'd been thinking of it as a tomb-like place, damp and austere. Instead it was full of color and texture, like nothing she'd ever seen. Arlene had hinted something like that, but Tollie had been too distracted to give it much thought. She wished she had the peace of mind to appreciate it properly. There were interesting fabrics everywhere, cottons and some that were maybe silk, she couldn't tell for sure. They were mostly red with bold foreign-looking designs, like you'd imagine wrapped around a member of a tribe somewhere, or on a magic carpet flying through the sky. They covered walls, tables, pillows, bits of the floor. They were spread across chairs and the sofa where she and Lily were sitting. Most interesting of all, the whole ceiling was covered with fabric. It dipped down over your head so that sitting in the low room was like being in a tent. Like the desert sands of Arabia were shifting around in the wind outside, underneath a blue Oriental moon.

Tollie had felt more and more weird as she'd passed Madame Lucretia's painted hand outside and taken the last steps to the house. The Cape Fear River had seemed like something let loose from a vein, or the Black Lagoon. The moon had appeared to mottle right before her eyes, like some invisible somebody was walking across it, leaving his tracks. The trees had turned spookier, like old Halloween movie trees.

She'd stepped through the door feeling weak. Dis-located from herself, that's how she'd felt. Dis-oriented and dazed—Tollie in 3-D.

Now she was in The Creature's lair. She felt dislocated from the world as she had known it: like she'd left Earth and arrived on a Forbidden Planet. Her senses weren't up to all that was fluttering against them.

The room was too warm from the heat of the wood cookstove, the fabric ceiling billowing too close to the stove's rusty surface for comfort. An iron kettle—Madame Lucretia had just set two more kettles beside it on the stove—was sending steam up into the fabric's folds, releasing a vague, uncategorizable smell. Tollie guessed it must be dye, or accidental spices that had gathered in the cloth as it had waited for somebody to buy it, in a Casbah faraway.

Come with me to the Casbah. Boys used to say that to you in grade school and run off laughing, like they'd got away with something dirty. Maybe they had, Tollie thought, her mind swirling. Maybe the roots of her situation went all the way back to stuff like that, letting them get away with saying Casbah. But how was she to know? She'd looked it up in the dictionary and it only meant the old part of a town. The boys couldn't have known that. It meant whatever they thought it meant, something they thought was dirty, and they used it to make you feel dirty too, while they ran away, free. Where was Ramírez tonight? Even with Lily Jones hot on his tail for the last couple of weeks, he'd been nowhere to be found.

She held onto the sofa's arm and tried to sit up straighter. She was shocked and grateful when Lily gave her hand a hard squeeze, so quick it could almost be denied—that was Lily—but a gesture of undeniable comfort anyway.

Tollie let her eyes roll onto the woman who had just stepped in front of her. I'd been imagining her too, she realized. She'd been imagining her as black-black-black and red-eyed, like something from a movie, a Voodoo queen from an island in the Caribbean or somebody huge and grasping, with no sympathetic feelings, like Bloody Mary in South Pacific. But she wasn't like that at all. She was tall and thin, the color of Sugarbabies candy or the square caramels that came wrapped individually in cellophane. She looked like she could be a model in *Vogue* magazine, if they'd let a Negro woman be that.

She had a smooth, almost citified voice, Tollie had noticed right away. She had been talking to them like they'd come for the hocus-pocus, ever since they'd entered the room. "I'm going to Orient you to the Mysteries of the East," she'd said, giving Tollie a playful look. In spite of how she felt, Tollie had smiled; she liked somebody with a sense of wit. Maybe Madame Lucretia did have powers: how else could she have known that Tollie, not Lily, would understand her jokes? As she'd made them tea ("the magic potion," she'd called it, winking at Tollie), she'd been talking, talking, talking—about the "mysteries," about seeing the past and reading the future. Now she was talking about something that sounded to Tollie like days-of-voo, the words uncharacteristically slurred: Madame Lucretia seemed to speak very precisely, otherwise. I need to see it written down, Tollie thought, straining her ear at it. Even tonight, she wouldn't want any exotic words or phrases to slip by her. Madame Lucretia said it had to do with time beginning to lap over itself. Oh. Lily's *déjà vu.* Lily said it differently, probably wrong. It was an idea Tollie found interesting, but spooky: she'd been counting on time stretching out in a neat line, if she survived tonight, always a new day. That was one thing in life that could give you hope. But Madame Lucretia said you could suddenly see yourself from the outside and sense yourself inside at the same time and it was like you were somewhere and some time that you'd been before, time and place stirred up together and you repeating yourself and some previous time in your life.

That gave Tollie the creeps. Maybe it was meant to, but why? You'd think Madame Lucretia would be trying to make her calm and relaxed. After all, she—Tollie—was the customer here.

Madame Lucretia's voice was dramatic, and careful enunciation was its most noticeable feature. She said Miss Arr-lene, careful with the "r." She said Or-ri-ent, and Mys-terr-ies.

Tollie watched her set an odd brass pot and two china cups on the table (or box: she couldn't tell) draped with fabric. She acted like they were real company.

"You have to drink it plain," she said to Tollie now. "You can put milk and sugar in yours if you want to," she told Lily. "It needs to sit a minute first."

"I don't want to drink any," Lily said.

"Why not?" Madame Lucretia asked, giving her a wise half-smile and a look. Suddenly she was speaking in a different voice: "Fred it gone start you rockin' and rollin' like a wild voodoo nigger?"

Tollie felt her face burn with the shock. Then it scared her. Under all that talking and winking, her cool tone, Madame Lucretia did

271

have it in for white people. It came through in her voice now and a small hard thing in her eyes. Bitter.

While the tea steeped, Madame Lucretia checked the water on the stove, then got a can of Pet milk out of the cupboard and set it on the table, unopened. Tollie figured she didn't want to waste it if Lily wasn't going to drink her tea. Even with all the elaboration of the house's inside, you could tell life here was a struggle: no electricity, no visible plumbing. Even if you were rich, you probably couldn't get the town to run wires and pipes down to A, B, or C Street, just for you, and there weren't many other areas of town a Negro could live in.

Tollie watched the woman in her movements. She seemed about Janice's age. She was wearing a kimono, the kind you saw for sale in the windows of the pawn shops. Soldiers brought them back from Korea and Japan for their wives and daughters, but they ended up pawned, along with the shiny jackets they'd brought back for their sons, the ones with tigers and dragons on them and "Yokohama" or "Seoul" stitched in bright thread across the back. Madame Lucretia's kimono was deep blue, with gold trim, embroidered with gold thread. Tollie found herself staring at the embroidery. Over and over, the thread made the image of a stunted tree that grew out, not up. Its stylized branches were warped and twisted. Yet there was something pleasing abut it. Tollie stared at the tree that lay flat on Madame Lucretia's almost-flat chest. The stunted thing was beautiful after all, Tollie decided. Was that because it was displayed in gold thread? Would such a thing look beautiful in the real world? Tollie blinked her eyes to refocus them on the whole woman in the kimono. Who could say?

You couldn't see Madame Lucretia's hair. It was pulled back under a turban. She reminded Tollie of something out of long ago: Ava Gardner in "The Snows of Kilimanjaro," which Les had taken them all to see, thinking it would be more about Great White Hunters shooting exotic African animals than it had turned out to be. It seemed like Ava Gardner had worn something like a kimono, something like a turban, but they were pink, or flesh-colored.

White-flesh-colored, that is, Tollie thought, questioning the phrase for the first time in her life. She'd never been in a Negro person's house before.

"Why are you got up like that?" Lily said rudely. "Why have you hung all these rags all over the place? It's like a carnival in here. I keep expecting you to take off that robe and have a man's body, or a snake's."

272

"I might," Madame Lucretia said coolly. "You'd better be careful."

"People expect it, right?" Tollie said.

"They do!" Madame Lucretia said, pleased with the perception. "This and more."

Unlike the Ava Gardner Tollie thought she remembered from the movie, Madame Lucretia wore big loops dangling from her ears and, incredibly, she was wearing a gold charm bracelet, Tollie noticed. It jangled happily as she held Tollie's steaming cup out toward her—jingled like it was attached to the cheerful movements of any high school girl. When Tollie took the tea cup from the woman's long hand, she noticed that its palm was pale as her own, but in the odd light of the room, it seemed etched with dark lines. Like the Negro in her, coming out, Tollie thought, before she thought. It was a figure of speech she'd heard used all her life. It surprised her to hear herself think it in such a literal way, like Madame Lucretia's black blood was seeping out of her hands. Which wasn't very literal after all, she didn't guess, since nobody really had black blood. Mostly people said that about behavior: That's the nigger coming out in you.

Tollie pondered this while she blew on her tea and Madame Lucretia squabbled a little with Lily—anything to distract herself from why she found herself enfolded in Madame Lucretia's red room. People said That's the nigger coming out about white people, behind their backs; or they teased them to their faces, if they liked them. They said it about and to Negroes, sometimes teasing them too, if they liked them. Negroes said it to each other. She'd heard Negro women scold their children that way. She'd also heard Negroes use it to tease each other, if they liked each other, and if they didn't.

She looked up at Madame Lucretia's creamy face. The woman was smiling down on her a little, maybe sympathetic, or maybe perplexed, she couldn't tell.

"Drink it all now," Madame Lucretia said. Her hand was still in the air in front of Tollie, gracefully poised inches from her face. Tollie could see that the charms on the bracelet were not gold after all. Most were plastic or gold-painted metal, hearts and crosses, adjustable diamond-rings, little spinning discs, Cracker Jack things.

She looked back at the woman's interesting palm. People said that was how it was hard for Negroes to pass for white. The dark creases of their palms would give them away. So would "something" in their eyes, and the tattle-tale kink close to the scalp where their straightened hair was being pushed away from the emerging true hair. Madame Lucretia's palm lines looked like she'd drawn them on, on purpose, with black ink, like the lines in her advertisement. She was a pretty woman, Tollie decided. She actually looked a lot like Ava Gardner, now that she thought about it. Who was rumored to be part-Negro after she'd gone out in public with Sammy Davis, Jr. The pictures and the story were all over Lily's movie magazines. It was funny: once that rumor was started, you could look at a picture of Ava Gardner and begin to see the evidence, whether or not it was true. The seed had been planted. Your attention couldn't help going to her full lips and curly hair, to the "something" in her eyes with their gold-tinted irises.

Tollie took a sip of her tea. It didn't taste too bad, but it was unfamiliar, with a bitter after-taste. She looked up at Madame Lucretia, but the woman wasn't looking at her anymore. Just then, she moved away, still looking at some obscure point in the room, which told you she was thinking about something. Maybe she was preoccupied with the future, Tollie thought, which she must live with night and day. Even if you couldn't see the future, which she didn't believe Madame Lucretia necessarily could, if it was your business, it must give you a strange perspective on life.

"What do you think this is?" Tollie whispered to Lily.

"God knows," Lily said. Her cup was still sitting on the table. Lily seemed to be drifting off into thought too, Tollie observed. She felt like she was in the tent by herself, but she felt calmer. The tea seemed to be having that kind of effect. She gave into it and waited for instructions, trying to keep her mind off the immediate future, inching nearer moment to moment.

The magazines said Ava Gardner was ruining her reputation and career . . . worse, even, than Ingrid Bergman had ruined hers with bastard children. Abandoning her nice blond doctor for a dark Italian that wasn't even goodlooking, throwing away her life on the silver screen. Ingrid had been exiled to the half-life of Europe, until America forgave her. Ava was exiled to the half-life of Spain. America would never forgive her, not for Sammy Davis, Jr.

Why in the world am I thinking of movie stars at a time like this? Tollie wondered. I feel so weird.

She sipped the bitter tea.

"It will make you drift some," Madame Lucretia said. "That's all. It will make it easier."

Madame Lucretia picked up the other cup and held it out to Lily, smirking a little. It was an elegant smirk, Tollie decided.

"You might want to drift some too," the woman said to Lily. "For the fun of it."

"What is it?" Lily said warily.

"Fred it ol' chicken blood?" Madame Lucretia teased, shifting into Negro-talk again. Tollie could see that Lily brought out something in the woman, all right.

"I'm not afraid of a goddam thing on this earth," Lily said, taking the tea cup.

"Horse-*shit*. You fred o' the tea, fred o' the cup, and the spoon, that they been nigger-lipped. That's a saying y'all use, ain't it—'nigger-lipped?'"

"Well, we don't mean *that*," Lily said indignantly. "It just has to do with cigarettes."

Madame Lucretia laughed, tilting her head back. Tollie found herself trying to look inside her mouth, for a gypsy's gold tooth. She couldn't see one. Where was her crystal ball? She didn't see one of those either. She felt like she was drifting along Heaven's own shore, or Hell's.

"A white person gets white spit all over a white cigarette," Madame Lucretia was saying, in her ironic voice. "And that's called nigger-lipped. I get it."

"Why don't you just do what we came for," Lily said.

"I'm waiting for you ladies to finish your nice tea," Madame Lucretia said. "I'm just being po-lite. Isn't that how you like us to talk, po-lite?"

"I don't like you to talk at all," Lily said, taking a quick sip at the cup. "This tastes like shit." She set the cup back on the table.

"How would you know, now? I don't think you could taste too much with your mouth that far away from my nigger-lipped cup."

"I don't owe you anything," Lily said furiously.

"Lily," Tollie said woozily. All she needed was for Lily to tick off somebody who held her fate in her hands.

"Fred the milk's sour," Madame Lucretia said, walking over to a curtain made of the magic-carpet fabric, strung over the doorway to another room. "Fred it ain't pasteurized. Or it's from nigger cows. Fred the sugar ain't really sugar, or it's dirty sugar. You even think a nigger's dog is more of a dog than a dog. You can't tell me nothing I don't know already about white people. You 'bout ready?" she asked Tollie.

"I'm going outside to smoke," Lily said, getting up. "I don't want to set the place on fire. At least not till we're finished with what we came here for."

"Lily?" Tollie said. Was she going to have to walk the last few inches alone after all?

Lily hesitated. "I can't stay in here with you, Tollie. It wouldn't do either one of us any good."

Tollie felt Lily bending down near her. She felt Lily's hard lips swipe her forehead. "I'm sorry," Lily whispered. "Good luck."

"Sit yourself down," Madame Lucretia said to Tollie. They were in the kitchen now, which looked like an ordinary poor person's kitchen. Oil-cloth-covered table, two wooden chairs, a cupboard and a wash-stand with two big aluminum wash bowls on top, also on oil cloth. The only un-expected things were a small day-bed in one corner, covered with a dark blanket, and some galvanized water buckets—six or seven, Tollie couldn't count straight any longer—lined up, full of water, on the floor by the wall. There were several stacks of newspaper on the floor by the day-bed.

Tollie sat down in one of the chairs at the table. The oil cloth was covered with chickens, rooster-and-two-hens, over and over.

"How do you feel?" Madame Lucretia said. She sat down across from Tollie. She was doing something with her hands. It took Tollie a few seconds to realize that she was shuffling cards and had begun to lay them out on the table.

"A little drunk," Tollie said. "What was in that stuff?"

"Cotton root, mostly. Black locust seed-pods, belladonna, and rue, as in rue-the-day, which I guess you already do."

"I do," Tollie said. "With all my heart. I wish I could lie down over there." She inclined her head a little toward the day-bed. She felt so tired.

"First I have to read your palm. That's already paid for. Then I need to read your cards. You owe me fifty dollars for that."

Tollie stared at the woman's wavering face. "Oh," Tollie said. She took the money, two twenties and a five, four ones and a dollar in change, out of her skirt pocket and put it on the table.

"Give me your hands," the woman said.

Tollie put out her hands and Madame Lucretia took them in hers, turning them over to consult the palms.

"I see that they need a bath," she said.

"I fell," Tollie said.

Madame Lucretia got up and wet a cloth, bent in front of Tollie and washed her burning hands, the bracelet jingling like the sleigh bells on tv this time of year. Tollie couldn't see any signs of Christmas in Madame Lucretia's house, just like there hadn't been any anywhere on B Street, except for the natural-growing mistletoe. . . .

Suddenly Madame Lucretia seemed maternal. Her forehead wrinkled with concentration as she wiped at the cuts from Tollie's fall, evaluating their characteristics as though she was at her usual work of predicting things to come—"This one's going to get infected, you don't watch it," "This one might leave you a scar." She almost cooed her predictions, soothing you with the bad luck to come. Madame Lucretia, who spoke in tongues, out of her own complicated situation, Tollie guessed.

"I've got some cura-crome," she said finally, standing up and moving toward the cupboard.

Tollie smiled. In spite of the citified voice, certain things still slipped in from the past, unnoticed by the woman. It was like Janice, the way she'd say "frigidaire" for refrigerator.

Tollie sat quietly while the woman treated the cuts on her hands with Mercurachrome, tracing it on with a piece of cloth wrapped around a small stick of some kind. Tollie's palms looked lurid when she was done. Their true lines had receded, invisible behind her wounds, which were invisible under the blood-colored lines of the cure. This is worse than any movie I ever saw, Tollie thought woozily.

Madame Lucretia took up one of the hands. "I see you 'bout two months a-long." Tollie saw that Madame Lucretia was looking at her sharply, the dialect a ruse to disarm her. But it didn't disarm her. Tollie nodded and looked the woman straight in the eye. That's what Arlene said she'd have to do. That if Madame Lucretia knew how long it had been, she wouldn't do it.

"Then I see a rosy future for you, as you people like to say." She smiled broadly and put Tollie's hand down. "Let me read you your cards."

She turned over the bright cards and spoke quickly, perfunctorily— "I see you climbing every mountain," she said cryptically. "Fording every stream. Following every rainbow. Or as many as you can see, and in your own way."

She looked at Tollie and smiled quickly, then looked back down at her cards. She turned over another, then another.

"Is there any future for somebody like me?" Tollie half-whispered before she could stop herself. She could feel the tears starting up again. She'd been so emotional, every since her body got in this condition. She shut her eyes against the tears. She felt the Lonely Teardrop on her chest, imagined it shimmering in the oil-lamps' light, like it was a sign—of herself and her life and her future: Here's Tollie Ramsey, Past and Future, right here.

She could hear Madame Lucretia putting the cards down on the table, the jingling of her bracelet. Tollie opened her eyes. Madame Lucretia was looking into her face. The woman reached out and picked up one of her wounded hands, but she didn't look at the palm.

"I see you making the best of a bad lot," she said. "I see you as a girl with resources. . . ." She looked deep into Tollie's eyes, as if they were crystal balls. She spoke softly. "Unordinary riches, that's what you have, even if you don't know it yet. I could tell it the minute you came in the house. Unordinary riches, in your mind and in your heart."

"But how am I going to get through life," Tollie asked. "I feel like *everything* I have is inside myself. That nothing's coming from outside but junk, nothing to help me along and guide me. I always counted on that. And now, even people who might have loved me, a little, have been dropping away from me. Like rats jumping from a sinking ship."

"Don't worry. Rats can't swim that well," Madame Lucretia said with a little smile. "Your friend out there stuck by you. That's something. Love will come back to you, when you least expect it. Love does that. Kindness can crop up too, the Mystery of the East, West, North, and South, since it seems like Nature could take its course without it, pretty much. And you ought to remind yourself, every day, that in this world there is *good* luck. It falls where it falls, like the stars from the sky, favoring no one place over the other."

She was gripping Tollie's hand, her charm bracelet making a racket. It hurt. "Nobody, no-body, rich or poor, black or white, has a say in it—no say where those lucky stars will fall to earth and scatter their miracle dust!"

She let go of Tollie's hand. "Not that it's equally distributed. But almost everybody gets a little bit, sooner or later. Otherwise, you've just got to do for yourself, the best you can."

She was leaning back in her chair. Tollie knew she wasn't talking to her, especially, any longer. "We all got imagination when God passed out the brains. Inside, with all that shit, we can clear out a little patch and make it just like we want it, make it Paradise. There is the grace of God, giving you that ability. It can save your life."

"It can become your life," Tollie said groggily. "My friend outside is a good example of that." But she was pleased to see she and Madame Lucretia thought along some of the same lines.

"It's the grace of God from above," Madame Lucretia said firmly. "Imagination is. Trans-portation itself." Quickly and expertly, she gathered her cards into a pile, stacked them neatly and emphatically and set them in the middle of the table. She stood up, everything suddenly efficient. "I think my water must be boiled by now. You can lay down over there. Put some of that newspaper down under you, all right?"

She went back through the curtain and then carried in two of the kettles. Tollie went to where the newspapers were stacked. She picked up several and spread them out, trying to concentrate on their headlines, the news of the world outside herself, moments of time that had already passed her by. Castro Seizes Havana . . . Dalai Lama Flees Tibet . . . Lunik II Hits Moon . . . Girlfriend Mum on Errol Flynn Death . . . Migrant Workers Killed in Truck-Bus Mishap. . . .

Mishap. Hap meant luck. She'd learned a poem about it for class. Mishap. To miss luck? Un-luck? It was going to hurt. It was going to have consequences. She could feel it in the air, in the queerly spiced air of the narrow house.

She slipped off her loafers, relieved to see that she'd walked the clay off of them on the way here and wouldn't have to hear Madame Lucretia say her shoes needed a bath, like her Lady MacBeth hands. There wouldn't be any way to do a thing like this without it hurting a whole lot. Hurt your body, hurt your heart for life. Mishap. To miss luck. She was lying down now, her hands holding each other. They felt like they were on fire.

"You need to take off your underpants," Madame Lucretia said. She was as calm and efficient now as any nurse or doctor, the moment of her kind prophecy gone as if it had never been.

Tollie got up and slipped her underpants off and put them on top of her loafers. She lay back down.

Madame Lucretia had filled the pan with hot water. She had laid a towel on one of the chairs.

"How do you do it?" Tollie asked: the question she'd put out of her mind for days. "Do I drink something?" she said hopefully.

Madame Lucretia laughed a little on her way to the cupboard. "Wouldn't that be something. Do you feel like Alice in Wonderland? Don't worry. It's not a clotheshanger."

"Where'd you learn?" Tollie asked.

Madame Lucretia paused, her hand on the cupboard's knob. Tollie saw that she'd removed her bracelet. "Do you mean, where did I go to *medical* school?"

"No, I didn't mean that. I didn't mean anything by asking."

"I learned it in New York City," Madame Lucretia said, taking something out of the cupboard. "Where I went to be a singer and dancer, like Josephine Baker. Rode as far as New Jersey with a truck-load of migrant niggers, bribed the driver with all my cottonpicking money from down here, and a little something else he wanted, to let me out before they got to the place they were going. I *walked* across the bridge to New York in the dead of night, like I was a Displaced Person or a wetback Mexican. But mainly I ended up in the garment district, sewing."

"Is that where you got all your fabric?"

"Every bit of it. I stole it a yard or two or three at a time. By the end, I had a *little* of what I had coming to me, but not much."

"Did you ever sing and dance?" Tollie asked. Anything to keep her mind off the longest needle she'd ever seen, now in Madame Lucretia's hand. Tollie closed her eyes.

"Me and about a million other nigger-gals. I danced in a club, with men. That was my night job. You know, dime-a-dance? One of them gave me more than I bargained for and the woman who helped me out taught me how to do it. She was a nurse, but it was hard to get that work too, if you were a nigger-gal."

"Why did you come back here?" Anything to slow the woman's progress to the day-bed.

"My mamma got sick. She was already taking care of two of my kids, two of my dead sister's kids. I came on back home and took care of my mamma till she died. Right here in this house. Then it was too late to go back to trying to be Josephine Baker. I saw the future. So I stuck my palm up out there and got on with life. I sell a little bit of about everything folks take it in their minds to want, I guess. That you can't get at the store."

"Where are your kids now?"

"Grown. Your age. One married a soldier and is living in Europe. The other one's living with some drunk out on a tenant farm, picking tobacco and the last little bit of cotton that it looks like they're ever going to grow around here. You can't tell how life is going to go."

"You sure can't," Tollie said. Tollie watched Madame Lucretia reach back into the cupboard, then closed her eyes. "Is it a shot?" she asked, keeping her eyes squeezed shut. Then the mercurial voice was right by the day-bed.

"My nurse-friend sends the stuff down every month. She gets it from a doctor, along with some other stuff I need." Madame Lucretia laughed her low, ironic laugh. "I call the packages my monthlies."

"Do you give it in my arm or my hip?" Tollie asked.

"I give it where it's got to go. And even then I got to help things along some."

Tollie opened her eyes and looked up at her, not looking near the needle. "How do you feel about . . . your work?" she asked. She couldn't imagine doing this for a living, like she couldn't imagine people who pulled the switch for the electric chair or killed dogs at the County Pound.

"I like it better than laying on my back, or sewing for pennies," Madame Lucretia said matter of factly. "I like it better than ironing and cooking in somebody's hot kitchen and wiping up the dirt from their floors and off their babies' behinds. I've got to do something. I can't make a living by telling the future to poor niggers and a few crazy white women."

"Can you?"

"Tell the future? Why, *shore*! That's how y'all like us to say it, ain't it: Why, *shore*!" She gave Tollie one of her terrible looks. Tollie thought maybe she had one of those split personalities, like Eve White and Eve Black in the movie.

"I'll talk any way people want. I aim to please. A satisfied customer is a customer who'll come back. That was what my boss said when I dime-a-danced. He was right about that."

"I won't be coming back," Tollie said. Madame Lucretia was drawing something out of a vial and into the long needle. Tollie noticed that she'd tied an apron over her kimono. "I don't have to know how to tell the future to know that," Tollie said.

"I hope you won't," Madame Lucretia said. "But then again, I'm always happy to see an old customer."

"I don't know how you do it," Tollie said.

"Why, little white girl, don't you worry." Madame Lucretia was standing at the side of the day-bed now, smiling down on Tollie, not unkindly, but not kindly either. "Nigger-gals been doing dirty work for white women a *long* time."

"She's bleeding too much," Madame Lucretia was saying to Lily. "She's not supposed to bleed much till tomorrow. Not much is supposed to happen till tomorrow."

"You mean when you're out of the picture?" Lily said. "That's nice. You better know how to fix whatever's gone wrong here. Tollie? Tollie?" Lily bent over the daybed, shaking Tollie's shoulder.

"Lily?" Tollie looked up at Lily. She felt weak. She felt like she was breaking in half, down there. She could feel the sticky blood on her legs, seeping out from around the towel Madame Lucretia had put there, like a giant Kotex.

"You sure she's not more than two months gone?"

"It's been since summer!" Lily said.

"Lily. . . ." Tollie grabbed at Lily's hand.

"Then she lied," Madame Lucretia said. "I guess that's one of those white lies? Well, you get her out of my damn house, right now. I'm not going to jail over some white girl's white lie."

She bent down and looked at Tollie's eyes, studying them. She looked furious, her eyes empty of all sympathetic feeling, her nostrils flared with outrage. A clump of hair had escaped the turban and lay on her forehead, thick as moss and black as night. "She ain't going to die," she said to Lily. "If I thought she was, I'd kill her, and you too, cut you up like chickens. I ain't going to jail for no white-girls. Get her out of my damn house."

"She can't walk like that," Lily said. "I need to call a taxicab."

285

"No you ain't. If she can look me in the damn eye and lie, then cry about *her* troubles, telling a lie that could get me more trouble than I need, she can walk out of here. Get her out, or I'll cut you both up, chicken parts, I mean it."

Tollie tried to get up, failed, tried again. Madame Lucretia had her by the top of one arm. Her face was dark in its emotion. She pulled Tollie up and started pulling her toward the door. The bloody towel had fallen on the floor, like a babe in swaddling clothes. "Lily. . . ."

"At least give her something to catch the blood with!" Lily yelled. Tollie knew Lily was close to panic. She herself felt vague, propelled along, a ball of pain, disagreeable in its liquifying texture.

"You tell anybody, I'll come in the night and finish things, I mean it." Madame Lucretia threw a towel at Lily. Then Lily was squatting, bunching up the towel inside Tollie's underpants, helping her step inside them and pull them up under her bloody skirt.

"Look at this mess," Madame Lucretia smirked. "White blood, indeed!"

Lily led Tollie into the living room and helped her put on her coat. Tollie submitted to Lily's ministrations. Madame Lucretia's fabrics were blazing all around, like the flames of Hell.

"I'm sorry," Tollie said weakly to Madame Lucretia. "I didn't know anything else to do. It took a long time to find out about you."

"You blab it and you're done. I mean it. I done had all I can take from white people with one white lie after another one. I'm going to cut somebody up, I mean it."

"You old nigger!" Lily yelled as soon as she and Tollie had crossed the threshold and stepped into the dirt of the yard.

"I come get you like some old boogie man, I mean it, white girls. Tell that bitch Ah-lene she better not never come down here again, even to get her goddam fortune told."

A couple houses down, where there was a vacant lot, Lily helped Tollie sit down. "You stay put. I'll get back up to Ruffin Street and find a pay phone. You got to go to see a doctor."

"Call Raeford," Tollie said weakly. "At least he's discreet. I didn't go through all this to ruin my reputation. He's in the book under Rowen's name."

"Would he be home on a Friday night?"

"Then talk to Rowen himself. I guess he must owe me something. He's discreet too."

Tollie leaned back against a little mound of earth and watched Lily disappear in the direction of Ruffin Street. The Cape Fear River was coursing faster than it had been, it seemed like. Like blood running out, time running out.

Tollie reached under her coat and skirt and pushed the towel tighter against her, clamping her legs. Her hand was sticky when she put it in her pocket and laid it flat on her belly. Was it still in there or was it flying toward Heaven, a little angel on little wings? She wiped at her tears, forgetting the mess on her hand. When she licked her lips, she tasted the iron-taste, the baby's blood on her hands.

The moon had dimmed since they'd gone inside, and it had shifted its angle. A pine tree cast a shadow over the top of Madame Lucretia's sign, rising above her barge of a house. You couldn't even see the fingers.

The last thing Tollie saw as she slipped along the edge of something, toward slipping over, was the sign: the long wrist rising up to a hand with hidden fingers, a black fist.

3: New Year's Eve

In the kitchen, Tollie was washing collards, shaking them off and then laying them out on the counter, on a newspaper covered by three of her dead grandmother's tea towels that she'd found deep in a drawer. The towels were trimmed in rickrack and embroidered, one with roses, one with chickens, one with a dainty steaming teapot. Which nobody in Whiteville or Hope Mills would have had a use for, Tollie observed. Tea was a summer drink that you made in quantity. You just steeped it in a big pot, let the sugar melt in it, and poured it into pitchers with ice. Well. She guessed those things, cozy teapots and such, had a life of their own, in the lives of women, nothing you could do about it. She herself thought the towels were nice. It was hard to believe a woman would take such pains for a kitchen towel. Times sure had changed.

Time. Already it was New Year's Eve. She'd only been back home from the private hospital in Chapel Hill for a few days. Her mother would be getting out of Dix Hill this evening. Alone on their separate Hills, they'd missed Christmas altogether. Think of it.

At least Arlene had put them up a Christmas tree to enjoy late, one of the new artificial ones that until this year you only saw in department stores. "I bought it on sale for nothing," Arlene had said when she'd brought it over, its foil-like needles a hard glitter. "The day after Christmas. You just wait: by next year everybody will want them, paying top dollar. *I* strike while the iron is hot! I got myself one too."

Arlene had decorated the tree with whatever she could find around their house, ribbons and buttons and other "notions," little things

Janice had saved over time. Snowballs made out of the cotton that came in pill bottles, pieces of costume jewelry. The few Christmas cards that had come their family's way (one from Arlene herself, one from Marie, one from Aunt Gracie). Candy canes, some seashells, bows made out of fabric scraps; even—Tollie didn't know how to think about it—Janice's wedding band, tied on with a piece of red grosgrain ribbon.

Arlene had brought over some of the fruitcake her mamma had brought her. Arlene was sweet. She was also nervous: "Don't you tell anybody I told you where to go—you promise?"

Yes, yes, yes, I'll promise anybody anything right about now.

Tollie pinched a yellow spot off a collard leaf. Except for a very few spots, the collards looked perfect. She didn't know why Arlene's had failed when these were so pretty, unless these had been trucked in from some place else, not Hope Mills. These were silvery green, almost the color of money. The water rested on them in unstable beads, iridescent with the last bit of setting sunlight coming in the window over the sink. It was the right time of the year for collards. There had been several frosts, and the leaves would be full of their natural sugar. Sometimes the weather would be so warm near New Year's Day that you had to slip a spoon of sugar into the cooking water to make them taste right. Not this year. Not in *1960*, Tollie thought, full of the idea of a new decade. God. Was she ever going to put 1959 behind her! Try to.

"I'm off," Les said, stepping into the kitchen.

"I wish you'd let me go with you," Tollie said.

"Your mamma wouldn't want you to see her even getting out of that place," Les said firmly. "She'd want you to stay on home and work on the Hoppin' John. We're going to need some luck."

"I think things are looking up," Tollie said carefully, rinsing a leaf the size of a tropical frond.

"I'm going to take your mamma out to dinner. At one of those Angus places. Don't expect us back right away."

"That's a good use of *your* money," Tollie said, eyeing Les sternly.

"I'm going to feed her a big steak," Les declared, unfazed. "She needs to build herself up."

Les turned and started out of the kitchen.

"Get her a big baked potato, too," Tollie said. "With sour cream. And shrimp cocktail. Garlic bread." It was a good use of the money. Not that it was Les's!

Les had let it slip on the way home from Chapel Hill that Janice had told him about the money under the ironing board cover. "Did you know about that?" he'd asked Tollie suspiciously. Yes, Tollie had thought miserably. I thought I was going to burn it up with the iron all summer long. But I didn't know it was enough to pay a hospital bill. And after I had struggled not to even think of using a dollar of it, even in my darkest hour. . . .

"She had a whole stack of it," Les had said. Then he'd added quickly, "I just took what I thought we'd need for your bill, which I judged about right."

"Get her anything she wants," Tollie said to Les's retreating back. "Baked alaska. Crepes suzettes. It's that kind of place, isn't it?" She dried her hands on her clothes and followed him. "I wish we hadn't had to use it for my hospital bill."

"Me too," Les said, stepping over Lucky, who was sleeping in the middle of the floor. Les put on his jacket near the front door. "I should have known her mamma and daddy left her something."

"They had money?" Tollie asked, surprised. That must mean that Aunt Gracie had some money, too. Just yesterday Tollie had opened her aunt's late Christmas card to her alone and pulled out the usual puny dollar—!

At least the card was something pretty to add to that artificial tree, which Tollie had done: a card with a cherub on it.

"Well," Les said. "Compared to somebody like me they did. I wish she could have brought it out a little sooner. The way we've been living."

"Then she wouldn't have had it for an emergency!" Tollie said. "What's wrong with you?"

Les clammed up and searched his pockets for his keys. Tollie felt miserable. She'd blown most all of her mother's pin-money in a swoop. *Now* what stood between them and Fate?

"I just hope you've learned your lesson about soldiers," Les said. "Your reputation is probably safe. We don't know anybody in Chapel Hill."

Les, Tollie thought. He'll never change, no matter what he goes through. Less.

"We don't know anybody in Chapel Hill, and now it looks like we never will," Tollie said. She'd never forget how she'd felt when she woke up the day after that horrible night: *I'm finally in Chapel Hill,* she'd thought. *And I'm in a hospital!*

"Count your blessings," Les said.

"It's okay," Tollie said. "I'm probably not college material anyway. Even if a girl could go to school there."

"I'm off," Les said, reaching for the doorknob.

"Les?"

Les turned toward Tollie.

"Did she say what shock treatments were like?"

"I don't think she remembers much about it," Les said.

Tollie started to cry. When she imagined them putting electricity into Janice's brain, she imagined them imprisoning her mother's head in a hard steel cap, leaving her poor dry hair sticking out. She imagined how pathetic her mother would look, waiting for the pain. It made Tollie think about Caryl Chessman, in Heaven now too, or Hell, with everybody else.

Les touched her shoulder awkwardly. "She don't hold anything against you," Les said. "She told me so. I don't either."

"I'm not crying about that," Tollie said irritably, wiping her eyes with her hands.

"Come on, Boy," Les said to Lucky.

"You're not going to take that old dog?"

Lucky opened an eye.

"I think your mamma would like to see Lucky. Come on, Boy. Let's hit the road."

Lucky half raised up and then sank back to the floor, closing his eyes.

"It's just as well," Tollie told Les. "They'd probably commit him."

After Les was gone, Tollie stood at the sink and looked out, thinking. She supposed that she should count her blessings. She could have bled to death on the way to Chapel Hill, bumping through the night in Raeford's little car. She still hated to think of Raeford's face, grim in the light of the dashboard. Hated to think of the hopes she'd had for herself and that boy, even a little hope after he'd told her they were done with each other, at the restaurant. That was all definitely gone with the wind now. . . .

Count your blessings, girl! What if he hadn't known Randy, who had smoothed the way with the hospital and whoever it was at the hospital who'd advised state officials and law enforcers about her situation. Not that Randy hadn't been rude about it!

"How in the hell are you going to fuck up next, boy?" he'd asked Raeford. Raeford had shrugged and stayed mum, like Tollie was his trouble. "She's bleeding like a stuck pig," Randy had said.

Tollie guessed she *ought* to count her blessings that Randy hadn't made a stuck-pig joke at her expense, that he'd stopped at saying "fuck" in front of her, which pretty much said it all, how much she counted with those people.

She ought to count her blessings that Raeford had done this last favor for her, though he'd made it clear that she wasn't ever to call on him again. "Good luck," he'd said stiffly when the orderly wheeled her off to be examined by the doctor at the hospital. "I'll be gone when you get out of here. Your stepdaddy will have to come pick you up."

Which Les had done. Yep, she had to count her blessings that Les had come and picked her up, that her mother was coming home from Dix Hill, that her mother had had the money to pay her bill, that nobody much in Hope Mills knew about what she'd done, even that a nurse at the private hospital had been able to get the blood out of her only coat.

Lucky came into the kitchen and stood by her leg, licking his muzzle. "They're just collards," Tollie told him. "Nothing a dog eats."

She scratched his hard head. Les did love this old dog.

Les. She'd have to give him *some* credit. He'd come to the hospital to visit her three times on his swing by Dix Hill. He'd brought her a pizza pie, and a little fake leather purse, wrapped awkwardly for Christmas. "Where's my battery radio?" she hadn't been able to resist asking. "I think we ought to stop listening to the radio," Les had said. "It's all bad news. It's going to drive us crazy." There was something to that. And she had appreciated the purse he'd given her. It was a hopeful present. Not that anybody had given Les anything. Had anyone, ever? Tollie wracked her mind for memories of Christmases past, and she couldn't come up with one single memory of Les getting a present. She bet it had been that way his whole life.

He told her he'd bought Janice a nice watch. So what if it was with Janice's own money? Janice should have spent that money on herself anyway.

He'd talked to somebody in the police department about her, Tollie, when they'd cornered him. She didn't know what he'd had to promise them, but they hadn't sent her to jail. Les wouldn't talk about it, just that they'd made him feel like a piss-poor excuse for a family man. "Which I reckon I am," Les said. "But this family seems like it might be more trouble than most."

A state social worker had talked to them both, but separately, in Chapel Hill. Then they'd said she could go home, and then Dix Hill had told Les that Janice could go home. It was like the state had given up on them, thrown up its hands. Sent them back to Hope Mills to work everything out on their own.

Would they be able to? Tollie wondered. Would things work out? Or would the rest of her life be like it felt now? Wrinkled, like an old cotton skirt that had been balled up in the laundry bag so long you'd never get it straightened out. Well, at least they were going to be together again, the three of them. At least the phone was hooked up again, giving them a little connection to the normal world outside their troubled walls. Les, the only man she and Janice could count on even a little bit, turned out to be wearing a white hat after all. Sort of.

"What do you want?" she said affectionately to Lucky, who had begun to nibble at her fingers. "Just be patient. Old Les will probably bring you one of those Angus bones."

Tollie watched Lucky wander off, probably to drink out of the toilet. She turned on a light. The sun had gone down and the dark trees snaked against the lavender sky like a big vascular system. From this vantage, the Mill was only half in view, but black and dense as a rock. She looked back at the veiny trees, then down at her hands. At least she didn't have physical damage, a big blessing. No infection, nothing that wouldn't repair itself in time, the doctor had said, in between lectures on how girls ought to behave until they got married. Nobody had tried to make her expose Madame Lucretia. It was as if they recognized the need for the woman's services.

It was good they hadn't tried to force her, Tollie thought for the hundredth time. She would have cut out her tongue first. Madame Lucretia had helped her in her time of need. Tollie still felt bad about how things ended with her. To be exposed as a liar was one thing, but to be exposed as a selfish crybaby so blinded by her own trouble that she couldn't see an inch into somebody else's situation and act in an ethical way—that made Tollie burn, with a knowledge of her limitations, the limitations of her character.

Because that was exactly when you found out what people were made of! When they were pushed up against the wall, like Tollie Ramsey had been. Then they either did what they could see to do to save themselves, no matter what kind of risk it was to somebody else, or else they took it, because it was theirs.

Tollie understood she wasn't the last kind, but she was going to try to be. That was going to be her New Year's resolution.

Of course there wasn't much she could do about being a baby-killer.

Tollie turned on the water and went back to the collard greens. She wasn't going to think about that. It was easier to think of herself as an unethical and self-serving person in general.

Which was just the proof in the pudding! Tollie Ramsey, always taking the easier way.

She slapped a big collard frond against the sink. Madame Lucretia's life was harder than hers had ever been, and she was a Negro to boot. A resourceful woman. She didn't spend life tackling her hair and her skin, like most women and girls. She had imagination and spirit. Look at that little house! But she was a Negro, and poor, and in a dangerous profession. And her life had been made worse by Tollie Ramsey.

Tollie laid the last collard leaf on the counter and rinsed her hands. All the perfumes of Arabia wouldn't clean them now. She regarded the smooth white skin of her palms. The wounds of her fall were already healed, without leaving a sign. The body was fragile, but it was resilient too. The mind probably was too, and the spirit as well.

She looked out the window, craning at a cluster of bright winter stars rising over the dark Mill, its looms stilled forever now. Les said it had closed down right before Christmas, on the shortest day of the year. She certainly ought to count her blessings, all their blessings, that Les had got up off the couch and gone out looking for work. He *said* he had a job starting in January, collecting life insurance premiums from the Negros. "Twenty-five cents a week for each one, and I get to keep a nickel," he'd said. It didn't sound like much, but at least it was something. She'd better take a page out of his book. Go to Pandora's Box and try again.

She dried her hands and pulled the blind down. As for the mind, daydreaming was helpful. She was finally beginning to believe it. It wasn't just a frivolous thing that people like Lily selected. It was a practical activity to get you through hard times.

Madame Lucretia knew that, in her Sheik of Araby tent on B Street.

Maybe if you could just keep on imagining yourself on a camel somewhere, moving across the dunes, with date palms soaring into a starry sky and all the perfumes of Arabia sweetening your way, the moon reflected in the deep pool of a handy oasis, the area free of any dangerous animals or tribesmen, as you persisted through the night on an important quest. . . .

Dumb, but helpful. She wouldn't make fun of stuff like that again. It was a good capacity to have, even if you couldn't make it come to anything real.

She picked up a collard leaf and held it to the side of her ear, like it was a flower, then bent to glimpse herself in the stainless steel pop-up toaster. She guessed she was beginning to look like a normal person again. She'd better concentrate on her face, though. She didn't want to think about her breasts, still a little swollen with their thwarted mission. She didn't want to look into her eyes, either, she realized.

She distracted herself by waving the collard leaf behind her ear. She focused on her lips and smooched at herself, like Lily would sometimes do. Dumb. But helpful, a little.

She lay the leaf down and straightened up. Dumb-de-dumb-dumb. But then, how would someone like Les get through any day of his life if he couldn't relocate some part of himself to the South Sea Harem of Sgt. Red Wirkus? What had made her think she was any different from anybody else? Short-sightedness, that was what. Well. At least she wasn't moaning over the flight of Raeford Faircloth! Nor of Ramírez before him. Those were blessings to count, better believe it.

Tollie opened the cabinet and took out the bag of blackeyed peas for the Hoppin' John. Suddenly she was sad again. And so lonesome she could die.

Well, what had she expected? To be suddenly born again, like some holy-roller, all her sins washed away with the tide? She probably shouldn't get her hopes up about any little thing for the time being, even a minute of acting like a normal teenage girl kissing her own reflection. She wasn't a normal teenage girl. She was a Teenage Monster, the real thing, not a movie thing. She had slaughtered one of the Innocents, right there at Christmas time, and she would never be innocent again, never in this life. Tollie stared at the pea's dark eyes behind the bag's cellophane. She'd never be free of Madame Lucretia, either. That woman with the future in her bloody black hands would be holed up in some brain-cell of the Teenage Monster for the rest of her days, popping out when least expected, saying *Boo!*

The telephone rang loudly, making Tollie jump.

She hurried across the room. What if they weren't going to let Janice out after all? Or if Les were dead on the road, or the police had decided to put her in jail?

She stopped. What if the doctors in Chapel Hill had found something permanent, or even temporary, like blood poisoning, in all those samples they'd taken? She didn't feel sick, at least not that way. She put her hand on her heart. Like the something-something beat of the tom-tom, one of Janice's songs.

What if Madame Lucretia had tracked her down? If some jerk-kid from school *knew* and was going to make her suffer even more?

"Hello?" she said without hearing, her heart drowning her out.

"Tollie?"

"Lily?"

"Happy New Year!"

"Yes. . . ."

"Tollie?"

"Happy New Year!" Tollie said.

"It's a clean slate," Lily said sternly. "I hope you're going to see that."

"I expect I will," Tollie said. I won't, she thought. I never will.

"What are you doing?" Lily asked.

Every day, twice a day, since Tollie had come back from Chapel Hill, Lily had called to ask this question.

"I'm getting ready to dry off some collards and put them in the refrigerator. I'm trying to decide whether I need to soak some blackeyed peas overnight."

"Don't tell me y'all are going to make Hoppin' John for tomorrow? You're about as superstitious as Daddy!"

"We could use some good luck," Tollie said. "I don't really believe it myself. But it's sort of fun to think about."

"I think you might as well buy some of that old nigger woman's Bones of Bible Folk. Can you believe I don't have a goddam date tonight?"

"I thought you'd stopped worrying about that kind of thing."

"Well, I haven't. It's getting better though. Is your mamma home yet?"

"She's on the way. You could come over and watch Guy Lombardo with us later."

"I'd cut my throat first! Not that I don't appreciate the invitation. But watching New Year's Eve in New York City on *television*—That's the most depressing thing I've ever heard of. I'd rather die than feel like that would make me feel."

"Have you been crying?" Lily's voice sounded weepy to Tollie.

"I have not!"

"I didn't say you had," Tollie said defensively. How was it, after all they'd been through together, she and Lily could still end up bickering. "What are you going to be doing instead?" Tollie asked. "Listening to WMIL and hoping old Mack plays you a love song? Daydreaming about the Grand Opening of Rolando's Burger Quik?"

"Mean!" Lily exclaimed. "Mean as a snake! After all I've done for you lately. Which, by the way, caused me to ruin my own social life and have to ring in 1960 in my sleep. If I *can* sleep, with all those old cherry bombs they're setting off around here. Do you know that some fool soldier was celebrating early and set off a live grenade? This afternoon, right down on the Market Square. It was on the news."

"I think I'm going to give up the news," Tollie said. "It'll make us crazy if we don't watch out."

"What's wrong with the Army?" Lily said. "That somebody like Ramírez can ride into town and do what he did to you and just ride on out? Like he was the enemy, not the calvary!"

"*Cavalry!*" Tollie said. It was hard to believe Lily was almost a high school graduate. She couldn't afford to be as careless as she was. Neither one of them could.

"That somebody can take a live grenade into a civilian town?" Lily asked, ignoring the correction, or more likely, not even hearing it, Tollie thought. "Of course that fool blew his *own* hand off, can you imagine? If that's what the 1960s are going to be like. . . ."

"They're not," Tollie said firmly. "It's a whole new day."

"You sound like that old Pollyanna, just when misery needs company."

"You're the one who said it was a clean slate!"

"Well," Lily said.

"I hope we can be happy in 1960 and in all years beyond," Tollie persisted.

"I'm so depressed I'll be lucky if I can get myself ready to be in the Junior Miss by springtime. It's probably fixed anyway."

"There's no way to know, so you'll just have to get on out there and smile your head off," Tollie said.

"That's no comfort!" Lily said.

"If you want comfort, I think we ought to start planning to go to the Azalea Festival," Tollie said. "It'll give us something definite to look forward to."

"What are you talking about?"

"It was your idea! That day at Rolando's Beach."

"About a hundred years ago."

Tollie felt herself softening. She guessed she had given Lily a real burden to bear.

"You're doing fine," Tollie said. "You should have won Miss Hope Mills High. You're definitely going to be Junior Miss. I can't believe this is Lily talking."

"Believe it. I'm a new woman."

"Like your mamma."

"Jesus Christ in Tenny-Pumps!"

"At least she tries to make her circumstances interesting," Tollie insisted. "Instead of just running off or going crazy, like most people." She felt a swift stab of guilt. Janice hadn't wanted to go crazy.

"Yeah, she's a real special case," Lily said.

"Well, she's different."

"You're right about that," Lily said dismally. "Everywhere I look, *outside* of my own house, all I see is movie stars and beauty queens in the newspaper and, in real life, worn-out women with a string of rug-rats and some old boring guy with about two cents in his pocket. Or it's somebody who's got the money to go up to Women's College and meet some boy from Chapel Hill who's going to be a doctor, like those assholes you told me about. Those two will just have two rug-rats, since she'll be so busy getting her hair done and playing bridge and he'll be so busy screwing the nurses. He'll have more than two cents, but it all just about bores my head off anyway."

"Maybe we'd have been better off as boys," Tollie said. "I was thinking that the other day."

"Are you crazy?" Lily said. "How in the world would I get out of Mill Rat Heaven if I was a boy? Unless I was good at sports, which I'd sure as Hell make sure I was, if I was a boy. Do you know how hard all that sounds? If you were a boy Mill Rat, who couldn't even bleach your hair and show off your good body without somebody thinking you were a fairy, double-misery? You'd just have to go through life with your old dishwater hair, your bad skin from all that fried fat-back, no make-up.

Pretty soon you'd feel so low you'd just drive left of center and get it over with, like Eva Bledsoe."

"Lily—"

"Or you'd settle into Never-Never land, shootin-em-up inside your dishwater brain, waiting for the end, like your stepdaddy."

"Les is doing the best he can," Tollie said. "That's more than I can say for you. What a way to start a New Year."

Tollie hung up, flat. How was that girl going to get through life if she'd stopped dreaming this soon? With a personality as complicated as hers was, Lily was going to have a time of it, no lie.

Tollie had taken a break and was half-dozing on the couch when Lucky went to the front door and began to wag his tail. Tollie got up. She was nervous. Was Les right that Janice didn't hold her daughter's sins against her? More important, what would Janice be like, after all those shock treatments?

Les pushed open the door and helped Janice into the house. He closed the door.

"You sit over here on the couch, pretty girl," he said, guiding Janice around Lucky.

"Baby?" Janice said to Tollie.

Tollie was crying again. "Oh, Mamma."

"Come here, honey," Janice said, shaking off Les and holding out her arms. "This wasn't your fault. I wasn't paying attention."

"It wasn't your fault, Mamma," Tollie said, crying harder, moving into her mother's arms.

"Well, now that everybody's off the hook, let's watch some tv," Les said, moving over to turn the set on. He twisted the dial around. "It'll be time for Guy Lombardo before you know it. Though I hate that he's pre-empted 'The Lawless Years.'"

"How did you learn a word like that?" Janice said, pushing Tollie back and winking at her. Tollie could see bruise-like shadows under her mother's eyes, the faintly raised veins there. Her mother had been to Hell and come back, like Audie Murphy. Did Les realize that? She, Tollie, must never forget that. Her mother's moments of sweetness and understanding and humor were triumphs of her character, medals of honor.

"I'm not as dumb as I look," Les said. "I hate it that all these city crime shows are pre-empting the old westerns, though. They just go on and do anything they want to do at these television stations. Hey, Lucky Dawg. Dawgy-dawg." He scratched Lucky's head.

If anybody ever calls her a nut again, I'll pull their tongues out, Tollie vowed. *I'd like to see what variety of Hell they could go through and still come out with a drop of sweetness and forgiveness to give out to somebody else. My mother isn't a nut, my mother is a Hero!*

"What are you staring at?" Janice said to Tollie. "I guess I look like a wreck." She smoothed her hair.

The ravages of pain, they were her mother's medals, Tollie was thinking. Her signs of valor, and strength beyond most people's imagination. *For New Year's, I resolve to see all signs of my mother's trouble as Medals of Honor, amen.*

"You look pretty, Mamma," Tollie said. She kissed her mother on the lips. "Queen Janice."

"Poot," Janice said weakly.

"What time is it, exactly?" Les said.

Janice raised her arm to check her new watch. Tollie could see its thin band cutting right through the center of the x-mark on her mother's wrist. If you squinted, it looked like an asterisk. Or a snowflake or a star. It was all in how you looked at things. She resolved to have much more imagination in the coming year.

"Ten-thirty," Janice said. "More or less exactly." She winked at Tollie again. Then she looked sad. "I didn't even get you a Christmas present," she said.

"Me either," Tollie said.

"I meant to get you some new perfume," Janice said. "You must be out of Here's My Heart *and* Straw Hat by now."

"I meant to get *you* some," Tollie said. "I didn't get you one thing."

"It's all right," Janice said, patting Tollie's arm.

"Arlene put us up a tree, though." Tollie gestured at the tree, and Janice looked, then looked back at Tollie. "And gave us part of a fruitcake," Tollie said. "From her mamma, not Arlene!"

They laughed.

"Arlene's sweet," Janice said.

"I'll work at Kresge's next year and make it up to you, I promise," Tollie said. "Unless I get another job first. Then I promise to make it up to you sooner."

"You just promise to take as good care of yourself as you can," Janice said. "Your mamma's going to help. That's a promise." She hesitated. "I'm going to stop worrying you to death, too. Both of you."

"I got something in the car for you both," Les said, heading for the door. "Hang on."

"I know what I want for Christmas," Tollie said, when Les was out of hearing. "Something you can give me without spending a dime."

"What's that?" Janice said.

"My real Russian name."

Janice gave her a look.

"I mean it. I want to transform myself. I want to grow into whatever it was you had in mind for me in naming me that."

"It was just a name I saw on a marquee," Janice said nervously. "A ballerina's name."

Tollie smiled. "That's nice, Mamma. It really is."

Janice smiled back. "I'm glad you think so. Later, I thought it was a silly way to name a baby. And, of course, who could have predicted General Eisenhower and all that stuff about the Russians—"

"I like it," Tollie said. "I'm going to become my own 'I.' Tanya. At last. Separate myself from the junk in life. Starting on New Year's Day, 1960. Birthday of Tanya Ramsey."

"Here you go," Les said, coming in the house. "French champagne. Pink."

TANYA

I go into the kitchen and check the collards. Good. They're dry. I put the leaves one by one into the breadwrappers, which I've turned inside out so that no crumbs will get on the greens. Every leaf is so big and so luxurious. Every one looks like a natural fan that a person could use in the hottest weather and do herself some good. I think again how you could almost believe they're the leaves of a tropical plant, requiring the extremes of sun and the excess of rain that a tropical place gets, not something harvested in the dead of winter, maybe just down the road from Hope Mills. Amazing.

I put the collards in the refrigerator, fold up the tea-towels and throw all the wet newspaper in the garbage can, every story blurred into the next one. I wash the ink off my hands and get a big cooking pot out of the cabinet. Then I open the bag of black-eyed peas and pour them out on the counter, slowly, so they won't fall down on the floor and get lost. I want to cook every one. I pick up a fist full, then open my palm and sort through them with the fingertips of my other hand, moving them across the lines of my character and fate. You have to be careful or you'll get, not just pebbles, but little pebble-colored, pebble-sized clods of dirt. I flick the peas into the pot, a few at a time. They look pretty, dried like this. Each pea's body curves in on the black spot where it was attached to the pod. The separation has left its mark, like a wound or the lipstick print of a black kiss, dried in time. If you

305

overcook them, a lot of the black spots will float off on their own, but by then you'll have mush.

From the counter, I can see the tv against the living room wall. Old Lucky is all flung out in front of it, snoozing, happy in his dreams. Moving his paws a little. When he does that, Les says he's dreaming that he's chasing on the heels of rabbits. Les and Mamma are out of sight. I step around the counter's protrusion and look in on them.

"Hi," Mamma says.

"Hi," I say. I squint like I'm trying to see Guy Lombardo better. He's wearing a white jacket and moving his hands in a lively rhythm. Now and then he half-turns around and nods and smiles, at the audience at home. That's nice. Good evening, Mr. Lombardo, how-do-you-do. He seems to be playing in a fancy nightclub. I see the edge of a chandelier and there's a big potted palm over to the side. He's playing an oldie from Mamma's day: "A, You're Adorable." She's been singing that all my life, most of the time right to me, like a lullaby. It's like a gold thread in a piece of plain cloth. A gold thread running through my life.

"Music," Mamma says when it's over. "It keeps coming back like a song."

"Now there's a thought," Les says with a little cough. I sneak a look at: Mamma on the couch—sitting up, that's good—and Les in the chair. They seem okay. Comfortable. Just watching tv together, like other people do.

Somebody's singing on the tv now, thanking heaven for little girls, for the "delightful way" they grow up. *Innuendo*. Oldie and Baddie. Maybe the tv does brain damage too. I wish there were another atmosphere for girls to grow up in, but there doesn't seem to be. I guess we just have to tough it out.

Over in the corner Arlene's permanent Christmas tree is spending its last hours in the living room, for this year. We always take our tree down on New Year's Day. Since I'm pretending not to be looking at Mamma and Les, necessarily, I can see just a vertical half of the tree, with half a gold star at the top. Below that, a zigzag of piney branches and the decorations. There are three bells, two of them dull silver, the other pink and blue plastic. I hope Mamma doesn't see that: a crib decoration. Arlene must have been in outer space when she put that one up.

Before Grady died, Mamma decorated our Christmas tree with his toys. She said, I wish I'd saved your toys, Tollie. Then we'd have a tradition. She said I used to have a monkey-on-a-string that we could have glued angel-wings on. We laughed about that. The good old days.

After Grady died, I went through the decorations and took his toys out and put them in a box and put the box away. I must have missed the bell. Between the bells and the star at the top, I can see the cherub on Aunt Gracie's Christmas card, in its pose of flight, as if winging its way upward. Goodbye, I say.

It has to be said, and meant.

And so I say it, and mean it: goodbye . . . goodbye.

I go back to the peas. The orchestra's playing another Mamma-song, "It's Magic." She must have been singing *most* of the last fifteen years. Otherwise, I wouldn't know all these old songs. It's a real education, I can see that. Permanent. You never forget a song.

"That's purty," Les says. Talking Cowboy. Matt Dillon to Miss Kitty.

I rinse the peas and fill the pot with water, then put it in the refrigerator. If you soak peas overnight, they'll cook faster, and be easier on your system too. There's a see-through package of hog jowls in the refrigerator. They'll flavor the beans and the collards tomorrow. Everything should taste all right, even if I don't have any experience with this. Mamma says she'll cook it all, but I don't know. She says she'll make cornbread. She'll have to, if we're going to have it. I wouldn't have the first notion how to do that. We've got enough of Arlene's mamma's fruitcake left for dessert.

With everything ready for tomorrow, I do what I've known all the time I was going to do. I go to the phone and dial Lily's number. Marie answers.

"Happy New Year!" I say.

"Oh. Tollie. Happy New Year!"

"What are you doing?" (I let "Tollie" pass with Marie, *this* time.) I need to make conversation until Lily gets impatient and comes to the phone of her own accord, instead of my having to ask for her. *If* she'll come to the phone, after I hung up on her. This is all pretty delicate. "I'm working on Lily's dress for the county Junior Miss," Marie says, sounding fatigued. "I put these sweet little rosettes on it, to hold up these little—*simple, tiny*—flounces. Now she wants me to take off the rosettes and make the skirt plain as a sheet. She says they're 'too much.' The dress is so simple, Tollie, that it's almost not a plus anymore. But she's saying it's too fancy. And old-fashioned. I made the dress right after the pattern, printed in 1959. How much more up-to-the-minute would you want to be?"

"It sounds pretty to me," I say.

"Well, she says she won't wear it, so I'm ripping and discarding and tucking and trimming, though I tried to make it a lot simpler than her last dress. Maybe I *was* going by the girls of my time, what they would have wanted if they were going to have an elegant formal. I never had a formal myself, elegant or otherwise."

I don't say anything. I'm almost worn down to a nub, myself, by mothers who feel like they were deprived of every happy thing in life, and are duty-bound to pass that information on, at regular intervals. My mamma is on the right track. If I can stop worrying about her, I might pay more attention to what's happening to me.

"It's really hard to know what Lily wants sometimes," Marie says.

She's waiting for me to say something.

"It is, sometimes," I agree. "She's a complicated person." Marie doesn't say anything. "I don't think she knows, herself," I say. "Not yet, anyway."

"*That's* probably true. Do you think Janice would have time to help me make this dress more modern? I've got a couple of months. I thought that maybe Janice, living in New York and being such a good seamstress, might know what I ought to do. After she's recovered, of course."

"I expect she would."

"How is she, Tollie?"

"I think okay."

Les walks in the kitchen and gets a tray of ice out of the freezer. "Who you talking to?" he asks.

"Just Lily." I mouth the words. He's so inquisitive!

"Good Girl," he says, like I'm Lucky. He pulls up the lever on the ice tray and releases the cubes with a racket. I feel myself frowning. I put my hand over the receiver, not so much to keep Les's noise from distracting Marie as she goes on about the dress and how mysterious Lily is, as to try to make a point to Les. If this family's going to stay together, we ought to get a little more respectful. Which is why I don't tell Les outright to stop that noise.

Les gets a plastic container out of the cabinet and fills it with the ice-cubes. More racket. I'm missing everything Marie is saying. He takes the champagne out of the refrigerator and tries to force it down in the ice, like they do in the movies. Fails, lifts out some cubes, tries again. The bottle of champagne gets set in the ice at an angle, close enough to the movies, and Les gets out the metallic ice tea glasses. He puts one in his hand and secures the other two against his belly with his forearm, then picks up the ice container with his free hand and goes back into the living room.

"What are y'all doing tomorrow?" I ask Marie when she seems like she might be finished talking about the rosettes and Lily, who has changed from mysterious to stubborn while I was watching Les.

"Virgil's going to church, naturally. I thought I'd take the day off to read *Profiles in Courage*, Senator Kennedy's book? I don't know about my daughter, Tollie. She's a mystery to me in just about every category right now. She stayed home tonight listening to the radio. On New Year's Eve."

"Is she still awake?" I give up. Lily is stubborn, if anything.

"I think so. Let me go see."

After a few minutes Lily is on the phone. "I already wished you Happy New Year once tonight," she says. She sounds irritated.

"Well, Happy New Year twice," I say, jumping, because there's a loud noise when Les pops the cork of the champagne. For a second I thought it was a firecracker, or a grenade.

"I dyed my hair," Lily says as I lean out to look into the living room. Les and Mamma are both sitting on the couch. Les pours the champagne. It is almost midnight, and on tv, thousands of people are crowded into Times Square.

"Why?" I ask Lily absently. I'm watching Les and Mamma.

"I just wanted to tone it down a little," Lily says. "Not much. It looks more . . . subtle. I like it."

"I want you to come over here tomorrow and eat with us," I say.

"That old Hoppin' John? No thanks, Tollie."

"Tanya. I'm going to use my real name from now on. Like you, I've outgrown Tollie."

"Jeez-us. What next?"

"Why not? If I can indulge you in 'Lili Lorene'—"

"I'm done with that. Junk. Junk, and more junk. I'm either going to be Lily Ann Jones, like I guess I was doomed to be a long time ago, or I'm going to be somebody dignified. Like 'Lillian.' I'd like to know what it feels like to have a minute's worth of dignity in this world."

"Lillian is dignified," I say, encouraging her. "And it's some version of Lily Ann, so it's not like you're just pulling it out of a hat."

"I guess," Lily says. She sounds dejected anyway.

"We'll eat about three in the afternoon, since it's a holiday."

"I'm not going to eat that mess," Lily says.

"We need luck, Lily," I say, full of what I think I understand. Finally. "Without it, there's no hope for us. Not in this life. We'd better try everything there is."

"I don't believe Hoppin' John would bring me one bit of luck. In fact, I think it would do big damage to my skin. No, ma'am."

"I'll expect you a little before three," I say. "Bring your dress. Mamma will be able to see in a second how to modernize it for 1960."

Lily's quiet.

"I hear wood burning," I say. The crowd on tv is counting down, but you can't hear them distinctly, so the tv announcer is counting into a microphone to keep everybody involved.

" . . . 9 . . . 8 . . . 7 . . . ."

"I'm not going to touch a speck of hog jowl," Lily says.

I can't help but laugh. I know Lily like the palm of my hand.

"I mean it," she says. "I'm afraid I'll grow a jowl. Before my time."

"I thought you weren't superstitious," I say.

"I'll see you about a quarter till," she says and hangs up. I hang up too. I'm smiling: she *had* to do that: hang up without saying goodbye. And I had to let her.

" . . . 2 . . . 1 . . . Happy New Year!" the man with the microphone cries. "It's nineteen-sixty!"

Guy Lombardo's orchestra breaks into "Auld Lang Syne," and the ball Mamma's always talked about begins to descend to Times Square from on high, a big shiny ball that looks like the world in miniature, made of glass. Les and Mamma click their glasses and take a sip of the champagne. Les picks up Mamma's hand and puts it to his lips. Mamma takes another quick sip. She gives Les a smile, then quickly looks at the tv.

Les pours my champagne and waves me in. We all click our metallic glasses, bright as Christmas tree ornaments.

"Happy New Year, Ladies," Les says.

"To the nineteen-sixties," Mamma says.

"Hope springs eternal," Les says. "They say."

"I guess it does," Mamma says.

"At least it trickles eternal," I say, lifting my glass. "To the nineteen-sixties. And to nineteen-ninety-nine."

"Good god, Girl. I'll be dead and gone by *then*," Les says.

The champagne has a kind of skunk-taste, but it's good. I like how it bursts in your mouth. Everybody on tv is singing. I can hear cherry bombs going off all over the neighborhood outside. Old Lucky just keeps on snoozing, through all the noise.

"What does 'Auld Lang Syne' mean?" I ask Mamma. I should know that, as much as I've studied in 1959.

"I'm not sure," Mamma says, shrugging. "Old something."

"It's got 'Lang' in it," I say, writing it out on the blackboard in my head. "Long?"

"Long Ago and Far Away?" Les says. He winks at Mamma. "That was always your favorite."

The people in Times Square burst into cheers before the song is finished, and the ending is lost. When I can hear music again, it's new music. It's not a song I can place. Whole passages are lost in the racket of car-horns and paper horns, which people are blowing toward the tv camera every couple of seconds. The horns roll out like the tongues of a fantastic species, like the firebreath of dragons in comic books. The tongues seem to snatch something invisible from the air and bear it off in a motion that's not just quick but cunning too. Too fast for the eye to see. Ticker-tape drifts down from the tall buildings and collapses on cars. It coils around excited boys and young men. I feel funny: sad and . . . expectant, at the same time. Some of the young men are raising whole bottles of champagne up in a toast, then drinking right out of the bottle. You can see the air cloud with their breath when they laugh. Everyone seems to be rushing around, though they're jam-packed. Men and women are kissing each other frantically, as if they're kissing goodbye, or hello.

It seems familiar, like something I've seen somewhere else, but who knows where or when? Maybe in a movie. It's as if the people are getting ready to set off for some distant place, or coming home from a war.

7/97